A
GLENN
TUNE-UP
AND
REPAIR
GUIDE

GLENN'S

BASIC
TUNE-UP
AND REPAIR GUIDE

by

Harold T. Glenn

HENRY REGNERY COMPANY • CHICAGO

Library of Congress Cataloging in Publication Data

Glenn Publications.
    Glenn's basic tune-up and repair guide.

    1. Automobiles—Maintenance and repair.
I. Glenn, Harold T. II. Title. III. Title:
Basic tune-up and repair guide.
TL152.G564 1976   629.28'7'22   76-25337
International Standard Book Number: 0-8092-8194-5

**Cover illustration by
Wayne L. Kibar**

Printed in the United States of America
Library of Congress Card Number: 76-25337
International Standard Book Number: 0-8092-8194-5

foreword

This is a basic repair and tune-up guide for all automobiles. It is a completely usable repair guide for a car owner who wants to make his or her own repairs, those who are interested in keeping their autos running smoothly and economically, as well as saving money.

The four "roadmaps" in the second chapter ("Troubleshooting") are especially important in helping to pinpoint the trouble before beginning repairs. This feature also helps to save time while repairs are in process, because it shows what to look for as the unit is being disassembled. Many simple procedures are demonstrated that require no elaborate equipment for testing and that can be made by any interested car owner.

Among the many special features of this guide is the use of step-by-step illustrated instructions. Another is the use of "exploded illustrations" of major mechanical and electrical units. There are many photographs of worn parts so that the reader will recognize such wear when he sees it. These pictures take the place of years of experience.

acknowledgments

The author wishes to express his appreciation to all American motor car manufacturers for their gracious assistance in furnishing material for this Guide.

Special thanks are due to my wife, Anna Glenn, for her gracious and devoted assistance in helping to proofread the manuscript and galley proofs and to Mark Tsunawaki for his contribution to the artwork of this book.

HAROLD T. GLENN

Books by HAROLD T. GLENN

Youth at the Wheel — Safe Living

Automechanics — Glenn's Auto Troubleshooting Guide

Exploring Power Mechanics — Automobile Engine Rebuilding and Maintenance

Automobile Power Accessories — Glenn's Auto Repair Manual

Automotive Smog Congrol Manual — Glenn's Emission-Control Systems

Glenn's Foreign Car Repair Manual — Glenn's Triumph Repair and Tune-Up Guide

Glenn's Alta Romeo Repair and Tune-Up Guide — Glenn's Austin, Austin-Healey Repair and Tune-Up Guide

Glenn's Sunbeam-Hillman Repair and Tune-Up Guide — Glenn's MG, Morris and Magnette Repair and Tune-Up Guide

Glenn's Volkswagen Repair and Tune-Up Guide — Glenn's Volkswagen Repair and Tune-Up Guide (Spanish Edition)

Glenn's Mercedes-Benz Repair and Tune-Up Guide — Glenn's Foreign Carburetors and Electrical Systems Guide

Glenn's Renault Repair and Tune-Up Guide — Glenn's Jaguar Repair and Tune-Up Guide

Glenn's Volvo Repair and Tune-Up Guide — Glenn's Peugeot Repair and Tune-Up Guide

Glenn's Fiat Repair and Tune-Up Guide — Glenn's Toyota Tune-Up and Repair Guide

Glenn's Tune-Up and Repair Manual for American and Imported Car Emission-Control Systems

Glenn's Chrysler Outboard Motor Repair and Tune-Up Guide for 1 & 2 Cylinder Engines

Glenn's Chrysler Outboard Motor Repair and Tune-Up Guide for 3 & 4 Cylinder Engines

Glenn's Evinrude Outboard Motor Repair and Tune-Up Guide for 1 & 2 Cylinder Engines

Glenn's Evinrude Outboard Motor Repair and Tune-Up Guide for 3 & 4 Cylinder Engines

Glenn's Johnson Outboard Motor Repair and Tune-Up Guide for 1 & 2 Cylinder Engines

Glenn's Johnson Outboard Motor Repair and Tune-Up Guide for 3 & 4 Cylinder Engines

Glenn's McCulloch Outboard Motor Repair and Tune-Up Guide — Glenn's Mercury Outboard Motor Repair and Tune-Up Guide

Glenn's Sears Outboard Motor Repair and Tune-Up Guide — Glenn's Honda One-Cylinder Repair and Tune-Up Guide

Glenn's Honda Two-Cylinder Repair and Tune-Up Guide — Glenn's Suzuki One-Cylinder Tune-Up and Repair Guide

Glenn's Yamaha Enduro Tune-Up and Repair Guide — Glenn's Triumph Two-Cylinder Motorcycle Tune-Up and Repair Guide

Glenn's Chevrolet Tune-Up and Repair Guide — Glenn's Chevrolet Camaro Tune-Up and Repair Guide

Glenn's Ford/Lincoln/Mercury Tune-Up and Repair Guide — Glenn's Chrysler/Plymouth/Dodge Tune-Up and Repair Guide

Glenn's Pontiac Tune-Up and Repair Guide — Glenn's Pontiac Firebird Tune-Up and Repair Guide

Glenn's Oldsmobile Tune-Up and Repair Guide — Glenn's Buick Tune-Up and Repair Guide

Glenn's Complete Bicycle Manual — Glenn's Opel Tune-Up and Repair Guide

Glenn's Datsun 510/610/710 Tune-Up and Repair Guide — Glenn's Pinto Tune-Up and Repair Guide

Glenn's Mustang II Tune-Up and Repair Guide — Glenn's Capri and Capri II Tune-Up and Repair Guide

Glenn's Bobcat Tune-Up and Repair Guide — Glenn's OMC Inboard/Outboard Tune-Up and Repair Guide

Glenn's Volkswagen Tune-Up and Repair Guide — Glenn's Kawasaki-3 Tune-Up and Repair Guide

Glenn's Honda-4 (750) Tune-Up and Repair Guide — Glenn's Mazda Tune-Up and Repair Guide

Glenn's Basic Repair Guide — Glenn's Hornet Tune-Up and Repair Guide

Glenn's Flat Rate Manual

table of contents

1. INTRODUCTION   1
    Top Tuner Tips   1
    Money Saving Tips   1
Tools   1
  Screwdrivers   2
  Hammers   5
  Punches   5
  Chisels   6
  Pliers   6
  Wrenches   8
    Non-adjustable   8
    Adjustable   9
  Socket wrenches   10
  Handles   10
  Torque wrenches   12
Test equipment   15
  Compression tester   15
  Vacuum gauge   15
  Volt-Amp tester   16
  Timing light   16
  Continuity test light   17
2. TROUBLESHOOTING   19
Roadmaps   19
Roadmap one — emergency troubleshooting   19
Roadmap two — cranking system tests   21
  Battery test   22
  Cable connection test   22
  Solenoid test   23
  Current draw test   24
Roadmap three — ignition system tests   24
  Ignition circuit test   24
  Primary circuit test   24
  Contact point test   26
  Condenser test   26
  Secondary circuit test   27
  Rotor test   28
Roadmap four — fuel system tests   28
  Fuel pump test   28
Spark plugs   30
Emission control systems   33
Fuel and ignition system problems   33
  Rough engine idle   33

Inconsistent engine idle speed   34
Excessive fuel consumption   34
Acceleration stumble   34
Engine surge   35
Poor high-speed performance   36
Poor low-speed performance   36
Engine stalling   36
Engine starts hard   37
Engine misfire   37
Troubleshooting the engine   37
  Vacuum gauge   38
Engine noises   39
Excessive oil consumption   39
Overheating   40
Electrical system   41
  Battery and Charging system   41
  Noisy alternator   42
  Turn signals   43
  Constant voltage system   43
Troubleshooting the driveline   44
  Clutch   44
  Standard transmission   44
  Automatic transmission   44
Rear axle   45
Troubleshooting the running gear   47
  Quick checks   47
  Road test   48
    Vehicle leads to one side   48
    Shimmy   48
Power steering   49
Irregular tire wear   49
  Underinflation   49
  Overinflation   49
  Scuffing   49
  Camber wear   49
  Cornering wear   50
  Cup and flat spot wear   50
Service brakes   50
  Grabbing brakes   50
  Dragging brakes   50
  Fading   51
  Noisy brakes   51

Chatter	51
Low pedal action	51
Spongy pedal	51
Hard pedal	52
Disc brakes	52
Troubleshooting the disc brake system	52
Troubleshooting chart	52
3. PREVENTIVE MAINTENANCE	**53**
Engine	53
Lubrication	53
Changing the engine oil and oil filter	53
Drive belts	55
Cooling system	59
Checking the level	59
Inspecting the hoses	59
Replacing the coolant	59
Fuel system	61
Checking the throttle linkage	61
Checking the choke linkage	61
Checking the throttle-stop solenoid	61
Inspecting the fuel lines for leakage	61
Checking the heated-air system	61
Replacing the air cleaner filter	61
Replacing the fuel filter	63
Ignition system	63
Checking the distributor	63
Replacing spark plugs	63
Checking the secondary wires	64
Battery	65
Checking the state of charge	65
Checking the battery cables	65
Clutch and manual transmission	65
Adjusting the clutch pedal free play	66
Checking the transmission fluid level	66
Automatic transmission	66
Checking the fluid level	66
Checking the initial engagement	66
Checking the shift points	68
Adjusting the neutral-start switch	68
Rear axle	68
Checking the lubricant level	68
Steering mechanism	69
Checking the steering column lock	69
Checking the steering control	69
Inspecting the ball joints	69
Lubricating the ball joints	70
Inspecting the front wheel linkage	71
Lubricating the linkage	71
Checking the pump fluid	71
Adjusting the pump drive belt	73
Brakes	73
Inspecting the master cylinder fluid level	73
Inspecting the brake hoses	73
Checking the operation of the braking system	73
Inspecting the disc brakes for wear	73
Checking the parking brakes	74
Wheels and tires	74
Inspecting the wheels	75
Checking the tires	75
Rotating the tires	75
Body	76
Inspecting the drain holes	76
Lubricating friction points	76
Lighting and accessories	76
Checking the lights	76
Checking the horns	77
Checking the windshield washers	77
Replacing windshield wiper blades	77
Replacing a rubber blade element	78
Checking the heater/air conditioner	78
4. ENGINE TUNE-UP	**79**
Mechanical conditions	79
Testing the compression	79
Performing the test	81
Top Tuner Tip	**82**
Ignition system	83
Servicing the ignition system	83
Inspecting the ignition points	83
Installing ignition points and condenser	84
Top Tuner Tip	**85**
Adjusting the point gap	87
Dwell or cam angle	87
Top Tuner Tip	**87**
Spark plugs	90
Cleaning and gapping the spark plugs	92
Setting the ignition timing	92
Power timing the engine	94
Fuel system service	96
Air filters	97
Thermostatically-controlled air cleaner	99
Service procedures	101
Carburetors	101
Money Saving Tips	**102**
Service procedures	103
Carburetor kits	103
Carburetor circuits	105
Float system	105
Idle system	105
Main metering system	106
Power system	106
Accelerating system	107
Automatic choke	109
Carburetor adjustments	109
Emission-controlled engines	109
Lean-drop method	109
Emission-control systems	112
Crankcase emission-control system	112
System Quick Test	**113**

Service procedures	113
Exhaust emission-control systems	113
Transmission-controlled spark	114
System quick test	**115**
System isolation test	**116**
Spark-Delay systems	118
System Basic Test	**118**
Service procedures	120
Exhaust-gas recirculation	120
System Quick Tests	**120**
5. ENGINE SERVICE	**122**
Money Saving Tips	**122**
Engine theory	122
Intake stroke	123
Compression stroke	123
Power stroke	123
Exhaust stroke	123
Combustion	124
Valve timing	124
General engine service procedures	**124**
Cylinder block	124
Cylinder heads and manifolds	125
Crankshaft	127
Main bearings	128
Measuring the oil clearance	129
Connecting rods	130
Pistons	131
Rings	132
Valve mechanism	134
Valve guides	135
Valve springs	135
Valves	136
Valve seats	136
Hydraulic valve lifters	138
Measuring timing gear or sprocket and chain wear	139
Six-cylinder engine service procedures	**140**
Cylinder head service	140
Removing	140
Cleaning and inspecting	140
Rocker arm studs	142
Valve seats	143
Valves	144
Assembling the cylinder head	144
Installing the cylinder head	144
Valve lash	145
Piston and rods, R&R	146
Removing	146
Cleaning and inspecting	146
Cylinder block	146
Piston pins	147
Disassembling	148
Assembling	148
Piston rings	148
Installing the piston and rod assembly	149
Crankcase front cover, R&R	151
Removing	151
Installing	152
Engine service specifications	152
V-8 engine service procedures	**154**
Cylinder head service	154
Removing	154
Cleaning and inspecting	154
Valves	155
Valve faces	156
Valve seats	156
Rocker arm stud replacement	156
Assembling the cylinder head	157
Installing the cylinder head	157
Checking the valve lash	157
Completing the assembly	158
Pistons, rings, and rods, R&R	160
Removing	160
Cleaning and inspecting	161
Cylinder bores	161
Piston pins	161
Piston rings	161
Installing	162
Cooling system service	163
Overheating	163
Service procedures	163
Fan belt	163
Money Saving Tips	**164**
Adjusting the belt tension	164
Cooling system	165
Cleaning	166
Reverse-flushing the system	166
Oil leaks	168
Top Tuner Tip	**168**
Electrical system service	168
Money Saving Tips	**168**
6. DRIVELINE SERVICE	**170**
Clutch	170
Clutch, R&R	170
Installing	171
Clutch pedal free play adjustment	172
Automatic transmissions	173
Checking the fluid level	173
Checking the condition of the fluid	174
Money Saving Tips	**174**
Changing the transmission fluid	174
Troubleshooting	175
Automatic transmission diagnosis guide	175
Kickdown linkage adjustments	176
Service procedures	176
Neutral-start switch adjustment	176
Transmission band adjustments	178
Driveshaft	179

Removing 179
Universal joint removal 179
Assembling 180
Driveline vibration 180
Driveline angle check 180
Driveshaft runout check 181
Driveshaft balancing 181
Rear axle 183
Pinion-positioning shim 183
Pinion Bearing preload adjustment 183
Differential bearing preload adjustment 184
Tooth contact adjustments 185

7. RUNNING GEAR SERVICE **186**
Wheel suspension 186
Repacking the front wheel bearings 186
Cleaning and inspecting 187
Installing 188
Adjusting the front wheel bearings:
Ford & American Motors 190
Chrysler & General Motors 190
Shock absorbers 191
Checking 191
Money Saving Tips **191**
Replacing a shock absorber 191
Braking systems 192
Money Saving Tips **192**
Dual braking system 192
Dual master cylinder 193
Front drum brakes 193
Front disc brakes 193
Combination valve 194
Metering valve 194
Brakes not applied 194
Initial brake apply 194

Hold-off blend pressure 195
Failure warning switch 195
Proportioner 196
Normal brake stops 196
Proportioning action 196
Brake distribution switch 197
Drum-type brakes 197
Front-wheel brakes 198
Self-energizing action 198
Self-adjusting action 198
Rear-wheel brakes 199
Single-piston type disc brakes 199
Four-piston type disc brakes 200
Drum-type brake service procedures 201
Relining 201
Removing 201
Inspecting 203
Installing 203
Adjusting drum-type brakes 205
Single-piston type disc brake
service procedures 206
Removing the brake shoes 206
Cleaning and inspecting 207
Installing 207
Four-piston type disc brake
service procedures 210
Removing the brake shoes 210
Installing new brake shoes 210
Master cylinder service procedures 211
Removing 211
Disassembling 212
Cleaning and inspecting 212
Assembling 212
Bench bleeding 213
Bleeding the hydraulic system 213

1/introduction

This book is written for the average car owner who has some mechanical ability; the owner who is desirous of saving time and money in these days of high gas prices, shoddy mechanics' work, inflated parts costs, and the high cost of repairs. With this book, the average car owner can diagnose and repair the simpler systems of his car. No attempt will be made to overhaul an automatic transmission, engine, or rear axle. However, the step-by-step troubleshooting procedures in the second chapter of this book will assist the reader to trace out problems so that he can make the repairs or to be more knowledgeable when he has to deal with mechanics about major repairs.

This book is not a shop manual with precise specifications for all models and years, but rather a broad overall view of problems that can develop in your car and how to cope with them.

The four "Roadmaps" in the second chapter (Troubleshooting) are especially important in helping you to pinpoint the trouble before attempting repairs. This feature will also help to save time while repairs are in process, because it will show you what to look for as the unit is being disassembled. Many simple procedures will be shown that require no elaborate test equipment or special tools.

Chapter Three covers simple preventive maintenance repairs that you can do on your car to save time and money. Chapter four covers tuning your engine with inexpensive tools and equipment. You are shown how to take and interpret a compression test to determine the mechanical condition of your engine, how to install new points, condenser, and spark plugs, and set the ignition timing. Chapter five covers the common service procedures for the engine. You will be shown how to remove the cylinder head in order to service the valve system, and remove the piston assemblies so that you can install new piston rings and bearing inserts to reduce oil consumption. You will be shown how to check the electrical system to determine where a defect lies.

Chapter Six will cover the simple maintenance and repairs that you can do on the vehicle. By following these procedures, you will be able to check and replenish the fluids in the transmission (manual and automatic), rear axle, power steering and brakes. Also simple service procedures are described in the brake, lubrication, and tire sections which you can do and have the satisfaction of knowing that the job is being done right as well as saving money.

TTT

This book will include **TTT** (Top Tuner Tips). And when you see **TTT** in the heading, it describes detailed procedures to follow to obtain the maximum economy and performance from your engine.

MST

When you see **MST** (Money Saving Tips) in the heading, you will know that we have suggested procedures for saving money by using a "mechanic's mechanic," a skilled technician with expensive and accurate equipment set up to do special work for the mechanic. You, too, can use his services and, thereby, reduce your costs by dealing directly with him to cut out the normal trade mark-up.

TOOLS

While there are several publications extolling the virtues of "tuning your car without tools" or "overhauling your gas guzzler V-8 with a pair of pliers and a screwdriver," this author insists that a minimum number of tools are necessary to do the jobs efficiently, quicker, and earier. The remainder of this chapter will discuss the minimum number of hand tools and inexpensive test equipment that is necessary to troubleshoot and to make minor repairs.

SCREWDRIVERS

A screwdriver is designed for loosening and tightening screws. Although it is frequently misused as a pry or chisel, it must not be used for these purposes.

Screwdrivers are classified by the length of the shank and by the shape and size of the blade. The shank is usually made from round stock, but is sometimes square for extra strength so that a wrench can be applied for removing tight screws. Some round-stock screwdrivers have a hex on the shank for the same purpose.

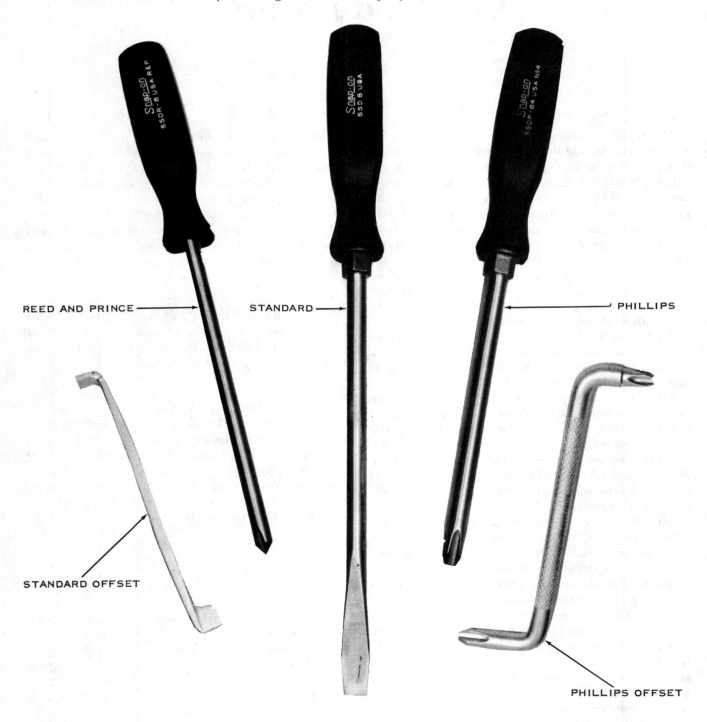

REED AND PRINCE ⟶

STANDARD ⟶

⟵ PHILLIPS

STANDARD OFFSET

PHILLIPS OFFSET

Examples of the various screwdrivers discussed in the text.

A *standard screwdriver* is made to fit screw heads having a single slot; it comes in a variety of blade widths and thicknesses. The blade should be as wide as the head of the screw and thick enough to fit the slot snugly. A blade that is too large or too small will damage the screw slot and may make it impossible to turn.

Phillips and *Reed and Prince screwdrivers* are often confused because both are made to turn screws having a four-way (or X-shaped) slot in the head. However, these two types of screwdrivers are not inter-

Details of the Phillips-head screw and screwdriver. Always select the screwdriver which fits the slot to keep it from slipping out.

When using a screwdriver, it is very important that the blade fits the screw head slot; otherwise, it can slip out and burr the slot.

STANDARD   PHILLIPS   REED AND PRINCE

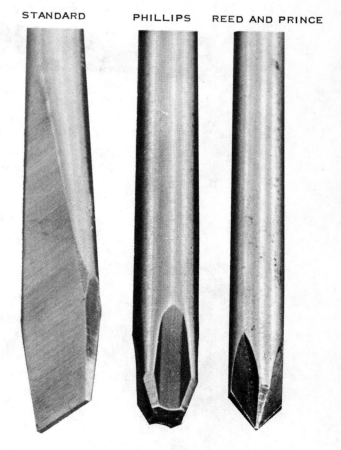

Three types of screwdrivers used by mechanics. Note the pointed end of the Reed-and-Prince blade compared with the Phillips.

Ball peen hammer.

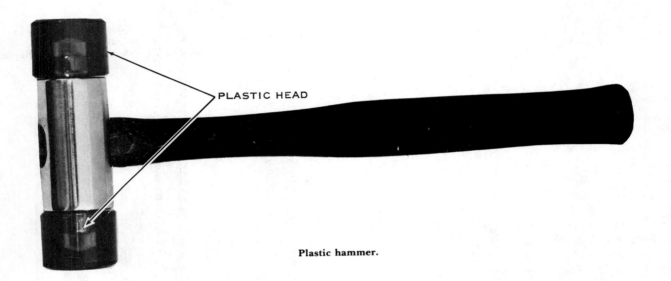

Plastic hammer.

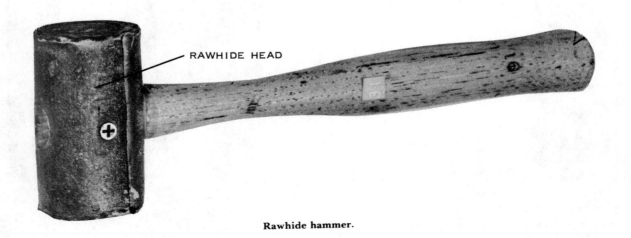

Rawhide hammer.

changeable. Reed and Prince screws have a different flute angle (45 degrees) than Phillips-head screws (30 degrees). Using an incorrect screwdriver will damage the screw. To distinguish the difference in screws, note that the slots in the Reed and Prince head are more sharply rectangular than those of the Phillips. The screwdrivers can be identified by comparing the more pointed end of the Reed and Prince with the blunt end of the Phillips.

Offset screwdrivers are angled for use in hard-to-reach areas and are available with various sizes of standard and Phillips blades. When using a screwdriver, always hold it at a right angle to the screw. **CAUTION: Never hold the work in your hand while using a screwdriver, because it can slip out of the screw head and cause a serious puncture wound.** It is safer to place the work in a vise.

HAMMERS

For automotive work, two types of hammers are required: (1) ball-peen hammers and (2) soft-face hammers. Ball-peen hammers are made in different weights, from 4 ounces to 2 pounds; 8 to 16 oz. are most commonly used. For safety and durability, a drop-forged steel head is preferable to one made of cast steel, which can chip or break in use. A good quality hammer should also have a handle of tough wood. The head is installed on the handle with a metal wedge driven into the end of the handle to expand the wood and hold it in place. **CAUTION: Check the hammer before using it to ensure the wedge is not loose or the hammer head may fly off when you swing it and cause a serious injury.**

The second type of hammer has a head made of plastic, brass, or tightly-rolled rawhide; brass and plastic hammers are also available with replaceable head tips. This type is used when there is danger of damaging the object being worked on, because its material is softer than steel and will "give" without rebound, even when striking a fairly heavy blow. An additional advantage is that the hammer will not give off a spark, and thus is useful in work where there is danger of fire, such as around fuel system areas.

Although a hammer is an elementary tool with which everyone is familiar, it is often used incorrectly. The hammer should be grasped near the end of the handle, and the thumb should not overlap the fingers. Holding the handle near the middle is acceptable for striking a light blow, but the hammer must never be grasped near the head. This is known as "choking," and it prevents striking at the correct angle. Always strike the object squarely, keeping the face of the hammer parallel to the piece being struck. This dis-

tributes the force of the blow over the full face of the hammer, protecting the face as well as the surface being struck from chipping or deforming. When striking a chisel or punch, the face of the hammer should be at least 1/2 inch larger than the head of the tool to lessen the chance of the hammer missing the tool and causing serious injury to your hand.

PUNCHES

Punches are made of tool steel and are used for a variety of jobs, depending on the shape of the point. The most useful are the center, prick, taper and pin punches.

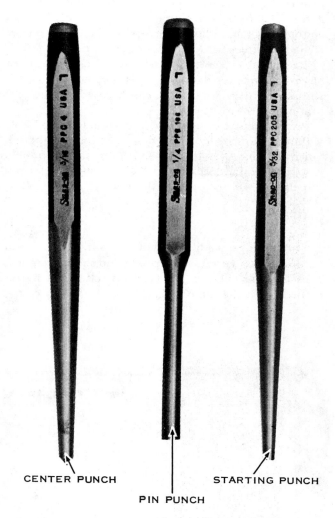

CENTER PUNCH   STARTING PUNCH

PIN PUNCH

Center punch (left) has a 60° angled point. The pin punch (center) has a straight shank. It comes in various size shanks. The starting punch (right) has a tapered shank, and it can be used to start to drive out a pin because of the strength of the shank, but a pin punch must be used to complete the job to keep the punch from binding in the hole.

CHISEL

A chisel is a cutting tool.

The *center punch* has a tapered end with a sharp point ground at a 60 degree angle. It is useful for punching an indentation in metal to start a drill bit, or for making corresponding marks on two pieces of an assembled unit so that they can be correctly aligned during assembly.

The *prick punch,* also tapered, has a sharp point ground at a narrower angle than the center punch, and is used for fine marking. It is sometimes called an aligning punch, because the tapered end can be used to line up holes in two pieces of sheet metal.

The *taper, or starting punch,* can also be used for aligning purposes. However, it is specifically made to withstand heavy blows, and can be used to free pins that are "frozen" in place.

Pin punches are designed to be driven through a hole without distorting it or jamming; they are not tapered. Once a pin has been loosened with the starting punch, it should be driven out with the largest-diameter pin punch that will fit through the hole.

CHISELS

The chisel, a wedge-shaped tool with a hardened cutting edge, is used for chipping and shearing metal. Chisels are usually octagonal, and are classified in sizes according to the length, diameter, and width of the cutting edge, all expressed in inches. Different point shapes are used for different cutting jobs.

Choose the correct size chisel and match it with the correct hammer. A larger chisel requires a larger hammer; otherwise, it will absorb the hammer blows and will not cut. When striking the chisel, hold it lightly near its upper end so that, in case the hammer slips, your hand can slide downward to lessen the effect of the blow. Strike the head squarely with the hammer, keeping the chisel at the proper angle to the object being worked on. An incorrect angle will cause the chisel to push rather than cut the metal. Keep your eyes on the cutting edge of the chisel, rather than the head. **CAUTION: Always wear safety goggles when using a chisel.**

PLIERS

Pliers are made in a variety of designs. They are divided into two main categories, solid-joint and slip-joint, with a few speciality styles in addition.

Solid-joint pliers come in several different jaw shapes, lengths, and widths. For general purposes, *duck-bill pliers* are the most adaptable. They have serrations inside the jaws, and are usually used for twisting wires together and for holding small objects that cannot be reached by hand.

Needle-nose pliers also have serrated jaws, but they are tapered to a point. They are available with angled jaws for especially crowded areas, and most types are also provided with a short cutting edge near the pivot. They are used to steady small items, bend wire, and to remove or install small cotter pins when such jobs cannot be done by hand.

Side-cutting pliers have two major jaw areas, a serrated gripping portion at the tip and a cutting

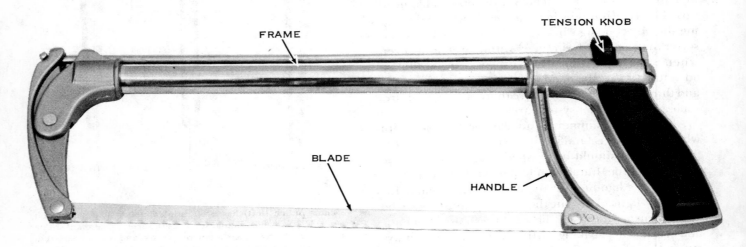

FRAME   TENSION KNOB

BLADE

HANDLE

A hacksaw is a handy tool for any mechanic's kit. It comes with various number of teeth on the blade, which can be replaced when worn.

portion near the pivot. They are used to hold or bend very thin materials, cut wire, or strip insulation from electrical wire.

Diagonal cutting pliers are made with a slanted face silhouette for cutting metal objects close to the surface. They have a hard steel edge designed only for cutting.

With *slip-joint pliers,* the pivot with which the two halves are fastened together can be moved to two or more positions for gripping objects of different sizes. When the handles are spread open as far as possible, the pivot can be moved to a different groove; at all other positions, the tool is operated in the same way as solid-joint pliers.

Combination slip-joint pliers are general-purpose tools. The jaws are fairly wide, have hardened cross-teeth for gripping, and adjust to two different positions. They are provided with a short shearing area for cutting wire as well, but are not designed to cut hard metal.

Channel-lock pliers are very versatile because they can be adjusted to many positions while the jaws remain parallel to each other. They have extra-long handles and are used when a more powerful gripping tool is required. When used to turn a nut or bolt, the large jaw of the channel-locks should grip the trailing edge of the object being turned. Channel-locks are useful for large or hard-to-reach objects, but it is always preferable to use a wrench specifically designed for the item.

Vise-grip© pliers are a special tool in that they have a clamp-type jaw which locks onto the piece. The jaw opening is adjusted by turning a knurled knob at the end of one handle. The object is gripped between the jaws and the knob turned until resistance is felt. Then the handles are squeezed together until a click occurs (this should require a fair amount of pressure). A lever on the other handle is pushed to release the pliers. These pliers can be used as a clamp, portable vise, or

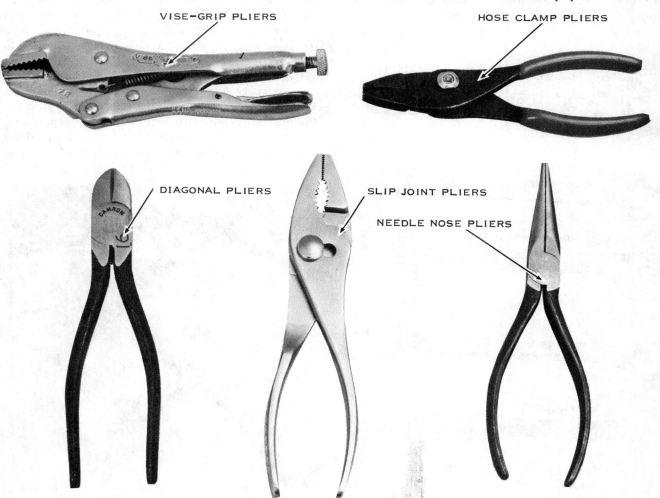

Various types of pliers that are commonly used, and should be part of any mechanic's kit.

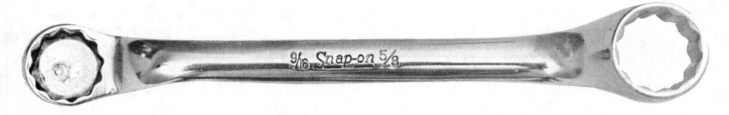

A box wrench is a handy tool to be used when loosening a tight bolt, because it cannot slip off the head of the bolt.

wrench. However, due to their powerful grip, they should be used with extreme caution on items that must be re-used.

Snap-ring pliers are a specialty tool, designed for removing internal and external snap rings. They have small tips called "tongs" which are inserted into the eyes of the snap ring; the handles are then squeezed to spread or compress the snap ring, depending on the type. They are available with different tong sizes and angles for convenience in close areas.

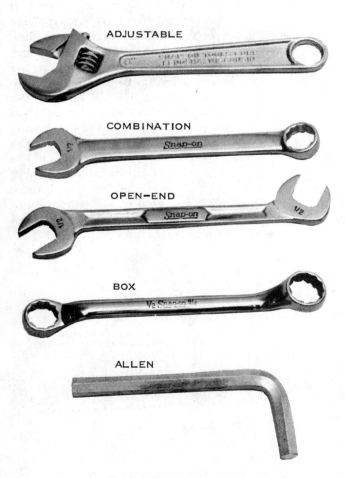

ADJUSTABLE

COMBINATION

OPEN-END

BOX

ALLEN

Different types of wrenches that are discussed in the text.

WRENCHES

Non-adjustable

The *open-end wrench* is a solid, non-adjustable turning tool, usually made of chrome vanadium steel. The openings at either end are usually of different sizes, each to accommodate a different size of bolt head, and markings are stamped near each face to indicate the size. An average set provides a wide enough range for most automotive purposes. The jaw opening of a standard open-end wrench is at an angle to the handle so that, when the wrench has been turned to its limit in close quarters, it can be turned over and repositioned on the bolt for additional swing.

Box-end wrenches are somewhat similar to open-ends, except that they grip the nut or bolt-head on all sides. Their openings have either six or twelve internal faces. The six-point type is stronger and is used for difficult jobs, while the twelve-point type can be positioned on

Always use two wrenches when undoing a fuel line fitting; otherwise, you will twist the pipe and possibly destroy it.

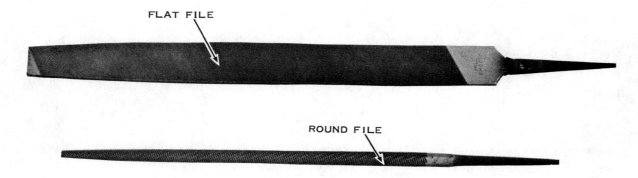

FLAT FILE

ROUND FILE

Flat and round files are handy to remove burrs and to fit parts.

the nut at a greater variety of angles for convenience in limited spaces. The head of a box-end wrench may be offset at an angle to the handle to provide hand clearance at the end for turning on flat surfaces and to reach recessed bolts. Box-ends, rather than open-end wrenches, should be used to break loose the fastener and to apply its final tightening.

The *combination wrench* has a box-type head on one end and an open-end head on the other, both accepting the same size fastener. It is available with a six- or twelve-point box end, and is a convenient, time-saving tool.

The *flare-nut wrench* is a special design meant to turn soft metal flare nuts which hold tubing in place. The jaws grip the nut around 270 degrees of its circumference to prevent distortion of the soft metal during removal or installation.

Allen wrenches are made to be used on headless screws provided with hexagonal holes for turning. The wrench has a six-sided L-shaped shank. The short end of the wrench is inserted into the screw recess for initial loosening; then it is removed, and the long end is inserted to turn out the screw.

Adjustable

The *adjustable wrench,* also known as a Crescent©, has a fixed jaw attached to the handle and a movable jaw positioned by means of a thumbscrew. It can accommodate a range of sizes and comes in different lengths depending on the capacity of the jaws. However, an adjustable wrench should never be used when the proper size of non-adjustable wrench is available; it is intended only for use on odd-size fasteners. Certain precautions must be observed when using an adjustable wrench: (1) never use a larger wrench than necessary; this can result in damaging the item or injuring the worker. (2) Be sure the jaws are snug against the faces of the nut. (3) Position the wrench as deep as possible in the throat of the wrench jaws. And (4) pull the handle toward the side having the adjustable jaw. **CAUTION: Never push on the handle of an non-adjustable wrench if it can be avoided.** The proper method of turning is by pulling towards you. If it is absolutely necessary to apply force by pushing, use the palm of your hand against the end of the handle, rather than gripping it to avoid smashed knuckles when the nut breaks loose.

An adjustable wrench is handy for odd-sized bolts, but it can slip unless it is securely tightened and turned in the direction indicated by the arrow.

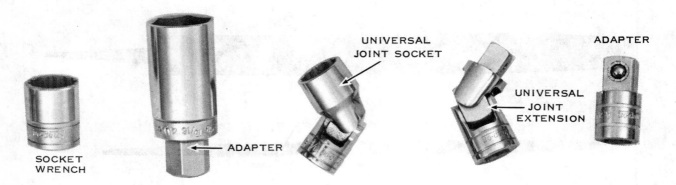

Different kinds of sockets and adapters for use with a ratchet, speed handle, or torque wrench.

SOCKET WRENCHES

Socket wrenches are available with a wide variety of handles and several styles of interchangeable sockets. Each socket is designed to turn only one size of fastener and can be obtained with either six or twelve points in the interior of the end accepting the bolt or nut. Sockets attach to the handle by means of a square hole in the other end, which fits onto the shank drive of the handle. They are held in place by a friction ball in the shank. Socket sets are available to match different sizes of drive handles, usually 1/4", 3/8", 1/2", and 3/4".

The standard socket has a shallow depth for maximum versatility in tight spaces. Another common style is the *deep socket,* used for removing nuts on protruding studs. The *universal, or "swivel" socket,* is used to turn nuts at difficult angles. In addition to these basic types, several special tools are designed to be used with the same handles. The *spark plug wrench* is a deep socket which slides over the spark plug and is partially lined with rubber to protect the ceramic insulator. Standard and Phillips screwdriver heads are also available with a square drive end for use with the handle assortment. For increased accessibility, all sockets and accessories can be fitted with various lengths of extensions. These components simply increase the vertical distance between the handle and the item being turned. A special case is the adapter which has a square hole of a given size on one end and a different size shank drive on the other. This converts the handle to accept a set of sockets of a different drive-end size. Adapters are available in all combinations of sizes.

HANDLES

The *reversible ratchet handle* is a general-purpose drive handle for socket wrench assemblies. A selector on the head is positioned to engage the desired turning direction, and the handle will swing freely in the opposite direction. This allows the fastener to be turned continuously without removing it from the socket. It is available in several lengths.

The *speed handle* is used much like a hand drill and saves time in removing fasteners that have already been loosened. The *hinge handle* (or breaker bar) has a flexible joint attaching a solid-shank drive to a long handle and is used for breaking loose tight nuts and bolts. When the handle reaches the limit of its travel, due to an obstruction, it can be swung on the hinge to its opposite position for additional turning. With the *sliding T-handle,* the drive head can be positioned at any point on an intersecting bar to obtain various degrees of offset, or used as a T-handle when at the center of the bar.

A ratchet handle is handy for removing or installing a bolt or nut, especially when working in tight quarters. The handle ratchets so that it can be moved in small increments.

A hinge handle provides great leverage to break loose a tight bolt or nut.

A sliding T-handle allows you to spin off a nut rapidly. It is especially advantageous when the adapter is centered so that an even torque can be applied, as when cutting out a piston ring ridge from the top of the cylinder bore.

An extension can be added between a ratchet and socket for working in tight quarters.

The ratchet handle has a latch which can be flipped to one side to change it from a tool for removing a bolt or to the other side for tightening a bolt.

Using a hinge handle with an attached socket provides great leverage.

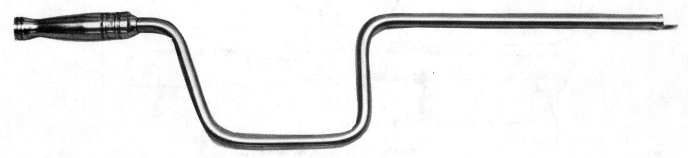

A speed handle is useful when a large number of bolts have to be installed or taken out. However, it does not provide leverage and so cannot be used on tight bolts until they are first loosened.

TORQUE WRENCHES

It is often necessary to tighten fasteners to an exact tension determined by the construction of the bolt (or nut) and its specific fastening role. To do this, the amount of twisting force (torque) applied must be measured with extreme accuracy. The *torque wrench* is a precision instrument designed for this purpose. It has a square drive to attach sockets, and a lever arrangement that may be any one of three kinds: deflecting-beam, dial-indicating, or audible-click type.

The *deflecting-beam type* has an indicator plate attached to the handle end of the beam and a long pointer attached to the drive end. When force is exerted on the handle, the beam bends and different indicating marks line up with the stationary pointer. This type is very durable and maintains its accuracy unless, through abuse, the pointer is bent away from its rest position at the "0" mark.

The basic construction of the *dial-indicating torque wrench* is the same as the deflecting-beam type. However, it is encased in a rigid frame, and its deflecting element rotates a pointer in a calibrated dial. The dial is turned to indicate "0" before force is applied.

An *audible-click type torque wrench* has an adjustable barrel at the handle end and a micrometer-type scale on the shank. The barrel is turned until it aligns with markings on the scale at the desired torque reading, then it is locked in place. When the proper amount of force is reached, a "break" occurs accompanied by an audible click. Whereas the first two kinds have indicators which must be read by sight, often difficult due to wrench position or close-working space, the audible-click type "signals" the correct amount of tor-

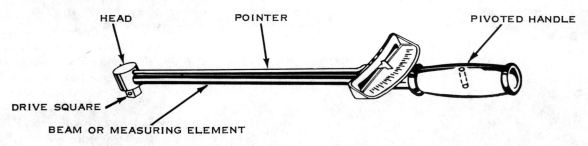

ROUND BEAM

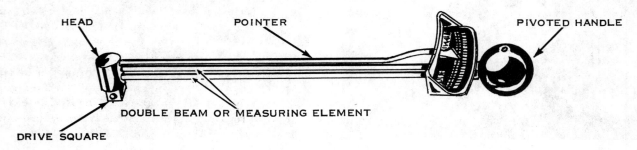

DOUBLE ROUND BEAM

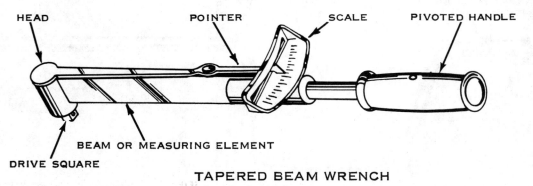

TAPERED BEAM WRENCH

Typical torque wrenches.

que. In addition, it has a ratcheting mechanism for tightening convenience. However, this type of wrench is delicate and requires special care. The barrel should be returned to the lowest torque setting on the scale when not in use; however, it must never be turned down below this setting.

Torque wrenches are calibrated in terms of units of force, usually inch-pounds or foot-pounds. In general, the units must be the same as those used in the work manual for the specific job. However, since twelve inch-pounds are equal to one foot-pound, a figure expressed in either unit can be easily converted to its value in the other. Some foreign manufacturers specify torque in meter-kilograms (m/kgs). Most torque wrench makers supply tables for converting these units; if this is unavailable, the figure can be derived by applying the following formula:

1 foot-pound = 0.14 meter-kilogram

Each torque wrench has a limited range of indicator marks or settings and must not be used to apply force beyond its maximum capacity. In choosing a torque wrench for a given job, it is best that the required torque value fall within the middle 80% of the torque wrench range, since accuracy tends to fall off at the top and bottom 10% of the scale. If the wrench is not used properly, the wrong amount of force can be applied, even though the indicator reading is correct. The length of the lever (handle) is taken into account when the calibrations are set. Therefore it is essential to grasp the center of the handle's gripping area; holding it too far towards either end will vary the torque value. Rapid or jerky motion will also result in error. Always pull the wrench smoothly.

Some jobs may necessitate the use of an adapter or extension on the torque wrench. A vertical adapter, that is one which extends straight downward from the square drive, does not affect the reading. However, if a horizontal adapter is used, it changes the effective length of the torque wrench, and a new value must be calculated taking this into account. The formula for this conversion is

$$TW = \frac{TA \times L}{L + A}$$

Where:

TA = torque desired according to specifications
L = length of wrench handle
A = length of horizontal adapter

If a torque specification is supplied for a given job, it must be assumed that the fasteners are critical. Special procedures must be followed to do the job correctly. Always torque the nut rather than the bolt-head when possible. If the fastener must be torqued at the bolt-head, tighten it towards the high end of the required range. When torquing two mating surfaces attached by a series of fasteners, follow the sequence specified for the job where available. If no diagram is provided, tighten the bolts in a circular pattern in pairs, first one, then the bolt 180 degrees opposite it, and so on. If the series is linear, tighten the center one (or two) first, then the bolts on each side of the one just tightened, working evenly from the center out to the ends. **CAUTION: Do not apply the full torque value on the initial tightening.** Snug all the fasteners first, then bring them to the desired torque in stages, tightening each one an additional amount with every stage. Never use a torque wrench on a bolt or nut that has already been tightened. The nut must first be backed off 1/2 turn, and then retightened to the proper torque.

Since the torque wrench is useless unless accurate, proper maintenance is essential. Dropping a torque wrench or using it as a loosening tool can damage it and result in incorrect indications. The tool should be tested and recalibrated at intervals to assure its precision.

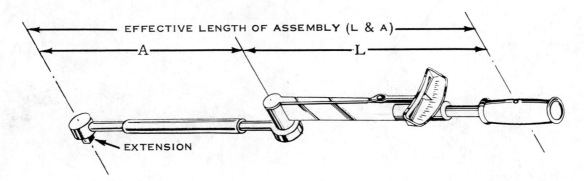

A torque wrench can be used with an extension to extend its range. For example, if the length of the extension is the same as the length of the torque wrench, you must multiply the torque reading on the scale to obtain the true value. Thus, a 100-ft-lb. wrench can be made to tighten bolts up to 200 ft-lbs. If you use an adapter half the length of the torque wrench, then multiply the reading by 1-1/2.

STEP TYPE FEELER GAUGE

Feeler gauges come in various thicknesses, as well as the step-type in which the blade is ground to two thicknesses. It can be used as a go/no-go gauge for adjusting the valve clearance, as shown here.

A compression gauge is essential to determine the mechanical condition of the engine.

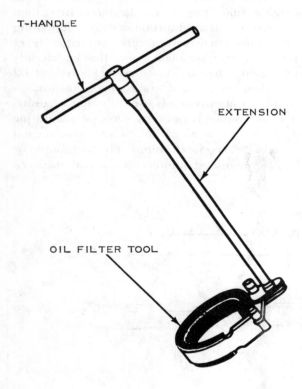

T-HANDLE

EXTENSION

OIL FILTER TOOL

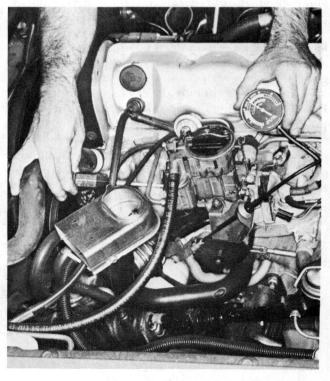

This special wrench is handy for removing and installing an oil filter without crushing the body of the filter.

A vacuum gauge is an excellent tool for adjusting the carburetor as well as making vacuum checks on your emission-control system.

TEST EQUIPMENT

Some test equipment will be extremely helpful in making basic repairs and, if you're going to do your own work, then you should invest in the following equipment: (1) compression gauge, (2) vacuum gauge, (3) volt-amp tester, (4) tach-dwell meter, and (5) timing light. The total cost for this equipment should not exceed $50.00 if you buy economy models. It can go to $125.00-$150.00 if you buy the better, more-accurate meters.

COMPRESSION TESTER

A compression tester is used to check the pressure in each cylinder of an engine. If the compression pressure is lower than normal in any or all cylinders the problem is mechanical, and a tune-up will not correct the problem.

The combustion chambers of an engine are sealed tight by piston rings and by the seated intake and exhaust valves. The pressure developed is expressed in psi (pounds per square inch).

The tip of the tester has a tire valve core in it to retain the highest reading. This pressure must be released before testing the next cylinder. On the least expensive testers, this is done by depressing the core, while on the better gauges, a button can be depressed to release the pressure.

An adequate compression tester should cost less than $10.00, and last many years.

VACUUM GAUGE

A vacuum gauge is essential to keep your engine in top tune. This gauge will allow you to power-tune your

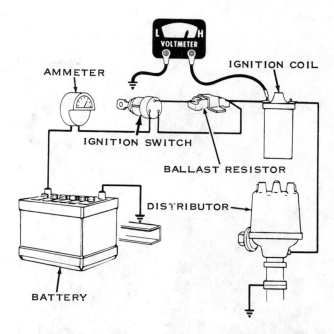

A voltmeter is handy for checking the voltages at various parts of the circuit. This inexpensive gauge is very important in any do-it-yourselfer's tool kit.

engine for maximum economy and performance. As discussed in Chapter 2, the actual reading of the vacuum gauge is not as important as the action of the needle and the relative readings obtained with the different adjustments made on the engine.

The least expensive vacuum gauge will run about $5.00 and do the job you want as well as one at the higher end of the price scale. In addition, it is possible to install a vacuum gauge in the dash to monitor the condition of the engine as well as your gas mileage driving skills.

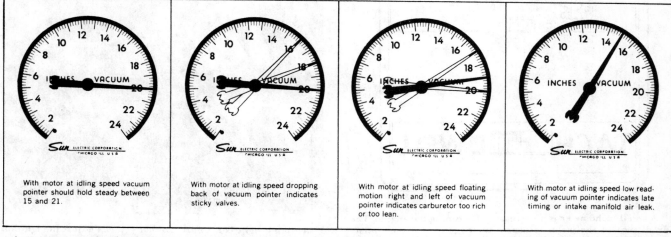

With motor at idling speed vacuum pointer should hold steady between 15 and 21.

With motor at idling speed dropping back of vacuum pointer indicates sticky valves.

With motor at idling speed floating motion right and left of vacuum pointer indicates carburetor too rich or too lean.

With motor at idling speed low reading of vacuum pointer indicates late timing or intake manifold air leak.

A vacuum gauge is a handy diagnostic tool for isolating troubles in an internal-combustion engine. The interpretations are shown under each of the gauge readings.

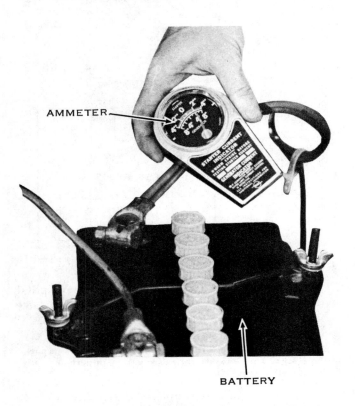

An induction-type ammeter can be used to measure the charging system output by holding the meter over the main wire to the battery with the engine running at a fast-idle speed.

VOLTAGE-AMPERAGE TESTER

A small hand-held volt-amp tester is a handy and inexpensive addition to your tool kit; it can simplify the checking of charging and starting circuits. In use, the tester is positioned over the cable of the circuit being tested while the alternator or starter is operated; the reading is read directly on the face of the tester. This test equipment can be purchased for less than $6.00.

TIMING LIGHT

A timing light is designed to "stop" the timing mark on a rotating part of the engine as the spark plug fires. It operates on the strobe light principle, where the light is on for only a fraction of a second as it is triggered by the firing of the spark plug to which it is attached. By hooking the pickup lead of the light to the #1 spark plug lead and running the engine at idle speed, the timing light will light each time #1 spark plug fires, which will freeze the action so that we can use this light to set the timing to the correct specifications.

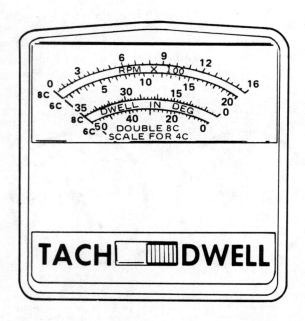

A dwell-tachometer is an accessory for tuning the engine. The dwell part of the meter measures the degrees that the contact points remain closed, and the tachometer can be used to determine engine speeds.

A timing light is a "must" so that you can adjust the ignition timing accurately. Every tool kit should include a good timing light.

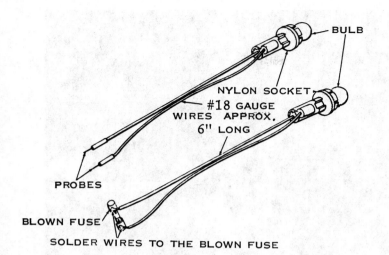

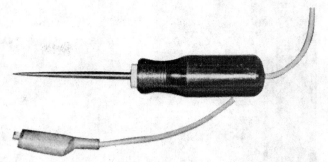

A continuity lamp that can be used for troubleshooting. The lamp will light when one probe is touched to a "hot" terminal and the other grounded.

A testing probe can be made with an old socket and a bulb. This device can be used to check terminals for current without blowing out the fuse. If a similar probe is soldered to a blown fuse (bottom), the fuse can be inserted into the fuse receptacle of a circuit for testing so that fuses are not blown out at each test.

Timing lights are available in a variety of price ranges from less than $3.00 for a small battery-operated type to more than $75.00 for a deluxe model that shows, in addition, the degrees advance of the vacuum and centrifugal advance units.

The lower-priced units generally have a dim light and are hard to see in daylight. In addition, the hook up usually means installing an adapter between the spark plug and the plug wire to attach the timing light. The more expensive versions have very bright strobe lights that are usable under difficult lighting conditions and have clamp-on attachments where the pickup is positioned around the spark plug lead without having to disconnect it. It is best to spend about 10-15 dollars and get an average quality timing light if your use is going to be minimal, but a more expensive unit, at a cost of 35-50 dollars, should be purchased if you intend to do a good deal of engine work.

CONTINUITY TEST LIGHT

A 12-volt test light is a handy tool to include in your tool kit because it will readily pin-point problems in the electrical system. A test light can be easily made with a lamp socket and two lengths of wire, as shown in the accompanying illustration, or it can be purchased at any automotive supply store at a cost of 2 or 3 dollars. A test lamp soldered to a blown fuse is handy for checking power to fuses and is an aid in locating shorts in the electrical circuits.

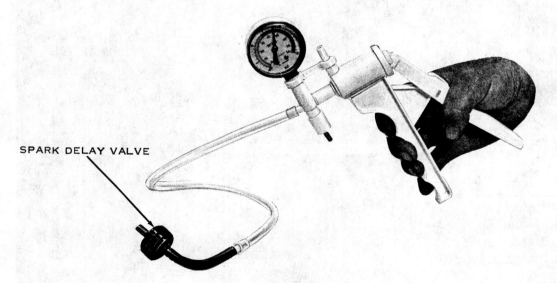

A Mityvac® hand-held vacuum pump kit is an extremely handy tool to test the vacuum-control valves on carburetors, distributors, air cleaners, emission-control valves, vacuum-switching valves, and transmission modulators. The tool can be purchased from Neward Enterprises, Inc., 9251 Archibald Ave., Cucamonga, CA 97130 at a prepaid cost of $20.00.

Top view of the Vega engine compartment, showing the placement of the various units.

2/troubleshooting

Troubleshooting must be a well thought-out procedure. To be successful with it, you must start by accurately determining the problem; then you must use a logical approach to arrive at the proper solution. Obviously, if the instructions are to be of maximum benefit as a guide, they must be fully understood and followed exactly.

ROADMAPS

When an engine does not start, the trouble must be localized to one of four general areas: cranking, ignition, fuel, and compression. Each of these areas must be systematically inspected until the trouble is located in one of them, and then detailed tests of that system must be made to isolate the part causing the starting problem.

To assist you, four roadmaps have been developed so that the testing program can be visualized in its entirety and the logical approach determined. ROADMAP ONE concerns EMERGENCY TROUBLESHOOTING, and it represents some quick and simple tests that can be made on the cranking, ignition, and fuel systems and the compression to determine which one requires further investigation. ROADMAP TWO deals with a detailed inspection of the various units which make up the cranking system. ROADMAP THREE details the various tests that are used for isolating ignition system troubles, while ROADMAP FOUR covers the tests that are used to pinpoint fuel system problems.

ROADMAP ONE—EMERGENCY TROUBLESHOOTING

In using this EMERGENCY TROUBLESHOOTING ROADMAP, proceed sequentially through each of the tests until a defect is uncovered. Then skip to the detailed testing procedure and roadmap for that system. For example, if, when using the EMERGENCY TROUBLESHOOTING ROADMAP, the first two systems, cranking and ignition, test OK, but the third test shows that there is trouble in the fuel system, then skip ROADMAPS TWO and THREE and proceed to the detailed tests under ROADMAP FOUR —FUEL SYSTEM TESTS.

①**CRANKING SYSTEM TEST:** Turn the ignition switch to the START position, and the starter should crank the engine at a normal rate of speed. If it does, it is an indication that the battery, cables, starting relay, and starter are in good condition and you should proceed with the testing program by going on to Test ② on the EMERGENCY TROUBLESHOOTING ROADMAP.

If the starter cranks the the engine slowly or doesn't crank it at all, the trouble is in the cranking system, and you should proceed to ROADMAP TWO— CRANKING SYSTEM TESTS for the detailed testing procedure that will help you uncover the starter trouble.

ROADMAP ONE — EMERGENCY TROUBLESHOOTING

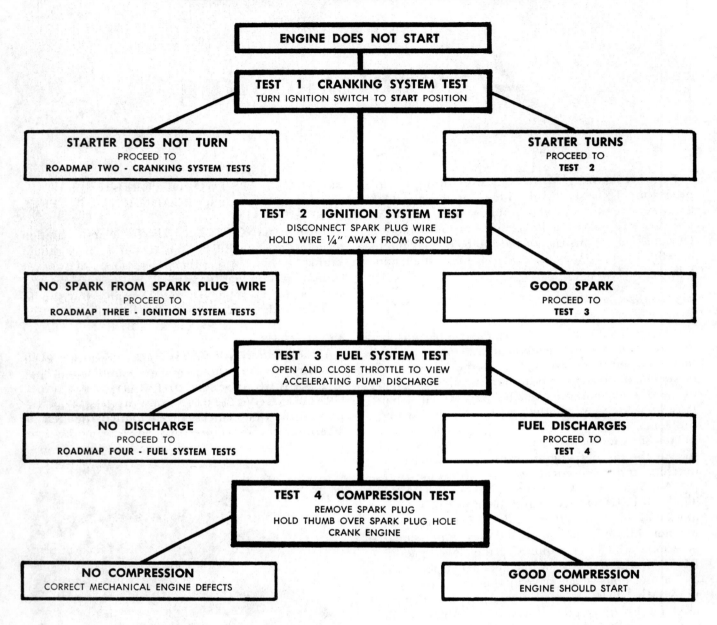

ENGINE DOES NOT START

TEST 1   CRANKING SYSTEM TEST
TURN IGNITION SWITCH TO **START** POSITION

STARTER DOES NOT TURN
PROCEED TO
ROADMAP TWO - CRANKING SYSTEM TESTS

STARTER TURNS
PROCEED TO
TEST 2

TEST 2   IGNITION SYSTEM TEST
DISCONNECT SPARK PLUG WIRE
HOLD WIRE ¼" AWAY FROM GROUND

NO SPARK FROM SPARK PLUG WIRE
PROCEED TO
ROADMAP THREE - IGNITION SYSTEM TESTS

GOOD SPARK
PROCEED TO
TEST 3

TEST 3   FUEL SYSTEM TEST
OPEN AND CLOSE THROTTLE TO VIEW
ACCELERATING PUMP DISCHARGE

NO DISCHARGE
PROCEED TO
ROADMAP FOUR - FUEL SYSTEM TESTS

FUEL DISCHARGES
PROCEED TO
TEST 4

TEST 4   COMPRESSION TEST
REMOVE SPARK PLUG
HOLD THUMB OVER SPARK PLUG HOLE
CRANK ENGINE

NO COMPRESSION
CORRECT MECHANICAL ENGINE DEFECTS

GOOD COMPRESSION
ENGINE SHOULD START

②**IGNITION SYSTEM TEST:** Disconnect a spark plug wire and hold it about 1/4" from a spark plug or ground. *NOTE: If the boot cannot be slid back, insert a screwdriver for the test.* Crank the engine with the ignition switch turned ON, and a good spark should jump from the wire or screwdriver to the spark plug or ground. If it does, go on to Test ③ on the EMERGENCY TROUBLESHOOTING ROADMAP.

If there is no spark or the spark is very weak, the trouble is in the ignition system, and you should proceed to ROADMAP THREE—IGNITION SYSTEM TESTS for the detailed testing procedure that will help you to uncover the ignition system trouble.

③**FUEL SYSTEM TEST:** This test is to determine whether or not there is fuel in the carburetor. Remove the air cleaner, and then look down into the throat of the carburetor. Open and close the throttle several times to see if fuel is squirted out of the pump jets as shown in the accompanying illustration. *NOTE: The top of the carburetor has been removed in this illustration for photographic purposes.*

HIGH TENSION LEAD

SPARK PLUG

②

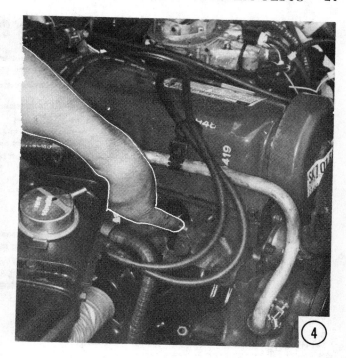

④

If fuel is discharged, it is an indication that there is fuel in the carburetor bowl and that the fuel system must be functioning properly; therefore, go on to Test ④ on the EMERGENCY TROUBLESHOOTING ROADMAP.

If no fuel is discharged from the pump jets, then the trouble is in the fuel system, and you should proceed to the detailed tests on ROADMAP FOUR—FUEL SYSTEM TESTS to isolate the trouble.

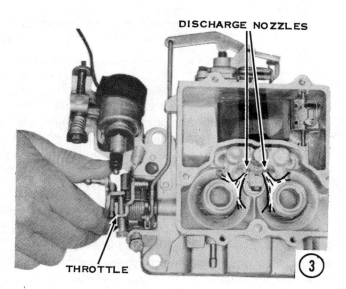

DISCHARGE NOZZLES

THROTTLE

③

④ **COMPRESSION TEST:** Remove a spark plug and hold your thumb over the spark plug hole. Have someone crank the engine. You should be able to feel pressure pulses as the piston comes up on each of the firing strokes. It is not necessary in this rough test to determine the exact pressure, as you only have to know whether or not there is compression. Strong pressure pulses indicate that the mechanical parts of the engine are sound.

ROADMAP TWO—CRANKING SYSTEM TESTS

This roadmap provides a sequential series of tests that can be made to isolate trouble in a cranking system that does not function properly. Obviously, an engine cannot be started properly if it cannot be turned fast enough to draw in a full charge of fuel, compress it properly, and have enough voltage reserve left for igniting the mixture. The cranking system includes the starter and drive, battery, starting relay, ignition switch, and the necessary wiring and cables to complete the various circuits. Vehicles with an automatic transmission have, in addition, a neutral-safety switch which prevents operation of the starter in all transmission selector positions except NEUTRAL or PARK.

Every cranking system problem falls into one of three situations: the starter does not turn at all, it spins rapidly but does not crank the engine, or it cranks the engine very slowly.

ROADMAP TWO — CRANKING SYSTEM TESTS

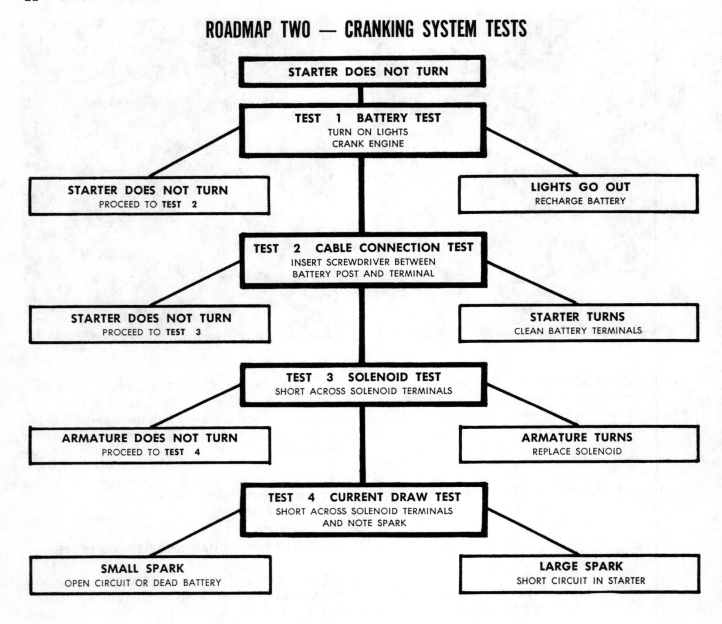

STARTER DOES NOT TURN

TEST 1   BATTERY TEST
TURN ON LIGHTS
CRANK ENGINE

STARTER DOES NOT TURN
PROCEED TO **TEST 2**

LIGHTS GO OUT
RECHARGE BATTERY

TEST 2   CABLE CONNECTION TEST
INSERT SCREWDRIVER BETWEEN
BATTERY POST AND TERMINAL

STARTER DOES NOT TURN
PROCEED TO **TEST 3**

STARTER TURNS
CLEAN BATTERY TERMINALS

TEST 3   SOLENOID TEST
SHORT ACROSS SOLENOID TERMINALS

ARMATURE DOES NOT TURN
PROCEED TO **TEST 4**

ARMATURE TURNS
REPLACE SOLENOID

TEST 4   CURRENT DRAW TEST
SHORT ACROSS SOLENOID TERMINALS
AND NOTE SPARK

SMALL SPARK
OPEN CIRCUIT OR DEAD BATTERY

LARGE SPARK
SHORT CIRCUIT IN STARTER

BATTERY TEST

①Turn on the headlights, and then crank the engine by turning the ignition switch to the START position. On a car with a normal electrical system, the lights will dim somewhat and the starter will crank the engine at a normal rate of speed. On a vehicle with a defect, there are several possible results, depending upon the amount of charge left in the battery or the condition of the cables. If the lights go out completely, or dim considerably, the battery is dead and must be recharged. If the starting relay clicks like a machine gun, the battery charge is too low to keep the relay engaged when the starter load is connected into the circuit. If the starter spins without cranking the engine, the drive is broken and the starter should be removed for repairs. If the headlights do not dim and the starter does not operate, then there is an open circuit. Go on to Test ②.

CABLE CONNECTION TEST

②If the starter is inoperative and the headlights do not dim, you should troubleshoot for a poor connection at the battery, starting relay, starter, or neutral-safety switch. The first test is to insert a screwdriver

blade tip between a battery post and cable while trying to crank the engine. If the starter now turns, the battery cable connection is corroded and must be disassembled, cleaned, and reassembled. Make this screwdriver test between each of the two battery terminals. *NOTE: This is a very common cause of trouble because of the corrosive nature of battery electrolyte.* If the

starter still does not turn with the screwdriver blade tip between the battery post and cable, try moving the transmission selector lever from NEUTRAL to PARK to see if the neutral-safety switch is out of adjustment or has a poor connection. Sometimes jiggling the selector lever will restore a connection temporarily so that the engine can be started. If the starter still does not turn, go on to Test ③.

SOLENOID TEST

③ The solenoid (sometimes called a starting relay) should be checked next by holding a pair of pliers so that the handles short across the two large cable terminals. **CAUTION: Make sure that the uninsulated pliers handles do not touch any other metallic part of the car, or sparks will fly.** You can use a heavy jumper cable or screwdriver in place of the pliers to short across the terminals. **CAUTION: Don't use thin wire, as it will get very hot under the heavy load and will burn your hands.** If the starter armature now turns, the trouble is in the relay, which should be checked to see if the circuit from the ignition switch to the starting relay is complete. Check out this circuit by holding a piece of wire from the heavy terminal (battery) on the starting relay to the small terminal, which is the energizing circuit wire from the ignition

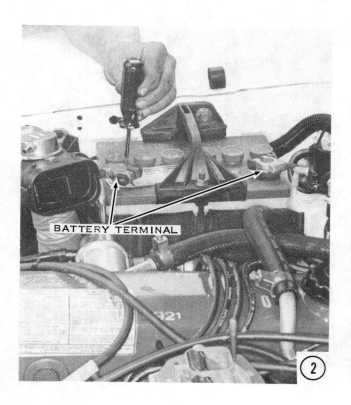

BATTERY TERMINAL

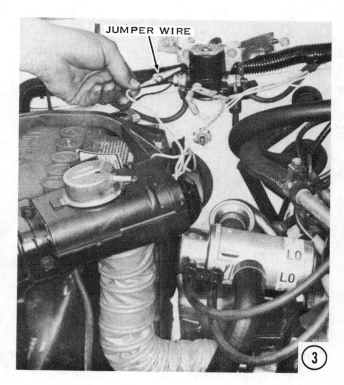

JUMPER WIRE

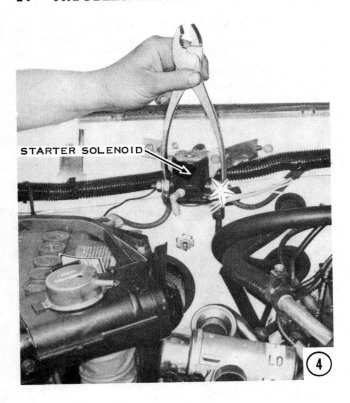

STARTER SOLENOID

④

switch. If the relay now operates, the trouble is in the circuit to the ignition switch. **CAUTION: The ignition switch must be turned to the START position in order to energize this circuit.** If the starter still does not turn, go on to Test ④

CURRENT DRAW TEST

④On some engines, it must be noted, shorting across the two large terminals of the starter relay (solenoid) will cause the starter armature to turn, but it may not crank the engine because the relay is not energized to pull the drive into engagement with the flywheel ring gear. In such a case, this test is still valuable in determining the current draw of the starter. With a normal starter, the size of the spark across the plier handles should be rather small. If you do get a large spark, it indicates that there is a short in the starter, which must be removed for service.

ROADMAP THREE—IGNITION SYSTEM TESTS

This roadmap provides a series of tests that can be used to isolate trouble in a conventional breaker-point type ignition system. You must make the tests and repairs in the sequence given below to arrive at a

solution to the problem. A large majority of starting troubles are caused by defects in the ignition system, and fully 90% of these troubles are the result of defective contact points.

IGNITION CIRCUIT TEST

① Disconnect the high-tension coil wire at the center of the distributor cap and hold it about 1/4″ from a good ground. *NOTE: If the rubber boot cannot be pushed back enough, insert a paper clip or use a screwdriver.* Turn the ignition switch to the START position and crank the engine. If there is no spark here, proceed to Test ②. If there is a good spark, and the trouble has been isolated to the ignition system, proceed to Test ⑤.

PRIMARY CIRCUIT TEST

② Remove the distributor cap, and then lift off the rotor. Turn the crankshaft until the contact points close. Use a small screwdriver to open and close the contact points with the ignition switch turned ON. With the high-tension coil wire held about 1/4″ from a ground, a good spark should jump to the ground if

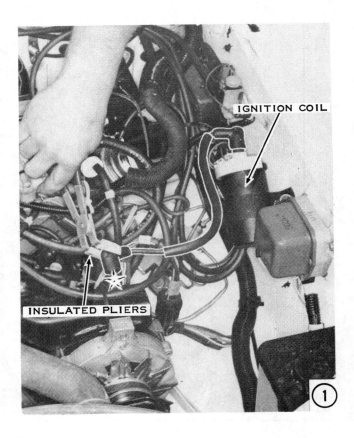

IGNITION COIL

INSULATED PLIERS

①

ROADMAP THREE — IGNITION SYSTEM TESTS

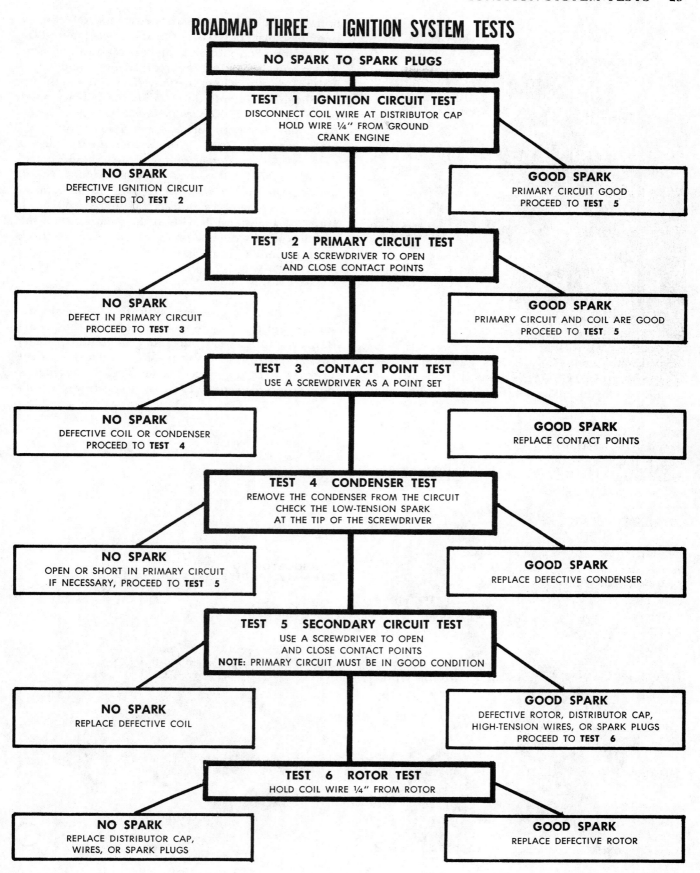

NO SPARK TO SPARK PLUGS

TEST 1 IGNITION CIRCUIT TEST
DISCONNECT COIL WIRE AT DISTRIBUTOR CAP
HOLD WIRE 1/4" FROM GROUND
CRANK ENGINE

NO SPARK
DEFECTIVE IGNITION CIRCUIT
PROCEED TO **TEST 2**

GOOD SPARK
PRIMARY CIRCUIT GOOD
PROCEED TO **TEST 5**

TEST 2 PRIMARY CIRCUIT TEST
USE A SCREWDRIVER TO OPEN
AND CLOSE CONTACT POINTS

NO SPARK
DEFECT IN PRIMARY CIRCUIT
PROCEED TO **TEST 3**

GOOD SPARK
PRIMARY CIRCUIT AND COIL ARE GOOD
PROCEED TO **TEST 5**

TEST 3 CONTACT POINT TEST
USE A SCREWDRIVER AS A POINT SET

NO SPARK
DEFECTIVE COIL OR CONDENSER
PROCEED TO **TEST 4**

GOOD SPARK
REPLACE CONTACT POINTS

TEST 4 CONDENSER TEST
REMOVE THE CONDENSER FROM THE CIRCUIT
CHECK THE LOW-TENSION SPARK
AT THE TIP OF THE SCREWDRIVER

NO SPARK
OPEN OR SHORT IN PRIMARY CIRCUIT
IF NECESSARY, PROCEED TO **TEST 5**

GOOD SPARK
REPLACE DEFECTIVE CONDENSER

TEST 5 SECONDARY CIRCUIT TEST
USE A SCREWDRIVER TO OPEN
AND CLOSE CONTACT POINTS
NOTE: PRIMARY CIRCUIT MUST BE IN GOOD CONDITION

NO SPARK
REPLACE DEFECTIVE COIL

GOOD SPARK
DEFECTIVE ROTOR, DISTRIBUTOR CAP,
HIGH-TENSION WIRES, OR SPARK PLUGS
PROCEED TO **TEST 6**

TEST 6 ROTOR TEST
HOLD COIL WIRE 1/4" FROM ROTOR

NO SPARK
REPLACE DISTRIBUTOR CAP,
WIRES, OR SPARK PLUGS

GOOD SPARK
REPLACE DEFECTIVE ROTOR

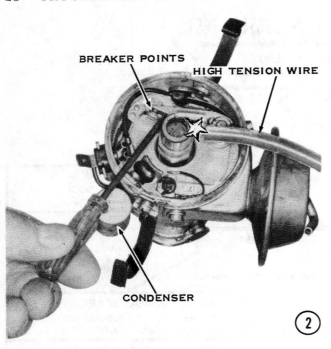

BREAKER POINTS

HIGH TENSION WIRE

CONDENSER

②

the primary circuit is OK. If it does, go on to Test ⑤. If there is no spark, there is a defect in the primary circuit, which you will be able to isolate by going on to Test ③.

CONTACT POINT TEST

③ With the high-tension wire held in the same posi-

tion, use the tip of the screwdriver and the contact point base plate of the distributor as a set of points. Do this by inserting an insulator between the points as shown and then sliding the screwdriver up and down, with the shaft touching the movable point and the tip making intermittent contact with the contact point base plate. *NOTE: This test substitutes the screwdriver for the contact points.* If you now get a spark from the high-tension wire to the ground, then the trouble is a defective set of contact points, which should be replaced. *NOTE: If the contact points are oxidized enough, the illustrated insulator is not required, as the oxidized surfaces form their own insulator.* If there is no spark from the high-tension wire to the ground, then the trouble can be a defective coil or condenser. To check out the condenser, go on to Test ④.

CONDENSER TEST

④ Condensers give very little trouble in general service, but there is always the possibility that a condenser might short out and ground the primary circuit. There is also the possibility that one of the primary wires or connections inside of the distributor might short to ground. The most accurate way to test a

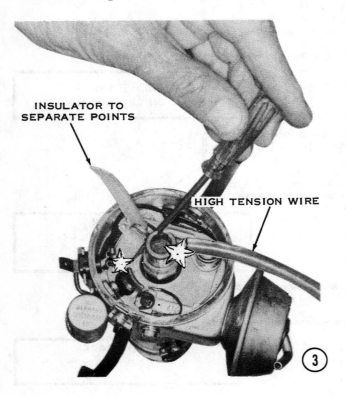

INSULATOR TO SEPARATE POINTS

HIGH TENSION WIRE

③

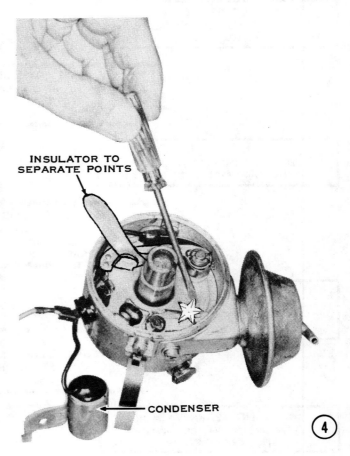

INSULATOR TO SEPARATE POINTS

CONDENSER

④

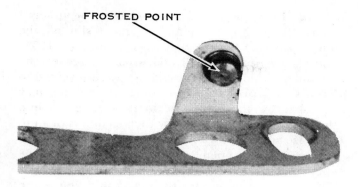

FROSTED POINT

Contact points with a frosted appearance are operating properly.

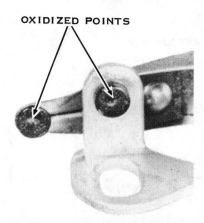

OXIDIZED POINTS

Contact points that have black oxidized surfaces cannot conduct electricity properly and must be replaced.

condenser is with a tester manufactured for that purpose. For emergency troubleshooting, however, it is possible to check the condenser and the primary circuit insulation for a short by removing the condenser from the system, and then making a few tests with a screwdriver. **CAUTION: Make sure that the metallic case of the condenser does not touch any part of the distributor while making the following tests.**

With an insulator between the contact points, slide the blade of a screwdriver up and down, with the shaft making contact with the movable contact point and the tip of the screwdriver making intermittent contact with the contact point base plate. This time check the low-tension spark between the screwdriver tip and the contact point base plate. You should have a spark here

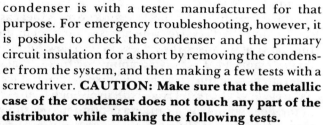

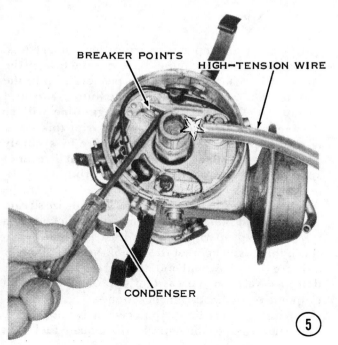

BREAKER POINTS   HIGH-TENSION WIRE

CONDENSER

⑤

indicating that the primary circuit is complete through the neutral-safety switch, primary of the ignition coil, ballast resistor, and primary wiring inside of the distributor. Reconnect the condenser and, if you **now** get no low-tension spark, the condenser is shorting the circuit to ground, and it should be replaced.

If you have no low-tension spark at the screwdriver tip without the condenser in the circuit, it indicates that there is no current flowing to this point, or that there is a short circuit to ground. In this case, it is necessary to check back along the primary circuit wiring to find the defective unit which is open circuited or shorted to ground. Check by using a jumper wire and shorting each unit in turn to ground, just as you did at the movable contact point. The defective unit is the one in which you get a low-tension spark at one of its terminals and no spark at the other. As mentioned before, this can be at the ignition switch, the primary of the ignition coil, the ballast resistor, or at the primary wires in the distributor.

If the condenser and the primary circuit are OK, but the engine still does not start, the trouble can be in the secondary circuit. Proceed to Test ⑤.

SECONDARY CIRCUIT TEST

⑤ **The secondary circuit cannot be tested by emergency troubleshooting techniques unless the primary circuit has tested OK so far or has been repaired as the defects have been uncovered.** If the primary circuit tests OK, use the same test procedures as in Test ②. Hold the high-tension wire about 1/4" from a good ground while using a screwdriver to open and close the contact points. A spark at the high-tension wire indicates that the ignition coil is good but, if the engine still does not start, the trouble must be somewhere else in the secondary circuit: in the rotor,

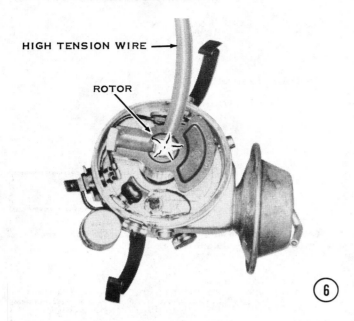

HIGH TENSION WIRE →

ROTOR

⑥

distributor cap, high-tension wires, or spark plugs. To test the rotor, go on to Test ⑥ .

If no spark occurs from the high-tension wire to ground, the ignition coil is defective and should be replaced.

ROTOR TEST

⑥ Replace the rotor on the distributor shaft. Hold the high-tension coil wire about 1/4″ from the rotor spring, and then crank the engine with the ignition switch turned ON. If a spark jumps to the rotor, it is shorted to ground and should be replaced. If no spark jumps to the rotor, its insulation is good and the trouble, if it still exists, must be found by inspecting the distributor cap for cracks, the high-tension wires for poor insulation, and the spark plugs for defects.

ROADMAP FOUR—FUEL SYSTEM TESTS

This roadmap details a series of tests to localize trouble in the fuel system. It is seldom that starting trouble can be caused by the carburetor itself. It is possible for an automatic choke to stick in the open position and cause starting trouble, but this can be overcome to some extent by pumping the accelerator pedal to discharge some fuel into the intake manifold. If the automatic choke sticks in the shut position, the engine will flood, and this will make it difficult to start. Depressing the accelerator pedal to the floorboard will cause the unloader linkage to open the choke enough for starting the engine in this case.

On the other hand, the fuel system can be a serious source of trouble when hard starting is encountered with a hot engine. When a hot engine is shut off, the temperature within the fuel bowl may rise to 150° - 200°F., and the fuel will boil which increases the pressure considerably. All carburetors are vented to bypass this pressure, but some of the fuel may percolate over the high-speed nozzle and overflow into the intake manifold. This raw fuel needs lots of air to vaporize and dilute it for a combustible mixture. The only remedy is to open the throttle wide and crank the engine until it draws in enough air to start. **CAUTION: Under no circumstances should you pump the accelerator pedal, or you will be adding fuel through the accelerating jets to compound the trouble.**

Too much fuel can also enter the intake manifold, causing hot starting trouble if the needle valve and seat assembly is leaking. After an engine is shut off, the residual pressure in the fuel line forces excess fuel past the leaking needle valve, which raises the level in the fuel bowl and causes the excess to overflow into the intake manifold. Excessive amounts of fuel can also enter an engine due to a "heavy" float, which reduces its buoyancy. The result is an excessively high fuel level in the float bowl, which causes a continuous overflow. Generally, fuel system troubles are caused by a plugged filter, defective fuel pump, or leak in the suction line from the fuel pump to the fuel tank. Oddly enough, the great majority of starting troubles in which the defect has been traced to the fuel system can be found to result from an empty fuel tank.

FUEL PUMP TEST

① Connect a jumper wire from the primary (distributor) side of the ignition coil to ground to keep the engine from starting. It is also possible to pull the high-tension wire out of the distributor cap and ground it. **CAUTION: Because gasoline will be flowing in the engine compartment during this test, it is very important to guard against fire by securely grounding the high-tension wire so that it cannot spark.** Disconnect the fuel line to the carburetor, position a container so that the discharged fuel can be caught, and then crank the engine. A good-size stream of fuel should pulse out of the line if the fuel pump is functioning properly. Catch at least 10-15 pulses to check the possibility that the size of the stream might decrese, which would indicate a restricted line or defective valve in the gas tank cap on vehicles with evaporative emission-control systems.

In case the fuel line is plugged, it is possible for the fuel stream to stop entirely. If adequate fuel flows

ROADMAP FOUR — FUEL SYSTEM TESTS

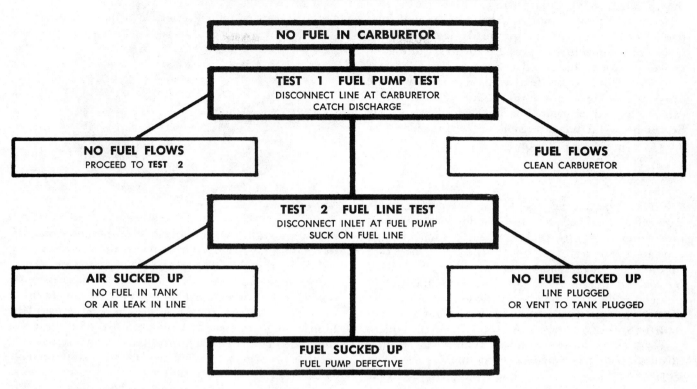

NO FUEL IN CARBURETOR

TEST 1   FUEL PUMP TEST
DISCONNECT LINE AT CARBURETOR
CATCH DISCHARGE

NO FUEL FLOWS
PROCEED TO **TEST 2**

FUEL FLOWS
CLEAN CARBURETOR

TEST 2   FUEL LINE TEST
DISCONNECT INLET AT FUEL PUMP
SUCK ON FUEL LINE

AIR SUCKED UP
NO FUEL IN TANK
OR AIR LEAK IN LINE

NO FUEL SUCKED UP
LINE PLUGGED
OR VENT TO TANK PLUGGED

FUEL SUCKED UP
FUEL PUMP DEFECTIVE

FUEL HOSE

①

HOSE

②

to the carburetor, and the engine still does not start, there is the possibility that a strainer in the carburetor inlet or fuel tank is plugged, or that the fuel inlet needle valve and seat are gummed together, which would not allows fuel to pass. Or it can be automatic choke trouble, as discussed before.

If no fuel flows, a defective fuel pump can be the cause or the line from the fuel tank to the fuel pump can be plugged or leaking air. In this case, no fuel will flow. Check out these possibilities by proceeding to Test ②.

FUEL LINE TEST

② The fuel line can be tested by sucking on it. Because of the inaccessibility of the line, it is necessary to disconnect it at the fuel pump and attach a rubber tube to it. Suck on the tube, and one of three conditions will occur: (1) air will be sucked up, (2) fuel will be sucked up, or (3) the fuel or vent line will be plugged and little or no fuel will be sucked up. If air is sucked up, there is a leak in the suction line from the tank to the fuel pump or there is no fuel in the tank. If fuel is sucked up, then the line is clear and the trouble must be in the fuel pump. If little or no fuel can be sucked up, then the suction line is plugged, the strainer in the fuel tank is clogged, or the vent to the fuel tank is not open. Without an open vent to the fuel tank, suction builds up and keeps the fuel from flowing to the fuel pump.

SPARK PLUGS

①By way of confirmation, carefully examine the spark plugs you removed from the engine. Line them up in the order of removal so that you can "read" the firing end of the spark plugs and thereby ascertain what has been going on in each cylinder of the engine.

②This is the way a normal spark plug should look after use. The deposits should be dry and powdery. The hard deposits inside the shell indicate that the engine is starting to use some oil, but the condition is

not serious. The most important evidence, however, is the light gray color of the porcelain, which is an indication that this spark plug has been running at the correct temperature. This means that the spark plug is one with the correct heat range and that the air-fuel mixture is correct. The combustion temperature is high enough to raise the temperature of the spark plug porcelain so that it burns off the small amount of oil that is normally present in the combustion chamber during the firing period.

③This black, sooty condition on both the shell and porcelain is caused by an excessively rich air-fuel mixture, both at low and high speeds. The rich mixture lowers the combustion temperature so that the spark plug does not run hot enough to burn off the deposits.

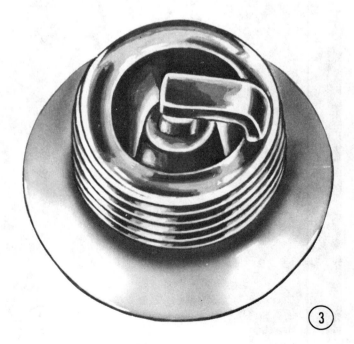

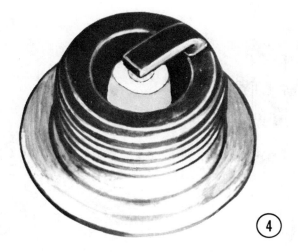

④ If the deposits are formed only on the shell, it is an indication that the low-speed air-fuel mixture is too rich. With a normal mixture at high speeds, the combustion chamber temperature is high enough to burn off the deposits on the insulator.

⑤ This dark insulator, with very few deposits, indicates that the spark plug is running too cool. This condition can be caused by low compression or by using a spark plug of an incorrect heat range. If the condition is isolated to one cylinder, low compression can be suspected. If all of the spark plugs look like this, they are probably of a heat range that is too cold.

⑥ Heavy carbon-like deposits are an indication of excessive oil consumption. This can result from worn piston rings, worn valve guides, or from a valve seal that is either worn or incorrectly installed.

⑦ This wet, fouled spark plug is not firing. Any combustion would have dried off the deposits until the spark plug looked like the one in the preceding picture. This fouled condition of the spark plug can be caused by the wet oily deposits on the insulator shorting the high-tension spark to ground inside the shell. Or the condition can be caused by ignition trouble, in which case no high-tension pulse is delivered to the plug to fire it.

⑧

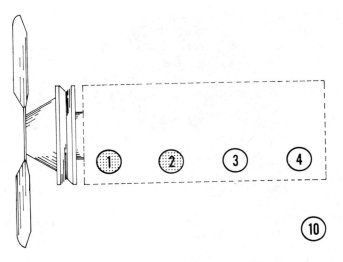

⑩

⑧Overheating and pre-ignition are indicated by a dead white or gray insulator, which is generally blistered. The electrode gap wear rate will be considerably more than normal and, in the case of pre-ignition, will actually cause the electrodes to melt as the ones in this spark plug did. Overadvanced ignition timing, detonation from using a fuel of too low octane rating, an excessively lean air-fuel mixture, or cooling system troubles can cause overheating.

⑨Excessive electrode wear results in a wide gap and, more important, the carbonized electrode surfaces form a high-resistance gap path for the spark to jump across. This condition will cause the engine to misfire under acceleration. If all of the spark plugs are in this condition, it can cause an increase in fuel consumption and a restricted top speed, especially so if the rest of the ignition system is not operating at maximum efficiency. The remedy, of course, is to replace the

spark plugs. However, it is possible to use this spark plug if the electrodes are filed to remove the resistance surfaces and then regapped to the correct specifications.

⑩If you find two adjacent spark plugs fouled, check for a blown cylinder head gasket or for incorrect connections of the high-tension wires to these plugs.

⑨

The spark plug insulator must be cleaned periodically of all foreign matter because this becomes a leakage path for the high-tension voltage to cross over.

EMISSION-CONTROL SYSTEMS

There are three kinds of emissions that must be controlled on a modern engine: crankcase, exhaust, and evaporative. The troubleshooting of these systems will be covered in Chapter 4.

FUEL AND IGNITION SYSTEM PROBLEMS

ROUGH ENGINE IDLE

A rough idle can be caused by any of numerous conditions and maladjustments of the engine. This problem is best approached by first doing a complete engine tune-up to take care of such possible ignition conditions as points and/or spark plugs burned, fouled, or improperly gapped, or the ignition timing set too far advanced or retarded.

Other engine conditions which can cause a rough idle are intake manifold air leaks, uneven compression, sticking valves, and troubles in the fuel system

Engine misfire is generally caused by ignition system defects. Worn-out spark plugs with corroded electrodes and an excessively wide gap can cause the engine to misfire on acceleration.

which can affect the idle mixture. These troubles include a high fuel level, a heavy float, a leaking needle valve and seat, a leaking power valve diaphragm, a

When the dirty insulator gets wet, flashover occurs, and the cylinder misfires. This condition causes hard starting in wet weather.

PLIERS

To check out the PCV system, clamp the hose shut, and the engine speed should drop about 60 rpm. CAUTION: If the hose is old, it is better to pull if off the valve and cover the end with your finger. Clamping off an old hose will often loosen particles from the brittle inside walls, which may then plug the valve.

restricted air filter element, an automatic choke malfunction, and poor idle mixture and/or speed adjustments.

With the advent of exhaust, evaporative, and crankcase emission control systems, the modern engine induction system has been designed with a calibrated amount of air leaking into the intake manifold. This is necessary to vent the crankcase of unburned vapors. Also, some of the late-model engines are passing intake manifold vacuum through calibrated bleeds to operate diaphragms for controlling valves in the power brakes, hand brake releasing mechanisms, heater and air conditioning door systems, and vacuum motors for regulating the temperature of the incoming air in the thermostatically controlled air cleaner. If an excessively large amount of air is bleeding into the intake manifold through a leak in one of the air hoses, by an improper vacuum connection, or by an incorrectly installed part with an improper air bleed, the result will be a rough engine idle. The only way to isolate troubles of this type is to pinch off one at a time the hoses leading to the intake manifold and to note the effect on a vacuum gauge and tachometer. In the case of a vent, such as the one to the PCV valve in the manifold, pinching it off should cause a drop in engine speed of about 60 rpm. If there is no drop then the PCV valve is plugged, and the calibrated air bleed is shut. If the drop is excessive, the PCV valve has an incorrectly calibrated air bleed.

Check for a vacuum leak in each of the other vacuum systems by pinching off each hose in turn and noting the effect of so doing on the vacuum gauge and the tachometer.

On engines with an Exhaust-Gas Recirculation (EGR) system, a valve that is stuck open can cause a very rough idle. See Chapter 4 for testing this system.

INCONSISTENT ENGINE IDLE SPEED

The most common cause of an inconsistent idle speed is sticking or binding in the throttle linkage and/or the automatic transmission throttle control and kickdown linkages. It is also possible for the carburetor throttle shaft to be either sticking or loose on the throttle lever, or to have a loose throttle plate which can shift in the body and cause this trouble.

If the carburetor is equipped with a dashpot, check the operation of the plunger for sticking or binding. Clean the end of the plunger and the plunger seat on the throttle lever. A dirty and gummy plunger and seat can cause a sticking condition.

EXCESSIVE FUEL CONSUMPTION

This condition can be the result of poor driving habits, a faulty condition of the vehicle, or inefficient engine operation. Quite often, it is a combination of all three. If the fuel consumption has been normal for some time, and then suddenly increases, defects other than the driver are indicated.

Preliminary checking should include an inspection for correct tire inflation, dragging brakes, or a fuel leak. Check for a fuel leak both with the engine running and not running. Fuel leaks show up more readily between the fuel pump and carburetor when the fuel pump is operating. On the other hand, a leak between the fuel pump and tank will not be evident when the fuel pump is operating. This is due to the vacuum that is created on the suction side of the system, which will keep the fuel from leaking.

Ignition performance can have a decided effect on gasoline mileage. Some of the factors which can adversely affect mileage are fouled or burned spark plugs, ignition system defects, and late ignition timing.

If the other factors check out or have been corrected and the fuel consumption is still excessive, then the carburetor must be overhauled. Check the power valve and the needle valve and seat for leaking. Care must be taken when making the adjustments which affect fuel consumption, such as those to the float level, automatic choke, vacuum-kick, and power valve. When checking the operation of the automatic choke, make sure that the heat tube is open and that the vacuum system works properly. Be sure to clean the filter element of the air cleaner.

ACCELERATION STUMBLE

A stumble on acceleration is generally caused by insufficient delivery of fuel during a stroke of the

If you get water in the gas tank through condensation or through the gas station hose, the filter at the end of the pickup tube in your gas tank will swell and restrict the flow of fuel, resulting in the carburetor running out of fuel during high-speed driving.

THROTTLE CONTROL LEVER   CHOKE VALVE

One way to check the air-fuel mixture is to speed up the engine and restrict the flow of air through the carburetor. This can be done by closing the choke valve partially or restricting the opening with the palm of your hand. If the mixture is too lean, restricting the air will cause the engine to speed up. If the mixture is too rich, restricting the air will cause the engine to slow down.

TIMING LIGHT

Improperly adjusted ignition timing has a decided effect on the performance of the engine, emissions, and gasoline mileage. Use a timing light to adjust the ignition timing to specifications.

A cracked fuel pump diaphragm (arrow) causes a leak of fuel into the engine crankcase, and this lowers the gas mileage considerably. You can smell the gasoline in the oil on the dipstick. It is necessary to replace the fuel pump, because they cannot be repaired on late-models.

carburetor accelerator pump. This deficiency could be the result of too short a pump stroke or leaking accelerator pump check valves. The remedy is to remove the carburetor, clean it thoroughly (paying particular attention to the parts of the acceleration system), and then reassemble it. Be sure to make the bench adjustments, paying special attention to those which are concerned with the parts of the accelerating circuit.

It is quite possible that other systems can cause a stumble on acceleration. If the manifold heat control valve is stuck in the open position, it can cause a stumble when the engine is warming up. Trouble in the ignition system secondary circuit will also cause a stumble, but this condition may better be referred to as a miss on acceleration.

ENGINE SURGE

A surging engine is one which runs as if the load on the car were being intermittently increased and decreased. This is best detected while maintaining a constant car speed. Surging can take place at any car speed. However, surging generally is detected in the mid-speed range and may not be in evidence at other speeds.

In general, surging is caused by a lean fuel condition, resulting from dirt or a restriction in the fuel system. A defective fuel pump or any condition that does not permit a normal flow of fuel mixture into the intake manifold can cause surging. Another cause, though quite remote, is a distributor vacuum-advance system that may be hunting or constantly changing the spark timing.

POOR HIGH-SPEED PERFORMANCE

This problem can be caused by either the fuel system or the ignition system. A fuel system that does not supply adequate fuel for high-speed operation usually causes the engine to cut out entirely as car speed is increased. As the car slows down, a speed will be reached where operation will again be normal.

An ignition problem is usually evidenced by the engine misfiring during acceleration, but it is possible for a malfunctioning ignition system, without sufficient reserve, to pass out at higher engine speeds. Generally, the feeling is one of rough engine operation rather than of a complete cutting out.

Other conditions which should be checked for poor high-speed performance are preignition and over-advanced ignition timing. Fuel system troubles include the following: a restricted air cleaner, restricted exhaust system, defective fuel pump, clogged fuel filter in the line, and partially clogged vent in the gas tank.

POOR LOW-SPEED PERFORMANCE

If the engine performance is sluggish at low speeds only and high-speed operation is normal, the fuel supply system must be operating satisfactorily. The spark plugs, distributor contact points, compression, and exhaust system must also be normal.

If the trouble occurs only at low speeds, it can be in the low-speed or range circuits of the carburetor, in an incorrect low-speed calibration of the distributor, or in a failure to set the ignition timing to specifications. Also, check the vacuum advance diaphragm of the distributor for a leak and passage in the carburetor to be sure it is open. An automatic transmission with a defective one-way clutch will aslo cause a loss of performance at low speeds.

ENGINE STALLING

When an engine starts normally but fails to keep running, the trouble is probably in the fuel system. If the temperature is below freezing, water in the fuel line or carburetor may have frozen, thereby restricting the flow of fuel. Stalling when cold can be caused by the fast-idle speed being too low, the choke plate sticking, an incorrect setting of the choke cover, or the choke plate pull-down adjustment being incorrect.

If a hot engine stalls and cannot be restarted, the trouble can be caused by vapor lock. Such an engine cannot usually be restarted until the vaporized fuel has condensed back into a liquid. If the hot engine stalling condition is general, the trouble can be caused by the idle speed being too low, the idle mixture being incorrectly adjusted, or the choke plate sticking partially closed.

Under certain weather conditions, an engine will run normally, both when it is cold and when it is hot, but will stall at idle or near-idle speeds during the engine warm-up period. This condition can be caused by carburetor icing, and it is most likely to occur when winter-grade gasoline (more volatile than summer grade) is used and when the atmospheric temperature ranges from 30° to 60°F. at relative humidities above 65%.

When carburetor icing occurs, moisture is drawn from the air passing through the carburetor. It condenses and forms ice on the throttle plates and the surrounding throttle body. When the throttle is almost completely closed for idling, this ice tends to bridge the gap between the throttle plate and body, thereby cutting off the air supply and causing the engine to stall. Opening the throttle for restarting breaks the ice bridge but does not eliminate the possibility of further stalling until the engine and carburetor are warmed up.

In some instances, an engine will run normally in all phases of its operation but will stall just as the car is brought to a stop. This condition usually is confined to cars equipped with an automatic transmission. Most cars so equipped have an anti-stall dashpot attached to the carburetor to control the closing rate of the throttle plates. A dashpot that is out of adjustment or one that is defective generally causes this type of engine stalling. However, if the stalling is accompanied by engine roughness, a contributing cause could be a high

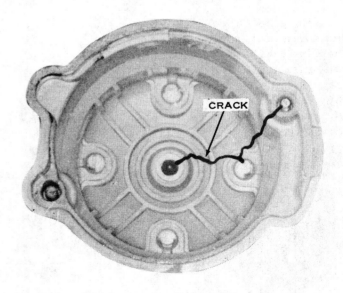

A cracked distributor cap can cause the engine to misfire or stop entirely if the crack runs from the center connector to any grounded point.

carburetor fuel level due to a leaking needle valve and seat or to a heavy float, or a combination of dashpot adjustment and high fuel level.

ENGINE STARTS HARD

When an engine is hard to start when cold but starts easily when hot, the trouble is usually caused by defects in the ignition system or by a lean supply of fuel through the carburetor. A choke coil that is set too lean, sticking choke plate, and binding choke linkage are the most common causes of this particular lean condition. If this cold-starting problem exists only when the temperature is below freezing, the most likely cause is water in the carburetor which freezes and restricts the flow of fuel.

Hard starting of a hot engine generally is caused by an oversupply of fuel through the carburetor, which results in engine flooding. The more common causes of flooding are a choke coil that is set too rich, sticking choke plate, and binding choke linkage. Flooding also can be caused by a dirty, worn, or leaking float valve needle and seat or by a sticking float. Another cause of flooding is percolation, whereby the fuel in the carburetor bowl boils over into the intake manifold. This condition, when it exists, is most likely to occur shortly after a hot engine is shut off. High fuel pump pressure occasionally contributes to flooding.

When an engine can be started, but keeps running only when the ignition key is held in the START position, the trouble is in the ballast resistor or its circuit.

ENGINE MISFIRE

In most instances, this condition is caused by spark plug troubles; the plugs can be fouled, have broken insulators, be improperly gapped, or offer high resistance at the electrodes, or the wrong type may have been installed. The condition can also be caused by other defects in the ignition system secondary circuit—in the ignition coil, rotor, distributor cap, or high-tension wiring. If the condition can be traced to the primary circuit, then the trouble can be burned contact points, incorrect point dwell, incorrect point spring tension, a defective condenser, or a corroded low-tenision wiring connection.

Hardened and cracked spark plug boots allow moisture to seep onto the spark plug insulator, and this can cause hard starting and flashover.

TROUBLESHOOTING MECHANICAL ENGINE CONDITIONS

Good compression is the key to engine performance. An engine with worn piston rings, burned valves, or a blown gasket cannot be made to perform satisfactorily until the mechanical defects are repaired. Generally, a compression gauge is used to determine the cranking pressure within each cylinder. However, today's big displacement engines generally have considerable valve overlap, and the resulting compression reading may be much lower than the manufacturer's specifications of around 150-170 psi. It is entirely possible to obtain a reading as low as 120 psi on a modern engine which is in good mechanical condition. Such an engine is said to "exhale" at cranking speed, even though everything is perfectly normal at operating speeds.

To make a compression test, remove the spark plugs and lay them out in the order of removal. This is extremely important so that you can "read" the firing end of each spark plug. After the spark plugs are removed, insert the rubber adapter of a compression

COMPRESSION GAUGE

For an engine to idle smoothly, it must have compression that does not vary over 15 psi for any cylinder. The actual reading is not as important as the amount of variance between cylinders.

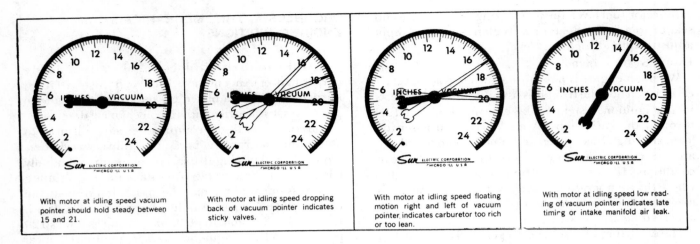

With motor at idling speed vacuum pointer should hold steady between 15 and 21.

With motor at idling speed dropping back of vacuum pointer indicates sticky valves.

With motor at idling speed floating motion right and left of vacuum pointer indicates carburetor too rich or too lean.

With motor at idling speed low reading of vacuum pointer indicates late timing or intake manifold air leak.

A vacuum gauge is a handy diagnostic tool for isolating troubles in an internal-combustion engine. The interpretations are shown under each of the gauge readings.

gauge into one cylinder and have a helper crank the engine. **CAUTION: Ground the primary terminal of the coil to prevent damage to it. CAUTION: The throttle valve and choke must be in the wide-open position in order to obtain maximum readings.** Crank the engine through several revolutions to obtain the highest reading on the compression gauge, or record an equal number of pulses for each cyliner.

The significance in a compression test is the variation in pressure readings between cylinders. As long as this variation is within 20-30 psi, the engine is normal. If a greater variation exists, then the low-reading cylinder should be checked by making a cylinder leak test to determine where the trouble lies. You can do this by introducing compressed air into the combustion chamber through the spark plug hole with the piston at TDC, firing position. If an exhaust valve is defective, you will be able to hear air escaping through the tailpipe. If an intake valve is burned, air will escape through the intake manifold, and it can be heard through the top of the carburetor.

VACUUM GAUGE

A vacuum gauge is a relatively inexpensive piece of test equipment that can be very handy in isolating trouble in an internal-combustion engine. As with a compression gauge, a numerical reading cannot be counted on. Instead, relative readings and typical actions of the needle provide clues to some types of troubles.

Normal idle vacuum in the intake manifold ranges from 15 to 22" Hg. On later-model engines, lower and

less steady intake manifold vacuum readings are becoming increasingly common because of the greater use of high-lift cams and the increase in the amounts of valve overlap. Also, altitude affects a vacuum gauge reading. In mountainous areas, a vacuum gauge will read about one inch lower for each 1,000' of elevation above sea level. It is also possible for a change in barometric pressure to affect a vacuum gauge reading, which emphasizes the fact that it is much more important to watch the needle action than its actual reading. With experience, you will come to recognize easily such conditions as sticking valves, a tight valve lash adjustment, or a restriction in the exhaust system.

This is part of an exhaust pipe that collapsed. This kind of defect can be checked with a vacuum gauge by accelerating the engine and allowing it to return to idle. A restricted exhaust will cause a momentary stop in the return of the needle when the throttle is closed quickly.

ENGINE NOISES

Noises are generally referred to as knock, slaps, clicks, and squeaks; they are caused by loose bearings, pistons, gears, and other moving parts of the engine. In general, the most common types of noises are either synchronized to engine speed or to one-half engine speed. Those that are timed to engine speed are sounds that have to do with the crankshaft, rods, pistons, and pins. The sounds that are emitted at one-half crankshaft speed concern valve-train noises. Whether or not the sound occurs at engine speed or one-half engine speed can usually be determined by operating the engine at a slow idle and noting whether the noise is synchronized with flashes of a timing light.

A main bearing knock is usually a dull thud that is noticeable under load. Trying to move the car under power with the brakes applied will bring out this noise. Pull the spark plug wires from the plugs, one at a time. If the noise disappears when a plug wire is removed, then it is probably coming from that cylinder. This category would include rod bearings, piston pins, and piston slap. If a rod bearing is loose, the noise will be loudest on deceleration. Piston pin noise and piston slap are, in general, louder when a cold engine is first started. **CAUTION: Don't pull off a spark plug wire on a vehicle with a catalytic converter, or you will destroy it.**

The use of a stethoscope or other listening device will often aid in locating the source of an unusual sound. However, a great deal of care and judgment must be used, because noise travels through other metallic parts as well as parts not involved in the problem.

Carbon build-up in the combustion chamber can cause interference with a piston. Fuel pumps can knock, belts can be noisy, distributors can emit clicking noises, and generators can contribute to unusual sounds. Flywheels, clutches, transmissions, water pumps, and loose manifolds can also cause noise problems.

A stethoscope is handy for determining the source of an engine noise. You can also use a screwdriver with the handle against your ear to determine the noise source.

EXCESSIVE OIL CONSUMPTION

High oil consumption complaints are often the result of oil leaks rather than actual consumption by the engine. Therefore, before assuming that an engine is burning oil, examine the exterior for evidence of oil leaks.

In analyzing a mechanical engine leak problem, consideration must be given to the fact that oil can enter the combustion chambers in only three ways: (1) past the piston rings, (2) through the valve guides, and (3) through the intake manifold. Evidence of excessive oil consumption usually is in the form of carbon deposits in the exhaust outlet pipe and oil-fouled spark plugs. The following items are generally responsible for internal oil consumption problems: (1) a clogged positive crankcase ventilation system, (2) piston rings not sealing, (3) excessive valve stem-to-guide clearance, (4) ineffective valve stem seals, or (5) a cracked intake manifold (the type that serves as a valve chamber cover).

A quick check to determine if the PCV (Positive Crankcase Ventilation) system is working can be made by removing the oil filler cap and placing the palm of your hand over the oil filler tube opening for 30 seconds with the engine idling. If there is suction when removing your hand, the system is working. If there is pressure against your hand, the system is inoperative and must be repaired.

OVERHEATING

WITHOUT THE LOSS OF COOLANT

Overheating can be caused by the front of the radiator being obstructed by leaves, bugs, and/or dirt. Restricted hoses in the cooling system can affect the flow of coolant, and this is also true if the pump drive belt is loose. Any restriction in the exhaust system, too, will cause overheating. This can be a bent exhaust pipe or an exhaust control valve that is stuck in the closed position.

Circulation can also be impaired by a loose or broken pump hub or impeller, or the thermostat can be defective. The thermostat can be checked by removing it from the engine and testing it in a pail of heated water.

When the thermostat is removed for checking, inspect the casting for a foundry flash inside the manifold. This can be done by a visual inspection or by probing through the thermostat opening with a piece of welding rod or heavy wire. If there is a flash, it will restrict the flow of coolant through the manifold, causing the coolant to boil after the engine is stopped. This condition can also cause the engine to overheat after long driving periods.

If the car is equipped with a fluid-coupling type of fan drive, check the operation of the unit as follows: (1) Run the engine at approximately 1,000 rpm until normal operating temperature is reached. This process can be speeded up by blocking off the front of the radiator with cardboard. (2) Stop the engine and, using a cloth to protect your hand, immediately check the effort required to turn the fan. If considerable effort is required, the coupling is operating satisfactorily. If very little effort is required to turn the fan, it is an indication that the coupling is not operating properly and that it should be serviced or replaced.

Retarded ignition timing and a lean air-fuel mixture

The pressure rating of the radiator filler cap can be checked with a pump and gauge arrangement as shown.

will also cause overheating.

WITH LOSS OF COOLANT

When it becomes necessary to add coolant to the system at regular intervals, the cause of the trouble should be investigated. Visually inspect the radiator, pump, engine, and hoses for leaks. Check the pressure rating and operation of the radiator filler cap.

If the loss of coolant is due to an internal leak caused by a crack in the combustion chamber, the coolant will be rusty and the engine will overheat. If this is the case, evidence of the crack can be determined by looking for bubbles in the coolant as the engine is accelerated. Do this by draining the coolant to the top of the block and then removing the top hose. Add coolant until the level is even with the top of the thermostat housing. Start the engine and accelerate it quickly. Check the coolant surface for evidence of bubbles.

If you suspect a crack in the combustion chamber, you can introduce air pressure into each cylinder while checking the coolant at the thermostat housing for bubbles. To do this, install an air hose adapter (an old spark plug shell to which a tire valve has been brazed)

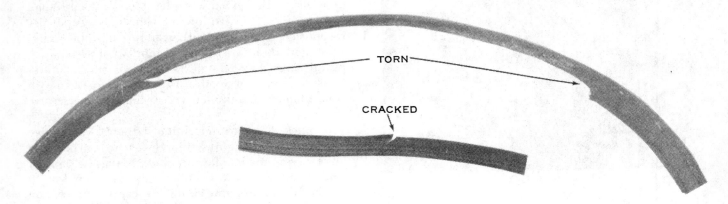

A broken or cracked fan belt or power steering pump drive belt will often cause a noise that is clearly audible from the driver's seat. Always replace belts with defects before they actually break.

A crack in the head or block can be checked by introducing compressed air into each cylinder with the piston at TDC firing position and checking for bubbles in the coolant at the thermostat housing, as discussed in the text.

ELECTRICAL SYSTEM

BATTERY AND CHARGING SYSTEM

The charging system consists of an alternator, a regulator, a battery, a charge indicator gauge, and the necessary wiring to connect the components. Many late-model alternators have the regulator built into one end cap.

Battery problems are not always due to charging sytstem defects. Excessive use of lights and accessories while the engine is either off or running at low speed, voltage losses, corroded battery cables and connectors, low water level in the battery, or prolonged disuse of the battery which would permit a self-discharging condition are all possible reasons which should be considered when a battery is run down or low in charge.

Charging system troubles such as low alternator output or no alternator output (indicated by the in-

in No. 1 spark plug hole. Start the test by rotating the crankshaft until No. 1 cylinder is at TDC, firing position. Check the distributor points, which should just be starting to open. Introduce air at full line pressure. Check each cylinder in turn by rotating the crankshaft until the breaker points start to open for the next cylinder in the firing order. Transfer the air hose adapter to that cylinder, and then repeat the test.

An induction-type ammeter can be used to measure the charging system output by holding the meter over the main wire to the battery with the engine running at a fast-idle speed.

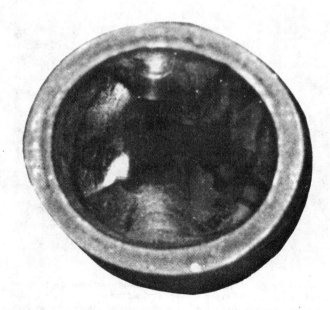

A clogged radiator hose is an indication that the rest of the cooling system is plugged in a similar fashion. The remedy is to reverse-flush the system and replace the hoses. It may be necessary to remove the radiator for cleaning by a speciality shop.

dicator gauge showing discharge while the engine is running) require testing of both the alternator and the alternator regulator. Alternator regulator problems usually do not make themselves known except by their direct effect on the alternator output and, of course, eventually by creating a battery problem. Proper adjustment of the regulating units contained in the regulator assembly is very important.

Test the alternator output at the battery with a voltmeter connected across the terminals. Start the engine, and the voltmeter reading should advance from the battery voltage of 12 to the regulated voltage of approximately 14. If it doesn't increase above the battery voltage (12 volts), then the alternator or regulator is defective.

Isolating The Trouble

To isolate trouble between the alternator and regulator, hold a screwdriver blade against the back plate of the alternator. Turn on the ignition switch (engine not running), and you should have magnetism, indicating that the regulator is exciting the field circuit.

If there is no magnetic attraction, then the regulator is defective. If there is a magnetic field, and the system does not charge, then the alternator is defective.

Noise Alternator

When investigating the complaint of alternator noise, first try to localize and pinpoint the noise area to make sure that the alternator is at fault rather than the drive belt or water pump or another part of the engine. Start the engine and listen for the area and the type of noise. Use a stethoscope or similar sound-detection instrument to localize the noise. An alternator bearing, pump bearing, or belt noise is usually a squealing sound.

An alternator with a shorted diode will normally whine (magnetic noise) and will be most noticeable at idle speeds. Perform an alternator output test; if the output is approximately 10 amperes less than specifications, a shorted diode is indicated. To eliminate the belt as the cause of noise, apply a light amount of belt dressing. If the alternator belt is at fault, adjust the betl to specifications or replace it, if necessary. If the belt is satisfactory and the noise is believed to be in the alternator or pump, remove the alternator belt. Start the engine and listen for the noise as a double check to be sure the noise is not caused by another component. If the noise is traced to the alternator, remove it and inspect the bearings for wear, scoring, or an out-of-round condition.

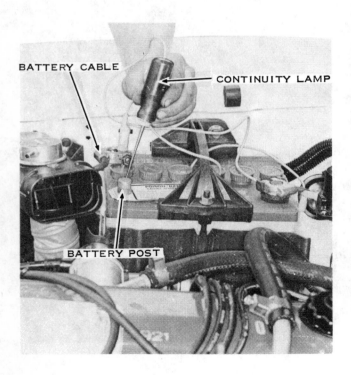

To check for a short circuit, connect a test lamp between the disconnected battery cable and the battery post. If the test lamp lights, then there is a short circuit.

A simple check to see if the regulator contacts are in good condition is to hold a screwdriver against the end of the alternator with the ignition key in the running position but with the engine stopped. If the regulator contact points are good, the field will be energized and the screwdriver will be attracted by the resulting magnetic field. CAUTION: Don't make contact at the positive diode heat sink which is at battery voltage, or sparks will fly.

TURN SIGNALS

The turn signal system includes a fuse, flasher unit, switch, front and rear signal lights, instrument panel indicator lights, ignition switch (accessory terminal is used as the power source), and the necessary wiring to connect the components.

As a visual aid in troubleshooting turn signal problems, connect an ammeter in series with the battery. Any indication of an excessive current draw can then be readily observed. **CAUTION: The ignition switch must be either in the ACC or ON position for the turn signal lights to operate.**

ONE SIGNAL LIGHT FAILS TO OPERATE

This type of trouble is most often the result of a burned-out bulb. If one bulb is burned out, the remaining bulb(s) will remain on but will not flash. Also, the respective right or left instrument panel indicator light will remain on. Switch failure, shorted or open wiring, loose connectors, or corroded bulb socket assemblies are other causes of inoperative signal lights.

ALL SIGNAL LIGHTS FAIL TO OPERATE

This trouble is most often the result of a blown fuse or a defective flasher unit. However, a turn signal switch failure or shorted or open wiring could also be contributing causes. As the fuse or turn signal power supply is fed from the accessory terminal of the ignition switch, check that other accessories, such as the radio, are operative. If other accessories are not operative, it is possible that the ignition switch may be defective.

A 12-volt test light can be substituted for a voltmeter. A voltage or test light indication should be obtained only at the connectors which lead to the lights in question. If there is voltage or a test light indication at connectors other than those for which the turn signal switch is positioned, then the turn signal switch or wiring has a short circuit. If there is no voltage at the connections, then an open circuit through the switch is indicated. In either case, the switch or wiring assembly must be removed for repair or replacement.

CONSTANT-VOLTAGE SYSTEM

The CV (Constant Voltage) system consists of the fuel level indicator gauge, fuel tank sending unit, temperature indicator gauge, temperature sending unit, and the oil pressure indicator gauge and sending unit except on cars equipped with an oil pressure indicator light.

If all gauge indicators read maximum, the condition is caused by sticking points or an open heater winding in the CV regulator. If all gauge indicators remain on the low end of the scale, an open CV regulator or an open circuit on the input side of the regulator is the probable cause. If one or two gauge indicators register incorrectly, a defective indicator or sending unit is the

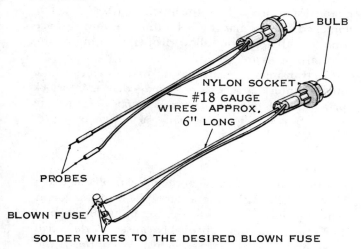

SOLDER WIRES TO THE DESIRED BLOWN FUSE

A testing probe can be made with an old socket and a bulb. This device can be used to check terminals for current without blowing out the fuse. If a similar probe is soldered to a blown fuse (lower), the fuse can be inserted into the fuse receptacle of a circuit for testing so that fuses are not blown out at each test.

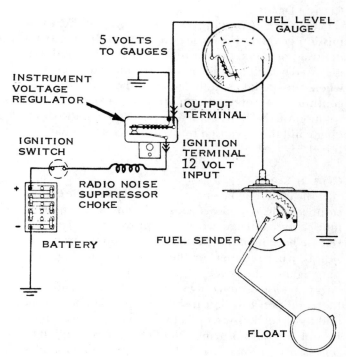

A constant voltage regulator is designed to furnish 5 volts for energizing the gauges. The battery voltage cannot be used for the gauge system because it varies with the state of battery charge and the charging rate of the alternator.

most probable cause. Substitute a new fuel tank sending unit to check out a suspected gauge. Disconnect the wire from the suspected sending unit and connect it to the test unit. **CAUTION: Be sure that the test unit is grounded properly to the metal of the car.**

If the gauge indicator operation is erratic, loose wiring connectors or a defective sending unit is the most probable cause. If all gauge indicators read higher than conditions warrant, the probable cause is a poor ground at the CV regulator. Clean and tighten the CV regulator ground connections, and then retest the system. If the gauge indicators still read higher than operating conditions indicate, replace the CV regulator.

TROUBLESHOOTING THE DRIVELINE

CLUTCH CHATTERS

Rapid gripping or slipping of the clutch assembly while the unit is being engaged will cause a clutch to chatter. Some of the conditions resulting in clutch chatter are release bearing binding, worn linkage, clutch pedal and assist spring being out of adjustment, loose engine mounts, and a warped or sticking clutch disc.

CLUTCH DRAGS

Clutch drag (spinning) causes clashing of the transmission gears and is most noticeable in shifting from neutral position to low or reverse gear. The condition is caused by a clutch disc that is not completely released when the pedal is fully depressed. Thus, the disc continues to rotate, being dragged around by the rotation of the flywheel. In most instances, the dragging condition is caused by excessive clutch pedal free travel.

CLUTCH NOISY

If the clutch pedal operation is noisy with the engine stopped, the trouble is caused by linkage requiring lubrication, linkage worn or improperly adjusted, release bearing burred and dragging on the transmission bearing retainer, or the pressure plate lugs rubbing against the cover.

If the noise occurs only when the engine is running, the condition can be caused by a misaligned engine and flywheel housing or by looseness or a worn condition of the pilot bearing. *NOTE: A faulty or dry clutch pilot bearing is characterized by a high-pitched noise when the clutch pedal is depressed with the engine idling.*

If the noise occurs only when the clutch pedal is partially depressed, the trouble is a defective release bearing. The pedal action brings the release bearing into contact with the clutch release fingers when the pedal is partially depressed, causing the bearing to spin.

CLUTCH SLIPS

Clutch disc slippage will be encountered if the friction surface of the clutch plate fails to hold the disc against the friction face of the flywheel. If severe clutch slippage exists, a greater than normal engine speed will be noticed in high gear when the accelerator is depressed to full throttle. If the slippage is slight but continuous, it may go unnoticed until excessive temperature caused by friction results in failure of the disc and/or friction surfaces.

In most cases, slippage is caused by insufficient clutch pedal free-travel. Normal clutch disc facing wear causes a gradual reduction in free-travel and when a point of no free-travel is reached, clutch slippage will begin.

STANDARD-GEARED TRANSMISSION

The problems related to a geared transmission are the transmission jumping out of gear, excessive noise, hard shifting efforts, clashing of gears when the transmission is shifted, and lubricant leakage.

TRANSMISSION JUMPS OUT OF GEAR

The gears will not slip out of low or reverse gear on cars that are equipped with a properly installed and adjusted exterior interlock linkage. This linkage has been designed to make certain the transmission low and reverse shift lever is locked in place after the clutch pedal has been fully released. If the linkage is not adjusted properly or the linkage parts are bent or damaged, there may be a binding or interference condition that will not allow proper meshing of the transmission gears.

The transmission gears may fail to stay in mesh if the internal interlock balls are damaged, the interlock spring is weak or broken, or the notches on the cam and shaft assemblies are worn, cracked, or broken.

TRANSMISSION NOISY

To determine the cause of the noise problem, drive the car and check the operation of the transmission in each gear ratio. If the noise is present only during one specific gear ratio, it is probably caused by defective gears pertaining to that respective gear ratio. If the transmission is noisy in each gear ratio, the noise could be caused by improper lubrication, damaged bearings, flywheel housing misalignment, loose transmission mount bolts, or a damaged mainshaft or cluster gears.

Check the synchronizers for damaged parts or improper operation. Make sure that the synchronizer parts are properly assembled. The insert springs should properly secure the inserts into the insert area of the hub. The sleeve and blocking rings should be free of nicks and burrs. The splines of the hub and shaft have to be free of burrs and nicks that could restrict the hub from moving on the shaft. The cam-and-shaft assembly of the gear-shift housing should be checked for restricted travel.

Check all the transmission and flywheel housing bolts for the proper torque. Start with the flywheel housing. **CAUTION: Make sure that the flywheel housing is properly positioned against the engine.** Check the torque on the engine rear mounting bolts and crossmember-to-body bolts. Loose mounting bolts allow misalignment of the transmission in relationship to the torque transfer from the engine to the transmission main drive gear. Misalignment between the flywheel housing and the engine will cause the same type of problem as loose mounting bolts.

Check the lubricant for proper level. If necessary, drain some of the old lubricant and make sure that it isn't contaminated with metal chips or dirt. The wrong type of lubricant can be a factor in causing noise.

Hard Shifting

Excessive shifting efforts are usually caused by an improperly adjusted clutch or transmission manual linkage. If the transmission has the exterior interlock type linkage, make sure that the cam or wedge parts are not binding and that the interlock is adjusted properly. The last items to be checked should be the internal shift linkage and synchronizers. If the problem exists only during cold weather, a pint of automatic transmission fluid can be added to the lubricant. Also, make sure that the transmission contains the specified lubricant.

If the linkage is not adjusted properly or bent, there will be a binding or interference condition when shifting from one gear to another. To check this out, disconnect the linkage at the end of the steering column and move the selector lever to check for any binding condition. Next, disconnect the linkage rods at the transmission shift levers, and then try the levers for freedom of movement.

If there are no linkage problems, then the transmission will have to be disassembled in order to check the synchronizers for proper operation. Check the splines on the sleeve and hub for nicks or burrs. Make sure that the synchronizer ring is not damaged and that the inserts are properly assembled and retained in the hub by the insert springs.

AUTOMATIC TRANSMISSION

The routine for diagnosing troubles in an automatic transmission requires that you follow certain procedures. Before any repairs or adjustments are made, certain checks must be made, and then the vehicle must be taken for a road test. For example, the transmission fluid level and the manual throttle linkage adjustment must be checked before any road test in undertaken.

See Chapter 6 for detailed tests and service procedures for automatic transmissions.

REAR AXLE

The most common axle or driveline complaint is noise. Excessive rear axle or driveline noise can indicate a malfunction. However, it must be noted that axle gears inherently make some noise and an absolutely quiet unit is seldom found. When evaluating the rear axle, make sure that the noise is not caused by the road surface, by a grounding exhaust system, by the engine, tires, transmission, or wheel bearings, or by some other external component of the car.

Road Test

Before a road test of the car is performed, make sure that there is sufficient lubricant of the specified type in the rear axle housing. Drive the car far enough to warm the lubricant to normal operating temperature before testing. A car should be tested for axle noise by being operated in high gear under the following four driving conditions:

1. DRIVE: Higher than normal road load power where the speed gradually increases on level road acceleration.

2. CRUISE: Constant speed operation at normal road speeds.

3. FLOAT: Using only enough throttle to keep the car from driving the engine. In float, the car will slow down with very little load on the rear axle gears.

4. COAST: Throttle closed—engine is braking the car. Load is on the coast side of the gear set.

When a rear axle is noisy, the following tests are to be performed to pinpoint the problem and eliminate the possibility that the noise is of external origin.

Road Noise

Road surfaces, such as those of brick or rough-surfaced concrete, can cause a noise condition which may be mistaken for tire or rear axle noise. Driving on a smooth asphalt surface will quickly show whether the road surface is the cause of the noise. A road noise usually has the same pitch on DRIVE or COAST.

Tire Noise

Tire noise can easily be mistaken for rear axle noise, even though the noisy tires may be located on the front wheels. Sounds and vibrations are caused by unevenly worn tire surfaces or ply separations. Also, some designs of non-skid treads on low-pressure tires, snow tires, and other assorted types cause vibrations. *NOTE: Temporarily inflate all tires to approximately 40 pounds pressure for test purposes only.* This will alter any noise caused by tires but will not affect noise caused by the rear axle. Excessive rear axle noise usually diminishes or ceases during COAST at speeds under 30 miles per hour. However, tire noise continues, but with a lower tone as car speed is reduced. Rear axle noise usually changes when comparing DRIVE and COAST. However, tire noise remains about the same.

Front Wheel Bearing Noise

Loose or rough front wheel bearing noises can be confused with rear axle noise. However, front wheel bearing noise does not change when comparing DRIVE and COAST. Drive the car through a series of left and right turns, which will put a load on the wheel bearings and emphasize a noisy condition, if it exists. A light application of the brake while holding the car speed steady will often cause wheel bearing noise to diminish. This action takes some weight off the bearings. If front wheel bearing noise is suspected, you can easily check it by jacking up the front wheels and spinning them while feeling and listening for roughness. Also, shake the wheels to determine if the bearings are loose.

Body Noises

The car body and/or one of the attached components can have a wind noise condition that sounds like a noisy rear axle. Items such as the grille, radio antenna, and hood can cause the condition which must be isolated. In some cases, loose body hold-down bolts or brackets can be a source of noise.

Rear Axle Noise

Sometimes a noise which seems to originate in the rear axle is actually caused by the engine, exhaust, transmission, or power steering. To determine which unit is actually causing the noise, observe the approximate car speeds and conditions under which the noise is most pronounced, and then stop the car in a quiet place to avoid interfering noises. With the transmission in neutral, run the engine slowly up and down through engine speeds corresponding to the car speed at which the noise was most pronounced. If a similar noise is produced with the car standing still, it is caused by components other than the rear axle or driveline assemblies.

If a careful road test of the car shows that the noise is not caused by the road surface or by components previously described, it is reasonable to assume that the noise is caused by the rear axle or driveline units. The rear axle should be tested on a smooth level road to avoid road noise. **CAUTION: It is not advisable to test the rear axle assembly for noise by running it with the rear wheels jacked up because the load distribution is different.**

Noises in the rear axle assembly can be caused by faulty rear wheel bearings; loss of pinion pre-load; faulty differential or pinion shaft bearings; worn differential side gears and pinions; or by a mismatched, improperly adjusted, or scored ring-and-pinion gear set. It is sometimes impossible to determine from a test exactly which internal repairs are required to correct a noisy axle unit. The needed repairs can best be determined by a careful inspection of wear on the individual parts when the unit is disassembled.

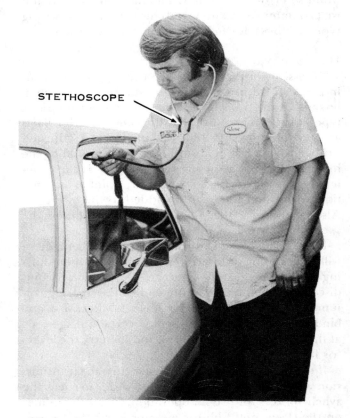

STETHOSCOPE

Wind noises can be traced by using a stethoscope with the indicating end removed. Close all windows and air vents and turn the ventilating fan to HIGH SPEED. Move the hose along the edges of all openings to trace wind noises caused by leaking seals. Some mechanics paint suspected areas with a soapy water solution and check for bubbles.

Rear Wheel Bearing Noise

A rough rear wheel bearing produces a heavy grinding or "growling" noise in DRIVE and CRUISE, which will continue when the transmission is positioned in neutral with the car coasting. A brinelled rear wheel bearing causes a knock or click approximately every two revolutions of the rear wheel, since the bearing rollers do not travel at the same speed as the rear axle shaft and wheel. To accentuate the noise of a suspected bearing, drive the car in a series of right and left turns to put a load on the bearings. Sometimes the bearings can be tested with the rear wheels jacked up. Spin the rear wheels by hand while listening at the hubs for evidence of rough or brinelled wheel bearings.

Differential Side Gears And Pinion Noise

Differential side gears and pinions seldom cause noise since their movement is relatively small on straight-ahead driving. Noise produced by these gears will be most pronounced on turns. As a rule, the noise heard will be a "chuckling" sound, similar to the sound given by two steel balls when rattled together. The noise can be attributed to excessively worn or loosely fitted differential side gears.

Pinion Bearing Noise

Rough or brinelled pinion bearings produce a continuous "whine" that starts at a relatively low speed. The noise is most pronounced on FLOAT between 20 and 35 mph. In most instances, pinion bearing noise can be pinpointed by raising the rear axle on a hoist and running it with the transmission in high gear. If the pinion bearing is bad, the noise will be obvious.

Ring And Pinion Gear Noise

Noise produced by the ring-and-pinion gear set generally shows up as DRIVE, COAST, or FLOAT noise. As the gears become worn or out of adjustment, a heavy "humming" sound will be noticed. The noise in DRIVE, COAST, and FLOAT will be very rough or irregular if the differential pinion shaft bearings are rough, worn, or loose, and will vary in tone with speed. As a rule, DRIVE noise is caused by a heavy heel contact, and a COAST noise is caused by heavy toe contact. Heavy face contact is usually the trouble when the rear axle is noisy in FLOAT or CRUISE.

Backlash

Excessive backlash ("clunk noise") can be caused by worn axle shaft splines; loose axle shaft flange nuts; worn, broken, or loose universal joint flange or slip yoke mountings; excessive play between the drive pinion and ring gear; excessive backlash in the differential gears; bearings worn or out of adjustment; or the engine idle speed is too high.

Vibration

Excessive noise or vibration can be caused by a lack of lubrication in the driveshaft U-joint bearings, worn bearings, a bind between the universal joint and the rear axle companion flange (universal joint not seated properly), a sprung or damaged driveshaft, or a missing driveshaft balance weight. **CAUTION: Undercoating carelessly applied to the driveshaft can destroy the balance and cause vibration.**

Vibration or shudder, which is noticeable either on fast acceleration in DRIVE or when in COAST, can be caused by the rear axle housing being loose on the rear springs or by an excessive driveline angle.

TROUBLESHOOTING THE RUNNING GEAR

When troubleshooting a front suspension problem, it is important to follow a pattern before and during a road test that will isolate the area or item that is causing the trouble. This is because several of the problems attributable to front suspension components are also common to steering gear and linkage, rear suspension, and wheel or tire problems. For example, wrong or uneven tire pressures can cause steering problems. Also, a misaligned rear suspension, a binding steering linkage, or an improperly aligned front suspension component has a similar effect on the steering ability of a car.

QUICK CHECKS

Check the attitude of the car for an unbalanced load condition or sagging springs. Jounce the front and rear of the vehicle to check for noisy, weak, loose, or damaged springs, and shock absorbers. After it has settled, check the front and rear of the car for obviously improper front or rear spring riding heights.

If the vehicle looks uneven, measure the riding heights at the same places on each side. Although sagging may be apparent at one or more wheels, the action of all four shock absorbers and springs must be checked. One or more binding shock absorbers or springs can hold other corners of the car abnormally high or low, causing uneven weight distribution, with resulting abnormal tire wear.

Check the air pressure in each tire and the tires for uniformity in size. Also, observe the tread wear pattern for signs of misalignment. Rotate the front and rear wheels to make sure that they turn freely without brake or bearing bind. Check the front wheel bearings for noise, looseness, wear, or improper adjustment. Spin the wheels again to check the tires for run-out, ply separation, or an unbalanced condition.

Inspect the steering column, steering gear, linkage, and stabilizer for loose mountings, wear, or damaged parts. Check the engine and transmission mounts for looseness or damage. Inspect the front and rear springs, shock absorbers, and suspension components for loose mountings, excessive wear, cracks, or damaged parts.

ROAD TEST

Perform a short road test over a smooth and level surface, rough surfaces, and a roadway with a series of small dips. On a level road, check the car for steering bind, side-to-side wander, looseness in the steering gear, shimmy, wheel tramp, pulling to one side, noisy conditions, excessive front-end vibration, and steering wheel vibration.

Drive the car over a surface that has roughness or dips and check for wander, rough ride, noisy conditions, excessive vibration at the steering wheel, weak or bottoming springs, and defective shock absorbers. Perform a series of quick stops in both forward and reverse gears and check for excessive dipping action, bounce, or bottoming, any of which is attributable to weak or damaged springs or shock absorbers. Perform a series of slow turns to the right and left and check the steering mechanism for excessive play, hard steering, and poor steering recovery. Check for excessive body sway, which can be attributed to weak springs, a weak shock absorber, or a loose stabilizer.

From a given point in a wide roadway, turn the steering wheel fully to the left. Then drive the car in a complete circle and observe the diameter of the turn. Perform a similar turn to the right. If the diameter is not the same on both turns, the steering mechanism is out of adjustment or the steering linkage or suspension arms are bent, worn, or damaged.

If misalignment or dog tracking of the front and rear suspension is suspected, drive the car straight ahead on a section of pavement, part of which is wet, and then stop about ten feet beyond the wet area. If alignment is correct, the rear tire imprints will overlap the front equally. If misalignment exists, it can be attributed to an improperly or loosely mounted rear axle or to damaged rear suspension components.

If the vehicle pulls to one side, the condition can be caused by faulty front-end alignment, defective wheel bearings, steering gear defects, or chasis misalignment. Specific defects which can cause the car to pull to one side are the steering gear off the center position, brakes out of adjustment, contaminated brake linings, drums out of round, damaged or worn interior brake components, restricted hydraulic line to one cylinder, or worn wheel bearings.

Abnormal tire tread wear indicates a front-end alignment problem. To check this out, drive the car on a fairly level road in a straight-ahead direction, and then momentarily release the steering wheel to observe if the car pulls to one side. Make a few normal stops to determine how much the steering or front-end alignment problem is related to the amount of direction that the car pulls when the brakes are applied.

VEHICLE LEADS TO ONE SIDE

Rear suspension misalignment is usually the cause of the vehicle leading to one side, and generally the trouble is the result either of bent parts or of a rear spring not being centered in a locating hole. To determine whether this condition exists, measure the distance between a locating hole at the rear of the spring mounting bracket common to both side rails and the forward edge of the axle. The dimension must be the same on both sides of the vehicle. Other causes of the vehicle leading to one side are front-end misalignment, uneven tire pressure, non-uniformity of tire sizes, a dragging brake, improperly adjusted wheel bearing, the steering gear out of adjustment, or binding of the steering linkage.

VIBRATION OR SHIMMY

This common complaint is generally due to an unbalanced condition of the front wheels. Low-speed vibration results from a static unbalanced condition, while high-speed problems are always caused by dynamic imbalance. Shimmy results from a combina-

Uneven tire wear can cause road noise that can be mistaken for rear axle noise. Uneven tire wear should always be investigated.

tion of an unbalanced condition and worn front-end parts. To check for an unbalanced condition during a road test, hold the steering wheel lightly and note the amount of vibration during various speeds.

Before balancing a tire, all foreign matter must be removed from the tread and bead. Check the wheels and tires for lateral and radial run-out, the total of which must not exceed 0.080", with a tolerance of 0.060" even more desirable. **CAUTION: Adding balance weights cannot counteract for wheel and tire run-out.** *NOTE: If excessive weight is required to balance a front tire, replace it with a new one or the spare.*

Other conditions which could cause vibration are damaged springs, inoperative shock absorbers, loose engine supports, worn universal joints, or a driveshaft that is loosely mounted or out of balance.

POWER STEERING

Power steering gear troubles generally include the following conditions: excess or loss of steering effort, partial steering assist or assist in only one direction, poor returnability, or leaks. Because the internal parts of the power gear assembly are always under high hydraulic pressure, lubrication and wear problems do not occur. However, because of the high pressures, seal problems and leaks are quite general.

Preliminary checks must include the drive belt condition and tension. Check the fluid level in the reservoir and add fluid if necessary. Start the engine and turn the steering wheel back and forth. Shut off the engine and recheck the fluid level. If the level is low, add fluid, but do not overfill.

A pressure check should be made on the pump, with and without the rest of the system, in order to isolate the trouble . This can be done by installing and closing a shut-off valve between the pump and the power steering gear unit. If the pressure builds up to specifications with the shut-off valve closed, then the pump is OK, and the pressure loss must be in the power steering gear assembly. If the pump does not build up to the specified pressure, then the pump is defective. *NOTE: The pitman arm must be disconnected from the sector shaft in order to perform steering gear checks and/or adjustments.*

Some of the conditions that could cause a loss of power assist are drive belt loose, worn, broken, or slipping; fluid level low or air in the system; fluid leaking or damage to the lines; pump pressure too low; and control valve and/or power steering gear assembly defective.

If there is a partial assist or an assist in only one direction, the condition causing this trouble could be the control valve out of adjustment; fluid level too low; air in system; drive belt loose, worn, or slipping; pump pressure too low; control valve defective; or power steering gear assembly defective.

Excessive steering effort and/or poor returnability can be caused by front-end misalignment, tire pressures too low, tires oversize, steering gear fluid low, steering gear out of adjustment, or steering linkage binding or bent.

IRREGULAR TIRE WEAR

Loose, worn, or bent front suspension parts and/or steering linkage can cause irregular tire wear.

UNDERINFLATION WEAR

Tires are designed so that, under a given load and with the proper air pressure, the tire will make a full pattern across the entire width of the tread, thereby distributing the wear evenly over the entire surface. When a tire is run underinflated, the side walls and the shoulders of the tread carry the load, while, due to the low internal air pressure, the center section folds in, or compresses. With the shoulders thus taking most of the driving and braking loads, they wear much faster than the center section.

OVERINFLATION WEAR

When a tire is overinflated, the outside or shoulder sections of the tread are lifted away from the road surface. The center section of the tread then receives most of the driving and braking loads, and this causes it to wear much faster than the shoulder sections.

SCUFFING WEAR

When the front wheels have an excessive amount of either toe-in or toe-out, the tires are actually dragged sideways when they travel straight down the road and a cross-wear or scraping action takes place, rapidly wearing away the tread. This scuffing action will produce a feather-edge on the ribs of the tread. In many instances, this can be detected by rubbing your hand across the face of the tire. If the feather-edges are on the inside of the tire ribs, too much toe-in is indicated. If the feather-edges are on the outside of the ribs, it indicates that the tires are being run with a toe-out condition.

CAMBER WEAR

Excessive wheel camber causes the tire to run at a slight angle to the road surface, resulting in more wear on one side of the tread than on the other. With too much positive camber, the outside of the tread will show the most wear. Too much negative camber will show a similar wear pattern on the inside of the tread.

CORNERING WEAR

Cornering wear can be identified by a rough, diagonal wear pattern across the face of the tread. This pattern is the result of the driver making high-speed turns, resulting in an abrasive action caused by tire slippage.

CUP- AND- FLAT SPOT WEAR

Cups and flat spots generally are the result of road tramp, caused by wheels and tires being out of balance. Wheel misalignment, along with the unbalanced condition, can cause unusually severe tire cupping. Cupped or spotty tread wear on a front tire cannot be corrected by wheel alignment or balancing. A cupped tire, if transferred to a rear wheel, will true itself up to a certain degree by absorbing the driving and braking loads.

SERVICE BRAKES

The function of the hydraulic system is to deliver equal pressure to each of the four wheel cylinders. This pressure must cause each of the wheel cylinder pistons to move outward to apply the brake shoe linings against the braking surface of each brake drum with equal force. It is also important to remember the effect of the tire treads; each tire must be capable of creating equal friction at the road surface. Another fact to remember is that power brakes do not stop a vehicle better than manual brakes; they only reduce the amount of effort needed to depress the brake pedal.

Some typical problems with service brakes are grabbing, dragging, fading, and noise. Problems associated with brake pedal action are low pedal, soft or spongy pedal, and hard pedal action.

GRABBING BRAKES

When one wheel brake grabs, the condition is caused by too much braking friction between the brake linings and brake drum of one wheel or unequal friction between the tread of one tire and the road surface. When all the brakes grab, the problem is at all four wheel brake assemblies.

If all four brakes grab, check the master cylinder piston for partially restricted movement. Check the push rod length adjustment if the car has power brakes. Also, check the internal parts of the power brake that could cause the problem; it could result from a sticking poppet valve, leaking reaction diaphragm, restricted diaphragm passage, or sticking actuating valve assembly.

Remove the brake drums and check the brake linings for defects or the wrong type of material. Wheel cylinder leakage and consequent lining contamination caused by improper overhaul or defective parts can also create a grabbing condition. Make sure that all of the internal brake parts are properly lubricated at the friction areas.

DRAGGING BRAKES

If the brakes are dragging at one wheel only, the trouble can be one wheel brake out of adjustment, a restriction in the hydraulic line, a front wheel bearing

	RAPID WEAR AT SHOULDERS	RAPID WEAR AT CENTER	CRACKED TREADS	WEAR ON ONE SIDE	FEATHERED EDGE	BALD SPOTS
CONDITION						
CAUSE	UNDER INFLATION	OVER INFLATION	UNDER-INFLATION OR EXCESSIVE SPEED	EXCESSIVE CAMBER	INCORRECT TOE	WHEEL UNBALANCED
CORRECTION	ADJUST PRESSURE TO SPECIFICATIONS WHEN TIRES ARE COOL			ADJUST CAMBER TO SPECIFICATIONS	ADJUST FOR TOE-IN 1/8 INCH	DYNAMIC OR STATIC BALANCE WHEELS

Uneven and excessive tire wear, causes, and corrections. The conditions are discussed in the text.

damaged or out of adjustment, weak return springs, or improper assembly of the brake shoes, causing their return to be restricted or the friction areas to be rusted or corroded. *NOTE: Rotate the defective wheel to determine just how much drag exists at the wheel, and then release the bleeder screw to determine if excessive hydraulic pressure is causing the shoes to be held against the drum.*

If a rear wheel brake is dragging, the trouble could be as described in the material just covered. In addition, check the parking brake adjustment and the operating linkage. If the brakes are dragging on all four wheels, the trouble could result from any of the following: restricted pedal return, a push rod of too great length, a defective residual check valve, a plugged compensator port, or a stuck piston or swollen rubber parts in the master cylinder.

If the vehicle is equipped with a power brake unit, see that all parts are free and allow the unit to return to the fully released position. Some of the following can cause trouble: a leak at the diaphragm assembly, sticking or unseated atmospheric check valve, sticking valve plunger, broken piston return spring, or a faulty check valve.

FADING BRAKES

Fading is generally due to an overheated drum expanding away from the brake linings after many hard stops. Fading is nonexistent with disc brakes, because the expansion of the rotor is against the friction pads. Any condition which causes overheating of the brake system can contribute to fading: riding the brake pedal, repeated panic stops, incorrect brake linings, glazed brake linings, thin brake drums, and weak brake shoe return springs.

NOISY BRAKES

Brake noises take several forms, one of the most annoying of which is squeal. This condition is caused by vibration due to loose parts or to misalignment of the brake shoes, which prevents the proper shoe contact with the drum.

When checking out noises, rotate each wheel. Noise related to defective or loose wheel bearings or incorrectly assembled and rubbing internal brake parts should be evident. Rotate the wheel again and have someone depress the brake pedal lightly so that the noise level can be determined with the linings contacting the drums or rotors. Check the drum surfaces for evidence of threads cut during a drum-turning process; cut threads could cause the linings to shift to the side and then snap back during a brake application.

CHATTER

The problem of brake chatter is caused by the brake lining's failure to maintain constant pressure on the braking surface of the drum. Make a road test: apply and release the brakes while checking for any clicking or other unusual noises that are audible at the four wheels. A noise indicates loose internal parts or parts that may not have been assembled correctly. Check to see if one particular wheel is causing the problem.

Brake chatter can be caused by loose backing plate retaining bolts; loose brake linings; oil, grease, or hydraulic fluid on the brake linings, causing unequal friction when the linings contact the drum; bent or distorted brake shoes; loose retaining springs; or distorted or out-of-round brake drums.

LOW PEDAL ACTION

With a low pedal, the brakes may be capable of stopping the car under normal conditions, but there may not be enough reserve left in case of emergency. Also, the depressed pedal height does not position the leverage at its most advantageous point.

A low pedal is generally caused by excessive brake shoe travel in relation to the distance that the brake pedal has to be depressed. Check for the following troubles: air in the hydraulic lines, low fluid level, or improper adjustment of the brake shoes.

If the car has self-adjusting brakes, first try a few firm reverse stops to see if the brakes will adjust themselves. If they won't, try adjusting the brakes by hand. You can determine which wheel is giving the trouble by the amount of adjustment required. If the trouble is a loose adjustment at one wheel, check the self-adjuster mechanism to see if the cable and springs are properly installed and if the adjusting lever and wheel are free from burrs.

A low fluid level in the master cylinder indicates possible fluid leakage. Add fluid and then check the complete system for improper assembly or defective parts. If the trouble is in the master cylinder, remove and disassemble it. Check the valve, valve seat, springs, cups, pistons, and cylinder bore for excessive wear or damage.

If the pedal action remains soft or spongy, check the complete brake system for leakage. Start at the master cylinder, and then check the brake lines and connections to each wheel. Check the backing plate and the wheel area for evidence of wheel cylinder leakage. A fluid leak can cause inconsistency in building up pressure in the brake lines.

SOFT OR SPONGY PEDAL ACTION

Soft pedal action is generally due to air in the

hydraulic lines. If the brake shoes are out of adjustment or if the shoes are bent or out of alignment, the entire face of the lining may not make full contact with the brake drum. Use of an improper lining, one that is too soft, can also cause this type of trouble.

HARD PEDAL ACTION

Hard brake pedal action can be caused by any mechanical restriction in either the brake pedal linkage or the brake shoe assembly parts. Or it can be caused by a restriction in the hydraulic system.

Remove the brake drums and examine the brake shoes for restrictions in travel. **CAUTION: Don't move the shoes out too far or you will pop out the wheel cylinder cups.** Make sure that the return and hold-down springs are properly installed. Lubricate all friction points. Tighten the backing plate bolts, as a loose backing plate will allow the shoes to be out of position in relationship to the braking surface of the drum. Brake linings that have hard or glazed surfaces will cause hard pedal action, because the cushioning effect between the face of the lining and the braking surface of the drum has been lost.

Check the hydraulic system for a restriction which could cause difficulty in moving the hydraulic fluid. Check the vent in the master cylinder cover and the compensating port for restrictions.

DISC BRAKES

The caliper-type disc brake saddles a rotating disc, often called a rotor. Frictional pads compress against the sides of the rotor. It is important to note the following advantages of a disc brake system: (1) Heat radiation is very efficient, making brake application very effective without fading. (2) Due to heat expansion, the rotor does expand radially, but the thickness does not alter, thus the pedal stroke does not change. (3) Pad replacement and system maintenance are relatively easy as compared with drum-type brakes. (4) Brake effectiveness-recovery from water occurs quickly due to dispersion by centrifugal force. (5) Disc brakes are self-adjusting. As the pads wear, the piston is returned by the stretch of the piston seal within the cylinder.

TROUBLESHOOTING THE DISC BRAKE SYSTEM

WARNING LAMP

The brake warning lamp and the parking brake lamp utilize the same bulb, which can be tested by depressing the brake pedal with the ignition switch turned ON. If it doesn't light, replace the bulb or check for an open circuit.

After checking the warning lamp, test the switch assembly by raising the car and loosening one of the wheel cylinder bleeder screws. Slowly depress the brake pedal with the ignition switch turned ON. The pressure differential should activate the switch and light the warning lamp. If the lamp does not light, replace the safety switch. To recenter the safety switch piston, tighten the bleeder screw, and then apply light brake pedal pressure. The piston will center itself automatically.

PROPORTIONING VALVE

A proportioning valve (brake pressure control valve) is connected into the rear brake hydraulic line, where it controls the rear brake line pressure on a fast, hard brake application to minimize rear wheel lockup.

A rough test can be made by making a hard brake application at about 40 mph. If the rear wheels lock up (skid), the trouble can be a defective proportioning valve.

CALIPER ASSEMBLY

Check the caliper seals and piston boots for evidence of leaks or damage. If any brake fluid leakage is evident, it is necessary to disassemble the caliper and install a new seal kit. Replace the brake pads when the lining is worn to 1/16″ thickness.

DISC BRAKE TROUBLESHOOTING CHART

Symptoms & Causes
1. **Insufficient braking action**
   1a. Fluid leaking
   1b. Pad wear excessive
   1c. Pad contact surfaces wet with water or oil
   1d. Rotor worn
   1e. Proportioning valve defective
2. **Noisy brakes**
   2a. Deposits on pad surfaces
   2b. Improper pad seating
   2c. Front wheel bearing adjustment loose
   2d. Lining material glazed
   2e. Backing plate bolts loose
3. **Car pulls to one side**
   3a. Pads wet with water or oil deposits
   3b. Tire inflation incorrect
   3c. Front end misaligned
   3d. Backing plate bolts loose
   3e. Wheel bearings loose
4. **Excessive pedal travel**
   4a. Air in hydraulic system
   4b. Excessive play at master cylinder push rod
   4c. Fluid leaking
5. **Rear wheel lockup**
   5a. Defective proportioning valve

3/preventive maintenance

Preventive maintenance means performing certain adjustments, lubrication, or replacement of the vital operating parts of your car on a scheduled mileage basis to prevent the part from failing and creating extensive repairs. Taking wheel bearings as one simple example, it is much more economical and safer to remove, clean, inspect, lubricate, and install the wheel bearings on a set schedule to ensure against failure than it is to have the bearings fail from lack of lubrication, seize on the spindle, and possibly cause an accident. An hour spent once a year, maintaining the wheel bearings, is a small price to pay against the probability of a $50-$100 repair bill.

The first step in initiating a preventive maintenance schedule for your car is to obtain a recommended mileage schedule for the various jobs that you can perform on your car. This is always available in your owner's handbook. It will appear similar to the schedule shown here so that you can use our schedule if you do not have one. Our schedule is applicable to most vehicles.

The value of preventive maintenance cannot be overstressed these days. With repair shops charging $20-$30 per hour in some parts of the country, any preventive maintenance you can perform as an owner will be returned many times in increased savings. By following the manufacturer's schedule of things to do at certain mileages, and performing these jobs yourself, you will extend your car's life and put money in the bank that you would have spent on unnecessary repairs.

ENGINE

LUBRICATION

Crankcase oil should be selected to give the best performance under the climatic and driving conditions in the territory in which the vehicle is driven. During warm or hot weather, an oil which will provide adequate lubrication under high-operating temperatures, is required. During the colder months of the year, an oil which will permit easy starting at the lowest atmospheric temperature likely to be encountered should be used.

When the crankcase is drained and refilled, the oil

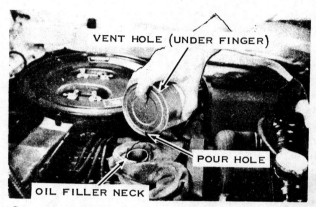

Cover the oil filler neck with a rag to catch the overflow. If you don't have a pouring spout, punch two holes in the cover of the can. Hold the can over the oil filler neck with your finger over the vent hole to control the flow of oil.

should be selected on the basis of the lowest temperature anticipated for the period during which the oil is to be used. Unless the crankcase oil is selected on the basis of viscosity or fluidity of the anticipated temperature, difficulty in starting will be experienced at each sudden drop in temperature.

CHANGING THE ENGINE OIL AND OIL FILTER

DRAINING

With the car raised, remove the oil pan drain plug,

A special tool is available to uncrews the oil filter. Position a drain pan under the engine to catch the drippings.

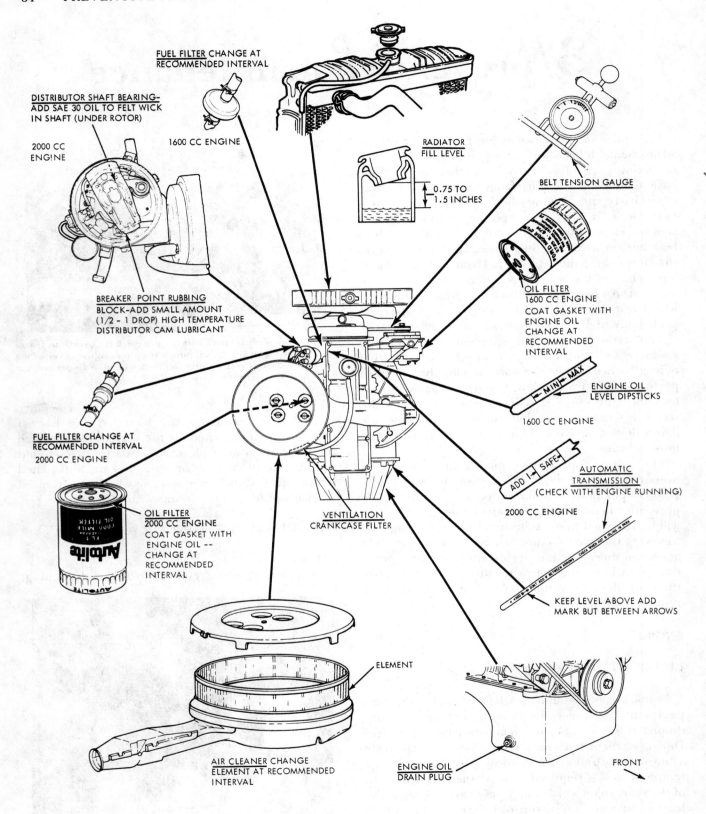

FUEL FILTER CHANGE AT
RECOMMENDED INTERVAL

DISTRIBUTOR SHAFT BEARING-
ADD SAE 30 OIL TO FELT WICK
IN SHAFT (UNDER ROTOR)

2000 CC
ENGINE

1600 CC ENGINE

RADIATOR
FILL LEVEL

0.75 TO
1.5 INCHES

BELT TENSION GAUGE

OIL FILTER
1600 CC ENGINE
COAT GASKET WITH
ENGINE OIL
CHANGE AT
RECOMMENDED
INTERVAL

BREAKER POINT RUBBING
BLOCK-ADD SMALL AMOUNT
(1/2 - 1 DROP) HIGH TEMPERATURE
DISTRIBUTOR CAM LUBRICANT

MIN   MAX

ENGINE OIL
LEVEL DIPSTICKS

1600 CC ENGINE

FUEL FILTER CHANGE AT
RECOMMENDED INTERVAL
2000 CC ENGINE

ADD   SAFE

AUTOMATIC
TRANSMISSION
(CHECK WITH ENGINE RUNNING)

2000 CC ENGINE

OIL FILTER
2000 CC ENGINE
COAT GASKET WITH
ENGINE OIL --
CHANGE AT
RECOMMENDED
INTERVAL

VENTILATION
CRANKCASE FILTER

KEEP LEVEL ABOVE ADD
MARK BUT BETWEEN ARROWS

ELEMENT

AIR CLEANER CHANGE
ELEMENT AT RECOMMENDED
INTERVAL

ENGINE OIL
DRAIN PLUG

FRONT

Four-cylinder engine lubrication and service points.

allowing the engine oil to drain into a container. *NOTE: The engine should be warm.*

Place a drip pan under the oil filter. Turn the filter counterclockwise, and then remove it from the engine.

REPLACING THE OIL FILTER

Clean the gasket surface at the cylinder block. Coat the gasket on the filter with a light film of oil. Thread the filter onto the adapter until the gasket contacts the sealing surface; then, advance it an additional 1/2 turn. **CAUTION: Do not overtighten the filter.** Remove the drip pan.

Replace the oil pan drain plug gasket if cracked or mutilated. Install the oil pan drain plug and torque it to 15 to 20 ft-lbs. Lower the car.

Fill the crankcase to the required level with the proper type and grade of lubricant. Start the engine and operate it at a fast idle. Check for oil leakage.

DRIVE BELTS

INSPECTING

Replace any belt that is broken, cracked, glazed, worn or stretched so that it cannot be sufficiently tightened. On a vehicle with matched belts, check both belts. **CAUTION: Use only the specified type of belt.**

COAT GASKET WITH ENGINE OIL

Motorcraft FL-1

To install a new oil filter, coat the gasket surface with engine oil and thread the filter onto the adapter until it contacts the gasket surface, and then tighten it an additional half turn.

Any belt that has operated for a minimum of 10 minutes is considered a used belt and must be adjusted accordingly.

When installing new belt(s), first adjust the belt to the new belt specification. Proper tension minimizes noise and prolongs belt service life. It is recommended that a belt tension gauge be used to check and adjust the belt tension.

ADJUSTING THE ALTERNATOR DRIVE BELT TENSION

Install the belt tension tool on the drive belt. Check the tension following the instructions furnished with the tool. If an adjustment is necessary, loosen the alternator mounting bolts and the alternator adjusting arm bolt. Move the alternator toward or away from the engine until the correct tension is obtained. **CAUTION: Apply pressure on the alternator front housing only.**

Remove the gauge. Tighten the alternator adjusting arm bolt first, and then the mounting bolts. Install the tension gauge and recheck the belt tension.

The condition of the drive belt should be checked every year, and the belt replaced every two years, or 24,000 miles. This is very important in today's engines with emission-control systems, where the underhood heat is much greater than ever before. Replace any belt with a crack or tear.

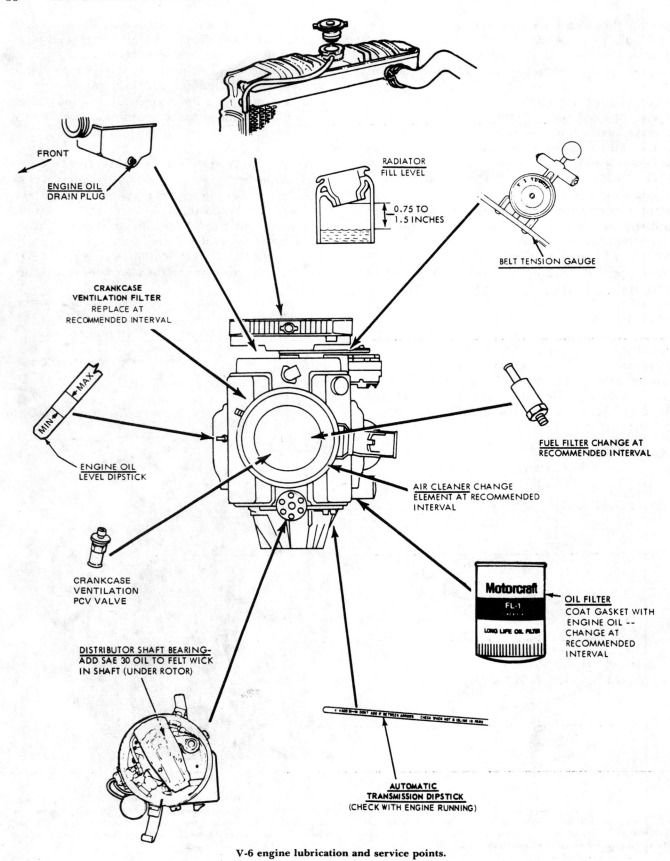

FRONT

ENGINE OIL
DRAIN PLUG

RADIATOR
FILL LEVEL

0.75 TO
1.5 INCHES

BELT TENSION GAUGE

CRANKCASE
VENTILATION FILTER
REPLACE AT
RECOMMENDED INTERVAL

MAX

MIN

ENGINE OIL
LEVEL DIPSTICK

FUEL FILTER CHANGE AT
RECOMMENDED INTERVAL

AIR CLEANER CHANGE
ELEMENT AT RECOMMENDED
INTERVAL

CRANKCASE
VENTILATION
PCV VALVE

Motorcraft
FL-1
LONG LIFE OIL FILTER

OIL FILTER
COAT GASKET WITH
ENGINE OIL --
CHANGE AT
RECOMMENDED
INTERVAL

DISTRIBUTOR SHAFT BEARING-
ADD SAE 30 OIL TO FELT WICK
IN SHAFT (UNDER ROTOR)

AUTOMATIC
TRANSMISSION DIPSTICK
(CHECK WITH ENGINE RUNNING)

V-6 engine lubrication and service points.

ADJUSTING THE POWER STEERING DRIVE BELT

Loosen the adjusting and mounting bolts on the front face of the pump cover plate (hub side) and the one nut at the rear. Attach a 9/16-inch open-end wrench on the projecting 1/2-inch boss and pry upward to correct tension on 4-cyl. engines.

To adjust the belt on an 8-cyl. engine, loosen the mounting bolt in the adjusting slot and the nut directly above the adjusting slot. Place a suitable pry bar between the cast boss on the pump cover plate; pry upward to correct tension. **CAUTION: Do not pry against the reservoir as it can be deformed and cause a leak.**

Recheck the belt tension. When the tension has been correctly adjusted, tighten the bolts to specifications.

ADJUSTING THE AIR CONDITIONING COMPRESSOR BELT

With A Rotary Compressor

Loosen the three belt tensioning adjusting screws; one at the compressor rear and two at the compressor front mounting brackets. Install the belt tension gauge on the compressor clutch drive belt. Insert a flex handle, having a 1/2-inch drive, into the belt tensioning pry bar slot, and then move the compressor toward or away from the engine to obtain the specified belt tension.

To check the belt tension, position a tension gauge as shown. The tension is correct when the indicator marks are lined up with the gauge body.

Tighten the three adjusting screws and recheck the belt tension.

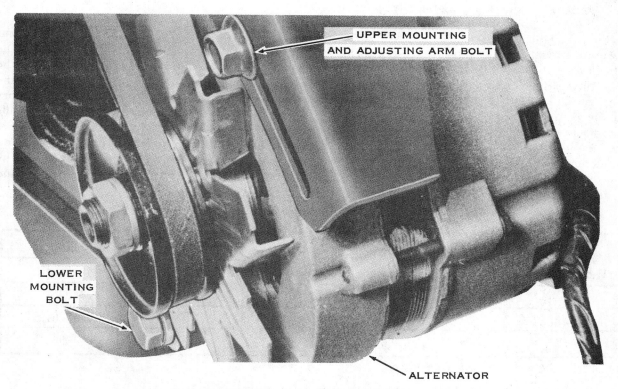

Typical alternator mounting and adjusting bolts.

The drive belt should be adjusted so that there is about ½″ free play when depressed in the center of the longest span.

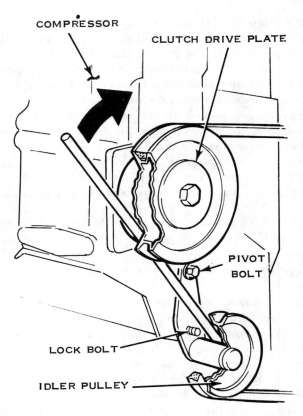

To adjust the air conditioner drive belt, it is necessary to insert a pry bar between the two pulleys, as shown. To increase belt tension, push upward on the pry handle.

With A Two-Cylinder Compressor

Adjust the belt by repositioning the idler pulley, if so equipped. Loosen the bolts attaching the idler pulley bracket to the engine block, reposition the assembly and retighten the bolts.

If not equipped with an idler pulley, adjust the belt tension by moving the compressor. To do this, loosen the bolts securing the compressor to the compressor mounting bracket.

Install the belt tension gauge on the compressor clutch drive belt. Move the compressor toward or away from the engine until the specified belt tension is obtained. Remove the gauge. Tighten the compressor-to-support bracket bolts. Install the tension gauge and recheck the belt tension.

ADJUSTING THE AIR PUMP DRIVE BELT

Install the belt tension gauge on the drive belt and check the tension. Adjust as necessary by loosening the air pump mounting and adjusting arm bolts. Move the air pump toward or away from the engine until the correct tension is obtained. Use a suitable bar and pry against the pump rear cover to hold belt tension while tightening the mounting bolts. **CAUTION: Do not pry against the pump housing or you will destroy it.**

Remove the gauge. Tighten the air pump adjusting arm and mounting bolts. Install the tension gauge and recheck the belt tension.

Belt Width	Minimum Tension (for use at maintenance interval only) (Hot Engine)	Installation Tension	
		Used Belt ①	New Belt
1/4″	30 lbs.	60 lbs.	80 lbs.
3/8″ and 15/32″	50 lbs.	110 lbs.	140 lbs.
1/2″	50 lbs.	110 lbs.	140 lbs.

① Any belt that has operated for ten minutes or more is considered a used belt.

Drive belt tension specifications.

COOLING SYSTEM

CHECKING THE COOLANT LEVEL

CAUTION: Avoid injury when checking a hot radiator. Muffle the radiator cap in a thick cloth and turn it slowly counterclockwise until the pressure escapes. After the pressure has completely dissipated, finish removing the cap.

Fill a vertical-flow type radiator only to the COLD FILL mark. **CAUTION: Check the level cold, the engine must not be running.**

If equipped with a constant-full (coolant recovery) system, check the level in the radiator COLD, and then add coolant as necessary to the radiator and to the overflow tank (plastic bottle).

Use the recommended mixture of permanent anti-freeze and water to maintain adequate protection against the temperatures to be encountered in the area of operation. To provide sufficient protection against corrosion and boiling, this level should be at least 0 degrees F.

To avoid chemical damage to the cooling system, do not mix different brands of anti-freeze. Use only those permanent anti-freeze brands which meet manufacturer's specifications.

CHECKING THE ANTI-FREEZE PROTECTION

Be sure the engine is at operating temperature. Check the anti-freeze in the cooling system by using a permanent anti-freeze test hydrometer. Standard protection is to -20 degrees F. (-35 degrees F. for Canadian and Alaskan vehicles) with a solution of water and permanent anti-freeze meeting your car's specifications.

CAUTION: Use extreme care when removing the cap from a hot radiator. Avoid rapid escape of pressurized fluid that can cause injury.

INSPECTING THE HOSES

Inspect the cooling system hoses for evidence of cracking, checking or weathering. Replace all cracked hoses. Check for leaking or porous hoses and tighten or replace. Make sure all supporting brackets for the hoses are in place and that the hoses are properly installed in the brackets.

Inspect the radiator core and tanks for seepage or leaks. Check all fittings to see that they are tight and in good condition. Examine the hoses at the fittings for cuts or weakness.

REPLACING THE COOLANT

To drain the radiator, open the drain cock located at the bottom of the radiator and remove the cylinder block drain plug(s). The 4-cylinder engines have one plug in the side of the engine block; the V-8 and V-6 engines have a drain plug on each side of the cylinder block.

To fill the cooling system, close the drain cock. Install the block drain plug(s). Disconnect the heater outlet hose at the water pump to release trapped air in the system. When the coolant begins to escape, connect the heater outlet hose.

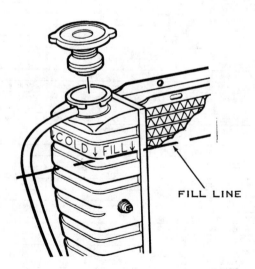

Fill a cross-flow type radiator only to the COLD FILL line. Fill a vertical-flow type radiator to one inch below the lower flange of the radiator filler neck.

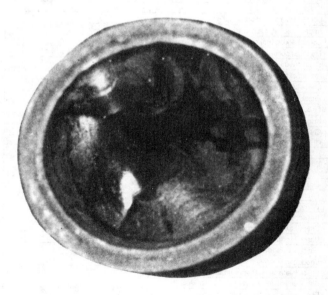

A rusted radiator hose is an indication that the rest of the cooling system is in a similar condition. Overheating and engine damage can result.

NON-EMISSION SYSTEMS SCHEDULED MAINTENANCE

Vehicles Designated Schedule "A" or "B" on Glovebox and Engine Emission Control Information Decal.	SERVICE INTERVAL — Time in months or mileage in thousands, whichever occurs first.									
MAINTENANCE OPERATION	5	10	15	20	25	30	35	40	45	50
Inspect Exhaust System Heat Shields (3)			AB			AB			AB	AB
Check Automatic Transmission Fluid Level	AB		AB			AB			AB	
Check Manual Transmission Fluid Level	AB		AB			AB			AB	
Check Rear Axle Fluid Level	AB		AB			AB			AB	
Check Brake Master Cylinder Fluid Level		AB	AB			AB			AB	
Inspect Clutch Linkage (2)		AB	AB			AB			AB	
Inspect Steering Linkage for Abnormal looseness or damaged seals			AB			AB			AB	
Adjust Automatic Transmission Bands (at 5,000, 15,000, 30,000 and 45,000 miles for severe service) (1)			AB							
Inspect Brake Lining, Lines, Hoses and front wheel bearing lube (2)					AB					AB
Lubricate Front Suspension and Steering Linkage						AB				
Drain and Refill Automatic Transmission Fluid — Continuous Service Only						AB				

Vehicles Designated Schedule "C" on Glovebox and Engine Emission Control information Decal.	SERVICE INTERVAL — Time in months or mileage in thousands, whichever occurs first.							
MAINTENANCE OPERATION	6	12	18	24	30	36	42	48
Check automatic transmission fluid level — add fluid if required	C		C		C		C	
Check brake master cylinder fluid level — add fluid if required	C	C	C	C	C	C	C	C
Check steering linkage for abnormal looseness or damaged seals		C		C		C		C
Lubricate front suspension, ball joints						C		
Check rear axle fluid level — add fluid if required	C		C		C		C	
Adjust automatic transmission bands (at 6,000, 18,000, 30,000, 42,000 for severe service) (1)		C						
Inspect brake lining, lines, hoses and front wheel bearing lube (2)				C				C
Check manual transmission fluid level — add fluid if required	C		C		C		C	
Check clutch linkage and adjust clutch pedal free play — adjust if required	C	C	C	C	C	C	C	C
Inspect exhaust system shields (3) (5)		C		C		C		C

NOTES:

(1)   Severe Service Operation — When vehicle is operated under any of the following conditions, observe severe service recommendations:
 - Extended period of idling or low speed operation such as police, taxi or door-to-door delivery.
 - Operation when outside temperature remains below +10°F. for 60 days or more and most trips are less than 10 miles.
 - Operation in severe dust conditions.

(2)   Adjust, repair or replace as required.

(3)   Remove accumulated debris or replace shield as required. Inspect for loose weld attachments, damage or deterioration.

(4)   Inspect at 5,000 mile intervals whenever the vehicle has been operated under the following conditions: a. On gravel roads   b. Off-road use   c. Severe road load conditions

(5)   Inspect at 6,000 mile intervals whenever the vehicle has been operated under the following conditions: a. On gravel roads   b. Off-road use   c. Severe road load conditions

Lubrication maintenance schedule. "Inspect" denotes a visual inspection, while "check" means an operational check to uncover defects and make repairs.

Items should be checked periodically and service performed when required. These services are not covered by the Warranty, you will be charged for the labor, parts and lubricants used.

MAINTENANCE OPERATION	WHEN PERFORMED
Inspect wheels and tires for damage and tighten lug nuts.	Periodically or if wheels are noisy.
Balance and rotate wheels and tires.	Tires show uneven wear pattern or vibrate.
Replace tires.	When tread wear indicator appears.
Front suspension check.	Abnormal tire wear.
Check front wheel alignment and steering linkage.	Abnormal tire wear if normal realignment is not required.
Check tire air pressure.	At least monthly.
Check power steering reservoir.	Each time engine oil is checked or when fueling car.
Inspect steering mechanism.	Hard steering, excessive free play, or unusual noise.
Check parking brake operation.	Excessive foot pedal travel required or will not hold car.
Check air conditioning system.	At beginning of warm weather season.
Check headlight alignment.	Light beam appears improperly aimed.
Inspect exterior lights and replace bulbs as required.	When performing regular car services (fueling, cleaning, etc.)
Check operation of turn signals, high beam indicator, and hazard flashers.	When performing regular car services (fueling, cleaning, etc.)
Check operation of engine warning lights.	Each time engine is started.
Check accelerator pedal operation.	If uneven pressure is observed or pedal does not function smoothly.
Inspect brake system components.	When brake light glows with engine running; if brakes are noisy or brake pedal travel is excessive.
Check and lubricate hood latches and auxiliary catch, hood, door, and trunk lid hinges and checks, and all lock cylinders.	When performing regular car service or when noisy or hard to operate.
Replace windshield wiper blade elements.	Blades do not properly clean windshield after wiper blades and glass have been properly cleaned.
Check windshield washers aim and reservoir level.	When insufficient solution is sprayed on windshield or improper cleaning is observed after function.
Clean body drain holes.	Improper water drainage from body is suspected.
Check locking of seatback latches.	Periodically (with doors closed.)
Check seat belt buckles, release mechanisms, and retractor locking.	Regularly.
Inspect seat belt webbing for cuts or broken fibers.	Regularly (replace if cut or broken).
Check horn operation.	Periodically or when malfunction is suspected.
Check for fluid leaks on pavement (water dripping from A/C after use is normal).	After car has been parked a while or when possible to observe underbody when vehicle is raised.
Lubricate transmission controls, kickdown linkage, and clutch linkage.	When moving parts and connections are sluggish in action.
Check engine coolant level and add as required.	When engine overheats, or once a month.
Check heater and radiator hoses.	Regularly (replace if cut or broken).
Check engine oil level and add as required.	When fueling vehicle.
Check battery water and add as required.	Every three months; more often in hot weather.
Lubricate door weatherstrips.	When squeaky or noisy during window operation or visual inspection shows need.
Test anti-theft alarm system operation.	Periodically or when malfunction is suspected.
Lubricate clutch (except cable) and transmission shift linkage.	When moving parts and connections are void of lube or sluggish in action.

Non-scheduled maintenance, which should be checked periodically and serviced when needed.

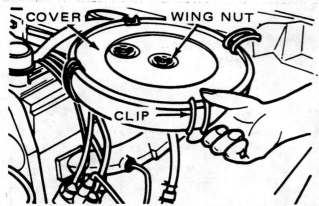

To gain access to the air filter, remove the wing nuts at the top, and then snap off the retaining clips.

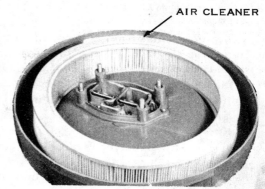

The filter element can be lifted out after removing the cover. CAUTION: If the filter has the word TOP molded into it, make sure that that side faces up.

To avoid overheating in very hot weather, use mixtures with not more than 50 percent anti-freeze, except in areas where anti-freeze protection below 35 degrees F is required. In this case, refer to the coolant mixture chart on the permanent anti-freeze container.

After the initial fill, the coolant level may drop approximately one quart after the engine has been operated about 20 minutes at 2000 rpm. This is due to the displacement of entrapped air. Refill to the proper level.

FUEL SYSTEM

CHECKING THE THROTTLE LINKAGE

Depress the accelerator pedal all the way to the floor and check to see that the throttle is fully open. Release the accelerator pedal and be sure the throttle lever and

pedal return to their original positions. Check all pivot points for binding. Check the throttle return springs for broken or damaged springs. Check the accelerator cable for kinks or other restrictions. Replace all broken or damaged parts. Lubricate the moving parts with engine oil.

CHECKING THE CHOKE LINKAGE

Examine the choke external linkage for free operation. If the linkage appears to be sticking or is dirty, clean it using a brush and common mineral-spirits type cleaning fluid. Operate the choke plate manually to make sure that it moves freely. Lubricate the choke plate shaft at each end and the choke operating linkage with engine oil if necessary.

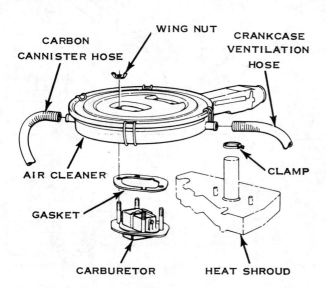

Always replace the gasket under the air cleaner assembly whenever it is removed. Failure to have a good seal at this point will allow unfiltered air to enter the engine.

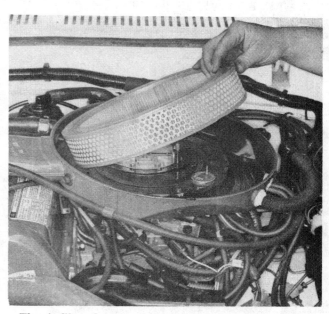

The air filter element can be replaced after taking off the top cover. It should be replaced periodically to minimize any restriction in the flow of air into the engine, which would cause the gas mileage to drop.

CHECKING THE THROTTLE-STOP SOLENOID

With the throttle solenoid connected and the engine running, open the throttle by hand. The solenoid plunger should follow the throttle lever until the plunger is fully extended. Disconnect the solenoid lead. The plunger should retract. If the solenoid does not operate properly, replace it.

INSPECTING THE FUEL LINES FOR LEAKAGE

With the engine off examine the fuel line connections for wetness, washed, or stained areas that indicate a fuel leak. Start the engine and observe all the connections for fuel seepage. Tighten or replace fuel lines as necessary.

CHECKING THE HEATED-AIR SYSTEM (VACUUM MOTOR TYPE)

Look into the snorkel to see if the heat door is wide open with the engine not running. Start the engine, and the door should move quickly to the heat-on position and remain there until the engine starts to heat. Then the door should move gradually to the heat-off position and should be wide open when the engine is fully heated.

REPLACING THE AIR CLEANER FILTER

Remove the wing nuts holding the air cleaner (and duct if so equipped) assembly to the carburetor. Disconnect the crankcase ventilation system hose at the air cleaner.

The fuel filter should be changed periodically to minimize the possibility of small dirt particles entering the carburetor and causing the float needle valve to remain partially open, thus raising the float level and lowering the gas mileage.

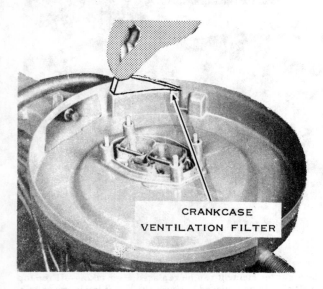

Replacing the crankcase ventilation filter.

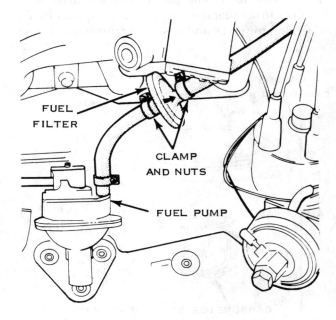

Some in-line filter elements are secured by means of clamps. Note the arrow to designate the direction of fuel flow. In some cases, the filter is screwed into the carburetor fuel bowl.

Remove the air cleaner and duct assembly from the carburetor. **CAUTION: To prevent dirt from entering the carburetor, the filter element must never be removed when the air cleaner body is mounted on the carburetor.**

Remove the air cleaner cover and filter element. Discard the air cleaner mounting gasket.

INSTALLING

Install a new air cleaner mounting gasket on the carburetor. **CAUTION: An air leak here will allow unfiltered air to enter the engine and cause excessive abrasive wear.** Install the air cleaner body on the carburetor, or position the air cleaner and air intake duct-and-valve assembly on the carburetor (and shroud tube if so equipped) so that the word FRONT faces the front of the car.

Place the new air cleaner filter element in the air cleaner body. **CAUTION: Make sure the filter is properly seated. If the word TOP is indicated on the filter element, make sure the word TOP faces up.** Install the cover and tighten the wing bolt. Connect the crankcase vent hose to the air cleaner.

REPLACING THE FUEL FILTER

The fuel filter used on all engines is of one-piece construction and cannot be cleaned. Replace the filter if it becomes clogged or restricted. Otherwise, replace it at the interval specified in the maintenance schedule.

To replace the filter, remove the air cleaner. Loosen

the retaining clamp(s) securing the fuel inlet hose to the fuel filter. Unscrew the fuel filter from the carburetor. Disconnect the fuel filter from the hose and discard the retaining clamp.

Install a new clamp on the inlet hose and connect the hose to the new filter. Screw the filter into the carburetor inlet port.

Position the fuel line hose clamp(s) and crimp the clamp(s) securely. Start the engine and check for fuel leaks.

IGNITION SYSTEM

CHECKING THE DISTRIBUTOR

Remove the distributor cap and inspect for cracks. Also check the inside of the cap for carbon build-up. Check the contact points for erosion. Also, remove the rotor and check for cracks or a bent or corroded contact arm.

Squirt a few drops of SAE 10W engine oil into the distributor oil cup, if so equipped.

REPLACING SPARK PLUGS

Remove the wire from each spark plug by grasping, twisting, and then pulling the moulded cap of the wire. **CAUTION: Do not pull on the wire because the**

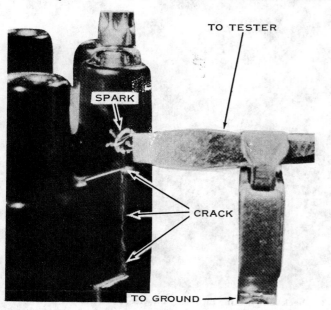

A cracked distributor cap can be checked by using a screwdriver and jumper wire that is grounded at one end. Move the tip of the screwdriver around the cap and along the high-tension wires with the engine running to determine cracks and leaks.

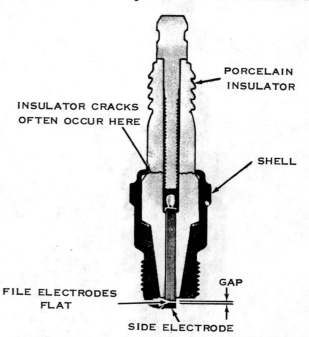

Details of the spark plug. You must file the electrodes to remove the corrosion that causes resistance, which leads to misfiring. Always bend the side electrode to adjust the gap; bending the center electrode will crack the porcelain. Insulator cracks in the area shown are always caused by tilting the socket when removing the spark plug.

After loosening the spark plug a few threads, it is good practice to blow away all dirt to keep it from entering the combustion chamber.

connection inside the cap may become separated or the weather seal may be damaged.

Clean the area around each spark plug port with compressed air; then remove the spark plugs.

Set the spark plug gap by bending the ground

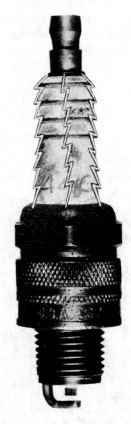

Dirty insulators cause flash-over and misfiring, especially in damp weather.

electrode. **CAUTION: Never bend the center electrode or you will crack the insulator.**

Install the spark plugs and torque each to 15 to 20 ft-lbs. Connect the spark plug wires. Check the wire position in the support brackets. Press the wires firmly into the proper bracket slots. Push the all-weather seals firmly into position.

CHECKING THE SECONDARY WIRES

A breakdown or energy loss in the secondary circuit can be caused by: fouled or improperly adjusted spark plugs; defective high-tension wiring; or high-tension leakage across the coil, distributor cap, or rotor resulting from an accumulation of dirt.

To check the spark intensity at the spark plugs, thereby isolating an ignition problem to a particular cylinder, proceed to check the spark intensity of one wire at a time.

When removing the wires from spark plugs, grasp and twist the molded cap back and forth on the plug insulator to free the cap. Use a tool to pull the cap from the insulator. **CAUTION: Do not pull directly on the wire, or it may become separated from the connector inside the cap to cause a loss of energy to that spark plug, which will result in a misfire.**

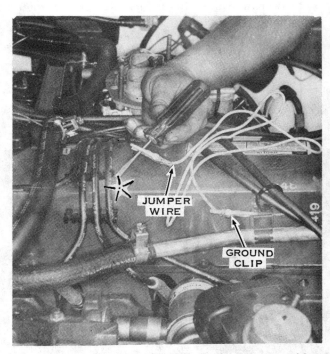

To check for a leaking high-tension wire, use a jumper with one end grounded. Disconnect the high-tension cable to the spark plug to increase the voltage in the cable and make the test more effective. If you draw a spark, you have a crack in the cable. In any case, replace the cables every two years to minimize hard-starting problems.

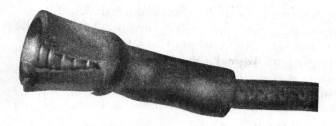

Spark plug wires that are old, dry out and crack, allowing moisture to leak through and this causes misfiring.

Install an adapter in the terminal of the wire to be checked. Hold the adapter approximately 3/16-inch from the exhaust manifold and crank the engine, using an auxiliary starter switch. The spark should jump the gap regularly. If the spark intensity of each wire is satisfactory, the coil, rotor, distributor cap, and the secondary wires are probably satisfactory.

If the spark is good at only some wires, check the resistance of the faulty leads with an ohmmeter, or replace the wire.

If the spark is equal at all wires, but weak or intermittent, check the coil, distributor cap, and the coil-to-distributor high-tension wire. The wire should be clean and bright on the conducting ends and on the coil tower and distributor sockets. The wire must fit snugly and be securely bottomed in the sockets.

BATTERY

CHECKING THE STATE OF CHARGE

With the battery temperature at 80 degrees F, the battery should have a specific gravity reading of not less than 1.230. **WARNING: Hydrogen and oxygen gases are produced during normal battery operation. This combustible mixture can explode if flames or sparks are brought near the vent openings of the battery. The sulphuric acid in the battery electrolyte can cause a serious burn if spilled on the skin or spattered in the eyes. It should be flushed away with large quantities of clear water.**

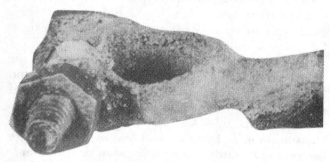

Corroded battery terminal which can cause all kinds of electrical trouble: hard starting, burned out alternator, and short lightbulb life.

Keep the fluid in each battery cell up to the level of the ring in the bottom of the filler well. Generally, tap water can be added unless it has a high mineral content or has been stored in a metal container. If the tap water is unsuitable for these reasons, distilled water should be used.

CHECKING THE BATTERY CABLES

Check the battery cable connections for clean terminals and tightness. Cables must be tight in the terminals and the terminals tight to the posts. A light coating of non-metallic grease can be applied to the terminals and posts to retard corrosion and oxidation.

CLUTCH AND MANUAL TRANSMISSION

LUBRICATING THE CLUTCH AND SHIFT LINKAGE

Clean and lubricate the shift linkage, trunnions, and external shift mechanism (floor shift) with lubricant meeting Ford Chassis and Ball Joint Lube specifications. If excessive shifting efforts are encountered, apply one or two drops of engine oil at the transmission shift arm pivot points.

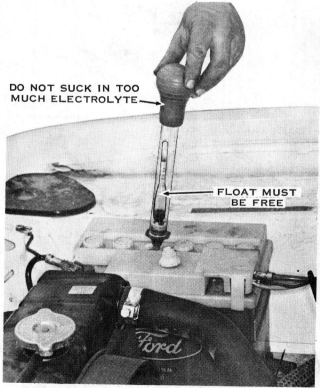

DO NOT SUCK IN TOO MUCH ELECTROLYTE

FLOAT MUST BE FREE

A hydrometer is needed to test the electrolyte of a storage battery. Keep the tube vertical and draw in only enough fluid to lift the float.

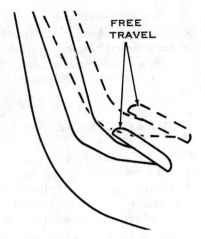

The clutch pedal free travel must be ½" with the engine running at about 3,000 rpm.

ADJUSTING THE CLUTCH PEDAL FREE PLAY

From under the car, loosen the cable locknuts and the adjusting nut at the flywheel housing boss. Pull the cable toward the front of the car until free movement of the release lever is eliminated.

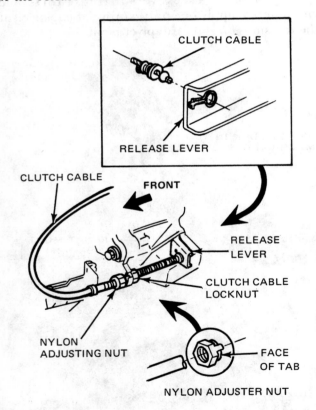

To make the clutch pedal free travel adjustment, loosen the clutch cable locknut, pull the cable to the front of the car until the tabs on the nylon adjuster nut are clear, and then rotate the nut to obtain ¼" clearance.

Holding the cable in this position, place a 1/4 inch spacer against the flywheel housing boss (on the engine side). Run the adjusting nut against the spacer fingertight. Tighten the front locknut against the adjusting nut, being careful not to disturb the adjustment. Torque the locknut to 40-60 ft-lbs.

Remove the spacer and tighten the rear locknut against the flywheel housing boss.

CHECKING THE TRANSMISSION FLUID LEVEL

Clean all dirt and grease from the area around the filler plug, and then remove the plug from the side of the case. If lubricant does not flow from the hole, fill the case with the specified lubricant until it is level with the bottom of the filler hole with the car in a level position. Install the filler plug.

AUTOMATIC TRANSMISSION

LUBRICATING THE LINKAGE

Lubricate all pivot points in the kickdown linkage with lubricant meeting Ford Chassis and Ball Joint Lube specifications.

CHECKING THE FLUID LEVEL

The automatic transmission is designed to operate with the oil level between the ADD and FULL marks on the dipstick at an operating temperature of 150 degrees F to 170 degrees F, and should be checked under these conditions. The operating temperature can be obtained by driving 15 to 20 miles of city type driving with the outside temperature above 50°F.

With the transmission in PARK, engine at curb idle rpm, foot brakes applied, and the vehicle on a level surface, move the transmission selector lever through each range, allowing time in each range to engage transmission units. Return to the PARK position and apply the parking brake.

Clean all dirt from the transmission fluid dipstick cap, and then pull the dipstick out of the tube. Wipe it clean, and then push it all the way back into the tube. Be sure it is fully seated.

Pull the dipstick out of the tube again and check the fluid level, which should be between the ADD and FULL marks. If additional fluid is required, add enough through the filler tube to bring the level between the marks. **CAUTION: Do not overfill the transmission, as foaming and loss of fluid through the vent can result in a transmission malfunction.**

Install the dipstick, making sure it is fully seated in the tube.

Throttle	Range	Shift	OPS–RPM	1	2
Minimum (10" - 15" Vacuum)	D	1-2	590-760	12-16	11-15
	D	2-3	820-1100	17-23	16-22
	D	3-2	680-800	14-17	13-16
	D	2-1	340-450	7-9	6-9
To Detent (Torque Demand)	1	2-1	1060-1570	21-32	20-31
	D	1-2	760-1070	16-22	15-21
	D	2-3	1480-2050	30-42	29-40
	D	3-2	1760 Max.	36 Max.	35 Max.
Through Detent (W.O.T.)	D	1-2	1790-2100	37-43	35-41
	D	2-3	3150-3490	64-72	62-69
	D	3-2	3200 Max.	66 Max.	63 Max.
	D	3-1	1180 Max.	24 Max.	23 Max.

Axle Ratio	Tire Size	Use Column No.
Pinto 3.40:1	BR70 x 13	1
	B78 x 13	1
	BR78 x 13	1
3.55:1	BR70 x 13	2
	B78 x 13	2
	BR78 x 13	2
	CR70 x 13	2

Typical shift points for a Ford four-cylinder engine.

The automatic transmission fluid level dipstick shows a pair of arrows to indicate the two levels which are acceptable. CAUTION: Don't overfill.

CHECKING THE TRANSMISSION INITIAL ENGAGEMENT

Initial engagement checks are made to determine if band and clutch engagements are smooth.

Run the engine until its normal operating temperature is reached. With the engine at the correct idle speed, shift the selector lever from N to 2, D1, and R. Observe the initial band and clutch engagements. Band and clutch engagements should be smooth in all positions. Rough initial engagements in D are caused by high engine idle speed or high control pressure.

Throttle	Range	Shift	OPS–RPM	1	2	3	4	5	6	7	8
Closed (Above 17" Vacuum)	D	1-2	370-440	8-10	8-10	8-10	8-10	7-9	7-9	7-8	7-8
	D	2-3	400-960	9-22	9-22	9-22	9-21	8-19	8-19	8-19	8-19
	D	3-1	370-440	8-10	8-10	8-10	8-10	7-9	7-9	7-8	7-8
	1	2-1	1470-1800	34-42	34-41	33-41	33-41	30-37	30-36	29-36	29-36
To Detent (Torque Demand)	D	1-2	840-1500	19-35	19-34	19-34	19-34	17-31	17-30	17-30	16-30
	D	2-3	1470-2220	34-52	34-51	33-51	33-50	30-46	30-45	29-45	29-44
	D	3-2	1380 Max.	32 Max.	32 Max.	31 Max.	31 Max.	28 Max.	28 Max.	28 Max.	27 Max.
	D	3-1 2-1	440 Max.	10 Max.	10 Max.	10 Max.	10 Max.	9 Max.	9 Max.	8 Max.	8 Max.
Through Detent (W.O.T.)	D	1-2	1720-2210	40-52	39-51	39-50	39-50	35-45	35-45	35-45	34-44
	D	2-3	3082-3800	72-89	71-88	71-87	70-86	64-79	63-77	62-77	62-76
	D	3-2	3270 Max.	76 Max.	75 Max.	75 Max.	74 Max.	67 Max.	67 Max.	66 Max.	66 Max.
	D	3-1 2-1	1950 Max.	45 Max.	45 Max.	44 Max.	44 Max.	40 Max.	39 Max.	39 Max.	39 Max.

Axle Ratio	Tire Size	Use Column No.
3.00:1	DR70-13	1
	CR70-13, B78-13	2
	175-13	3
	BR70-13, BR78-13	4
3.40:1	DR70-13	5
	CR70-13, B78-13	6
	175-13	7
	BR70-13, BR78-13	8

Typical shift points for a Ford V-6 engine.

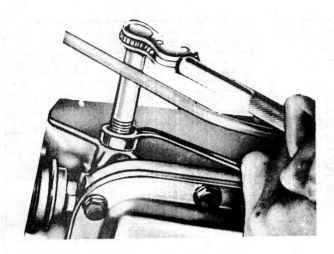

Adjusting the low-reverse band.

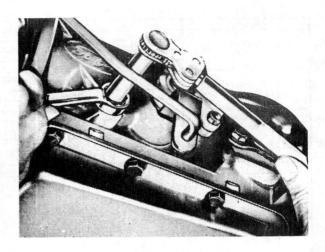

Adjusting the intermediate band.

CHECKING THE SHIFT POINTS

Check the light throttle upshifts in D. The transmission should start in first gear, shift to second, and shift to third within the shift points specified.

With the transmission in third gear, depress the accelerator pedal through the detent (to the floor). The transmission should shift from third to second, or third to first, depending on vehicle speed.

Check the closed-throttle downshift from third to first by coasting down from about 30 mph in third gear. The shift should occur within the limits specified.

CHECKING THE NEUTRAL-START SWITCH

Start the engine with the transmission selector lever in PARK and again in NEUTRAL. The engine should start in these gears only. Adjust the switch, if necessary.

ADJUSTING THE NEUTRAL-START SWITCH

With the manual lever properly adjusted, loosen the two switch attaching bolts. With the transmission manual lever in NEUTRAL, rotate the switch, and then insert the gauge pin (No. 43 drill shank end) into the gauge pin holes of the switch. **CAUTION: The gauge pin has to be inserted to a full 31/64 inch into the three holes of the switch.**

Tighten the two switch attaching bolts to 55 to 75 in-lbs. of torque. Remove the gauge pin from the switch.

Check the operation of the switch. The engine should start only with the transmission selector lever in NEUTRAL and PARK.

REAR AXLE

CHECKING THE LUBRICANT LEVEL

Clean all dirt and grease from the area around the filler plug, and then remove the plug at the location shown on the Lubrication Charts in this manual.

When checking the lubricant level, the axle must be in a normal curb position. If checked on a frame

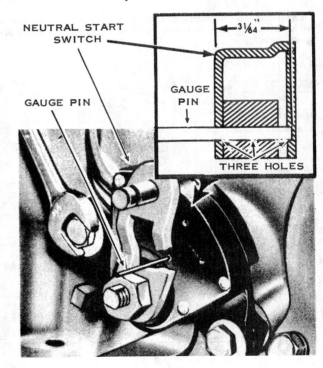

Neutral start switch adjustment. The gauge pin should be a No. 43 drill shank, as discussed in the text.

contact hoist, use safety stands to hold the axle in a normal curb position. Add the specified lubricant until it is level with the bottom of the filler hole. Replace the filler plug.

STEERING MECHANISM

INSPECTING THE STEERING LINKAGE

Check for looseness at the tie-rod ends. Looseness can affect the toe readings and adjustment.

Check the front suspension ball joints and mountings for looseness. Check the brake caliper attaching bolts. Torque all loose nuts and bolts to specifications. Be sure all cotter pins are correctly installed.

Check the steering gear mountings and all steering linkage connections for looseness. Torque all loose mountings to specifications.

CHECKING THE STEERING COLUMN LOCK

Place the transmission selector lever in PARK position on vehicles equipped with an automatic transmission; place it in REVERSE if equipped with a manual transmission.

Turn the key to the LOCK position. Some models are equipped with a lock button on the left side of the steering column, which must be depressed first. Turn the steering wheel left or right slightly until it snaps into the lock detent.

Check to see if the steering wheel is locked in both directions. *NOTE: The selector lever will remain locked only in the PARK position on the column-shift vehicles. The key can be removed from the ignition lock in the LOCK position only.* With the key in the ignition lock, open the driver's door to check the operation of the key removal warning buzzer.

CHECKING THE STEERING CONTROL

Road-test the vehicle and check it for harshness, noise, wander, or free play. Check the steering wheel return for stiffness or inconsistency in either direction.

If the steering is exceptionally stiff, put the vehicle on a hoist and disconnect the pitman arm. Check the steering effort with a scale on the rim of the steering wheel. The effort required to rotate the steering wheel should not exceed specifications. Adjust as required.

INSPECTING THE BALL JOINTS FOR WEAR

UPPER BALL JOINT

Raise the vehicle and place floor jacks beneath the lower arms.

Ask an assistant to grasp the lower edge of the tire and move the wheel in and out. Observe the upper end of the spindle and the upper arm.

ALIGNMENT MARKS

Straight-ahead alignment marks are located on the steering wheel rim and column tube.

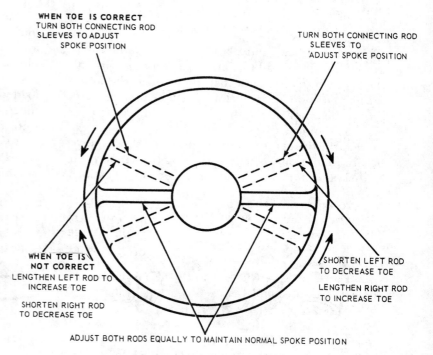

WHEN TOE IS CORRECT
TURN BOTH CONNECTING ROD SLEEVES TO ADJUST SPOKE POSITION

TURN BOTH CONNECTING ROD SLEEVES TO ADJUST SPOKE POSITION

WHEN TOE IS NOT CORRECT
LENGTHEN LEFT ROD TO INCREASE TOE
SHORTEN RIGHT ROD TO DECREASE TOE

SHORTEN LEFT ROD TO DECREASE TOE
LENGTHEN RIGHT ROD TO INCREASE TOE

ADJUST BOTH RODS EQUALLY TO MAINTAIN NORMAL SPOKE POSITION

Toe-in adjustments to keep the steering wheel aligned.

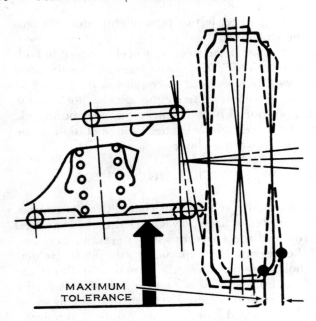

Measuring the lower ball joint radial play.

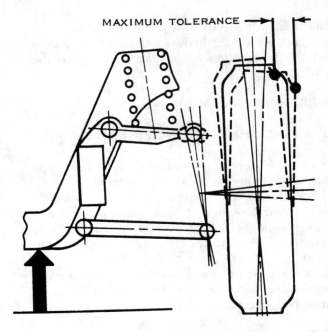

Measuring the upper ball joint radial play.

Any movement between the upper end of the spindle and the upper arm indicates ball joint wear and loss of preload. If any such movement is observed, replace the upper suspension arm. **CAUTION: During the check, the lower ball joint will be unloaded and may move. Disregard all such movement. Also, do not mistake loose wheel bearings for a worn ball joint.**

LOWER BALL JOINT

Raise the vehicle and place jacks under the lower arms. This will unload the lower ball joints. Adjust the wheel bearings. Attach a dial indicator to the lower arm and position the indicator so that the plunger rests against the inner side of the wheel rim adjacent to the lower ball joint.

Grasp the tire at the top and bottom and slowly move the tire in and out. Note the reading (radial play) on the dial indicator. If the reading exceeds specifications

replace the lower suspension arm. **CAUTION: During the check, the upper ball joint will be unloaded and may move. Disregard all such movement. Also, do not mistake loose wheel bearings for a worn ball joint.**

LUBRICATING THE BALL JOINTS

The plugs are located on the top of the upper ball joint and on the underside of the lower ball joint. Wipe all accumulated dirt from around the lubrication plugs.

Use a hand-operated, low-pressure grease gun, loaded with chassis and ball-joint lubricant which meets specifications. Force lubricant into the joint until the boot can be felt or seen to swell, indicating that the boot is full of lubricant. **CAUTION: Do not overlubricate until lubricant escapes from the boot, as this destroys the weathertight seal.** Install the

Details for making the spindle connecting rod adjustment.

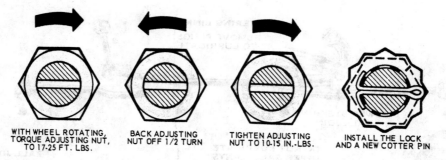

WITH WHEEL ROTATING, TORQUE ADJUSTING NUT, TO 17-25 FT. LBS.

BACK ADJUSTING NUT OFF 1/2 TURN

TIGHTEN ADJUSTING NUT TO 10-15 IN.-LBS.

INSTALL THE LOCK AND A NEW COTTER PIN

Making the front wheel bearing adjustment.

plugs. *NOTE: If the vehicle has been parked in a temperature below 20 degrees F, park it in a heated garage for 30 minutes, or until the joints will accept lubricant.*

INSPECTING THE FRONT WHEEL LINKAGE

Check for specified air pressures in all four tires. Raise the front of the vehicle off the floor. Shake each front wheel, grasping the upper and lower surfaces of the tire. Check the front suspension ball joints and mountings for looseness, wear, or damage.

Check the brake backing plate mountings. Torque all loose nuts and bolts to specification. Replace all worn parts.

Check the steering gear mountings and all steering linkage connections for looseness. Torque all mountings to specifications. If any of the linkage is worn or bent, replace the parts.

Check the front wheel bearings. If any in-and-out free play is noticed, adjust the bearings to specifications. Replace worn or damaged bearings. Spin each front wheel to check for balance.

Check the action of the shock absorbers. If the shock absorbers are not in good condition, the vehicle may not settle in a normal, level position, and front wheel alignment will be affected.

LUBRICATING THE STEERING LINKAGE

Wipe all accumulated dirt from around the lubrication plugs, and then remove the plugs. Use a rubber-tipped, hand-operated grease gun at low pressure, loaded with lubricant which meets specifications; to force lubricant into the joint until the joint boot can be felt or seen to swell, indicating that the boot is full of lubricant. **CAUTION: Do not overlubricate, until lubricant escapes from the boot, as this destroys the weathertight seal. Install the plug.** *NOTE: If the vehicle has been parked in a temperature below 20 degrees F, park it in a heated garage for 10 minutes, until the joints will accept lubricant.*

LUBRICATING THE STEERING ARM STOPS

Clean and lubricate all friction points. Steering arm stops are located on the inside of the steering arm and the upturned end of the front suspension strut, where it is attached to the lower control arm.

CHECKING THE POWER STEERING PUMP FLUID LEVEL

Run the engine until the fluid is at normal operating

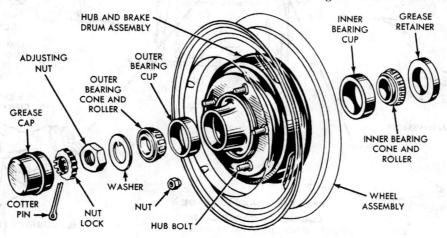

ADJUSTING NUT

HUB AND BRAKE DRUM ASSEMBLY

OUTER BEARING CONE AND ROLLER

OUTER BEARING CUP

INNER BEARING CUP

GREASE RETAINER

GREASE CAP

COTTER PIN

NUT LOCK

WASHER

NUT

HUB BOLT

INNER BEARING CONE AND ROLLER

WHEEL ASSEMBLY

Details of the front wheel and bearing assembly.

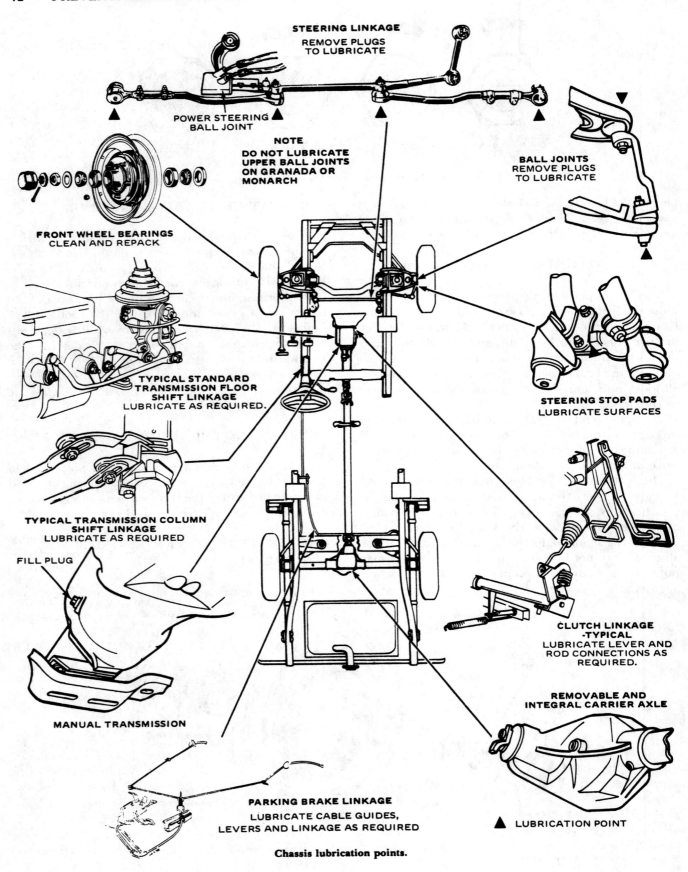

STEERING LINKAGE
REMOVE PLUGS
TO LUBRICATE

POWER STEERING
BALL JOINT

NOTE
DO NOT LUBRICATE
UPPER BALL JOINTS
ON GRANADA OR
MONARCH

BALL JOINTS
REMOVE PLUGS
TO LUBRICATE

FRONT WHEEL BEARINGS
CLEAN AND REPACK

**TYPICAL STANDARD
TRANSMISSION FLOOR
SHIFT LINKAGE**
LUBRICATE AS REQUIRED.

STEERING STOP PADS
LUBRICATE SURFACES

**TYPICAL TRANSMISSION COLUMN
SHIFT LINKAGE**
LUBRICATE AS REQUIRED

FILL PLUG

**CLUTCH LINKAGE
-TYPICAL**
LUBRICATE LEVER AND
ROD CONNECTIONS AS
REQUIRED.

**REMOVABLE AND
INTEGRAL CARRIER AXLE**

MANUAL TRANSMISSION

PARKING BRAKE LINKAGE
LUBRICATE CABLE GUIDES,
LEVERS AND LINKAGE AS REQUIRED

▲ LUBRICATION POINT

Chassis lubrication points.

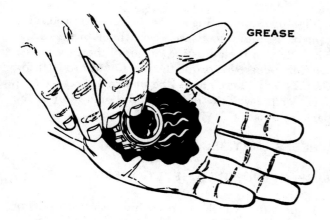

GREASE

Packing a bearing cone with grease.

temperature. Then turn the steering wheel all the way to the left and right several times. Shut off the engine.

Check the fluid level in the power steering reservoir. The level must show on the cross-hatching between the bottom of the dipstick and the full mark. **CAUTION: Do not overfill.** Remove excess fluid with a suction device.

ADJUSTING THE POWER STEERING PUMP DRIVE BELT TENSION

Loosen the adjusting and mounting bolts incorporated on the front face of the pump cover plate (hub side) and the one nut at the rear. Attach a 9/16-inch open-end wrench on the projecting 1/2-inch boss, and then pry upward to correct tension. To adjust the belt on 8 cyl. engines, loosen the mounting bolt in the adjusting slot and the nut directly above the adjusting slot. Place a suitable pry bar between the cast boss on the pump mounting bracket and the cast boss on the pump cover plate, and then pry upward to correct tension. **CAUTION: Do not pry against the reservoir because it can be deformed and cause a leak.**

Recheck the belt tension. When the tension has been correctly adjusted, tighten the bolts to specifications.

BRAKES

INSPECTING THE MASTER CYLINDER FLUID LEVEL

Push the master cylinder cap retainer to one side, and then remove the cover and cover gasket cap from the master cylinder. The gasket which seals the master cylinder should come off with the cap.

Fill the reservoir full or 1/4 inch from the top. Install the cover, making sure that the gasket is properly seated in the cap.

INSPECTING FLEXIBLE BRAKE HOSES

A flexible brake hose should be replaced if it shows signs of softening, cracking, or other damage.

When installing a new front brake hose, position the hose to avoid contact with other chassis parts. Place a new copper gasket over the hose fitting, and then thread the hose assembly into the front wheel cylinder. Engage the opposite end of the hose to the bracket on the frame. Install the horseshoe-type retaining clip, and then connect the tube to the hose with the tube fitting nut.

A rear brake hose should be installed so that it does not touch the muffler outlet pipe or shock absorber. Thread the hose into the rear brake tube connector. Engage the front end of the hose to the bracket on the frame. Install the horseshoe-type retaining clip, and then connect the tube to the hose with the tube fitting nut.

Bleed the hydraulic system to remove all trapped air. **CAUTION: Always check the fluid level in the master cylinder before performing the bleeding procedures.** If the fluid level is not within 1/4 inch of the top of the master cylinder reservoirs, add Extra Heavy Duty brake fluid for all brake applications. *NOTE: The extra heavy duty brake fluid is colored blue for identification purposes.*

CHECKING THE OPERATION OF THE BRAKING SYSTEM

Depress the foot brake pedal for good pedal height before road testing. Check and correct, if required, the following conditions: pull in either direction, harshness or noise, excessive pedal effort, spongy feel, and operation of the brake warning light. **CAUTION: Avoid sudden hard stops—make slow, gradual stops.**

INSPECTING THE DISC BRAKE UNITS FOR WEAR

Raise the vehicle until the wheel and tire clear the floor. Remove the wheel cover or hubcap from the wheel. Remove the wheel and tire from the hub and rotor.

Inspect the brake shoes and linings for wear. If a lining is worn to within 1/32 inch of the rivet heads or if there is more than 0.125" taper from end to end, or if the lining shows evidence of brake fluid contamination, replace all shoe-and-lining assemblies on both front wheels.

Check the rotor for scoring. If the rotor is excessively scored, refinish it or replace the rotor. Visually check the caliper. If the caliper housing is leaking, it should be replaced. If a seal is leaking, the caliper must be disassembled and new seals installed. If a piston is seized in the bore, a new caliper housing is required.

Check the brake hoses for signs of cracking, leaks or abrasion. Replace them if necessary. Install the wheel and hub assembly.

CHECKING THE OPERATION OF THE PARKING BRAKE MECHANISM

Check the operation of the parking brake and indicator light. When the parking brake is fully released, the cable should have no slack, and the rear brakes should not drag when the wheels are turned. Adjust as required with the vehicle on a hoist. If equipped with an indicator light, be sure it glows when the parking brake is engaged.

ADJUSTING THE PARKING BRAKES

Make sure the parking brake is fully released. Place transmission in NEUTRAL, and then raise vehicle.

Tighten the adjusting nut on the equalizer rod at the control assembly to cause rear wheel brake drag. Then, loosen the adjusting nut until the rear brakes are fully released. Torque the jam nut to 7 to 10 ft-lbs. **CAUTION: There should be no brake drag.**

Lower the vehicle and check the operation of the parking brake.

WHEELS AND TIRES

INSPECTING THE WHEEL COVERS

Inspect the wheel covers or hub caps for dents or looseness.

To install a wheel cover, center the tire valve stem in the wheel cover hole, and then position the cover on the wheel, with the valve stem side of the cover tight against the wheel. Use a rubber mallet to tap the cover into place, beginning on the outer perimeter opposite the valve stem. **CAUTION: Avoid damage to the wheel cover.** Be sure the cover is fully seated against the wheel all around the perimeter of the cover.

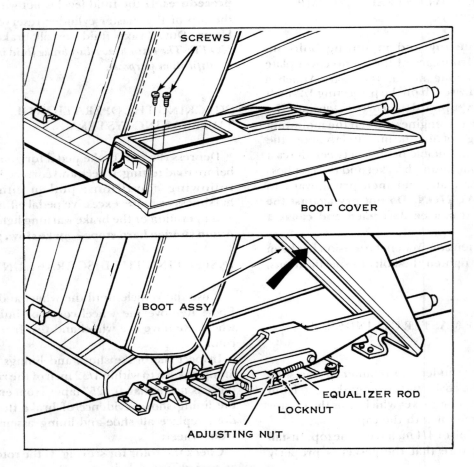

Parking brake adjustment.

INSPECTING THE WHEELS

Wheel hub nuts should be inspected and tightened to specifications. Loose wheel hub nuts can cause shimmy and vibration. Elongated stud holes in the wheels can also result from loose hub nuts.

Keep the wheels and hubs clean. Stones wedged between the wheel and drum and lumps of mud or grease can unbalance a wheel and tire.

Check for damage that would affect the runout of the wheel. Wobble or shimmy caused by a damaged wheel will eventually damage the wheel bearings. Inspect the wheel rims for dents that could permit air to leak from the tires.

CHECKING THE TIRES AND AIR PRESSURE

Inspect the tire treads and remove all stones, nails, glass, or other objects that may be wedged in the tread. Check for holes or cuts that can permit air leakage from the tire. Make necessary repairs. Inspect the tire side walls for cuts and damage. If internal damage is suspected, remove the tire from the wheel for further inspection and repair or replacement.

Check the tire valve for air leaks, and replace the valve, if necessary. Replace all missing valve caps. The tires should be checked frequently to be sure that air pressures agree with those specified for the tires and vehicle model, including the spare.

Inspect the tires for uneven wear that might indicate the need for front-end alignment or tire rotation.

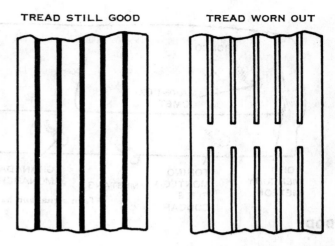

TREAD STILL GOOD **TREAD WORN OUT**

Modern tires have a built-in wear indicator, which shows a band across the tire (right) when the tread is worn to a dangerous condition.

ROTATING THE TIRES

Bias and bias-belted tires should be cross-switched as shown. If the vehicle is equipped with radial ply tires, they can be rotated from front to rear as shown in an accompanying illustration. *NOTE: Cross-switching is not recommended for radial ply tires.* **CAUTION: If the car is equipped with the optional Space Saver Tire, do not include it during rotation of the other four tires. CAUTION: Tires should not be rotated until the cause of unusual or uneven wear is located and corrected.**

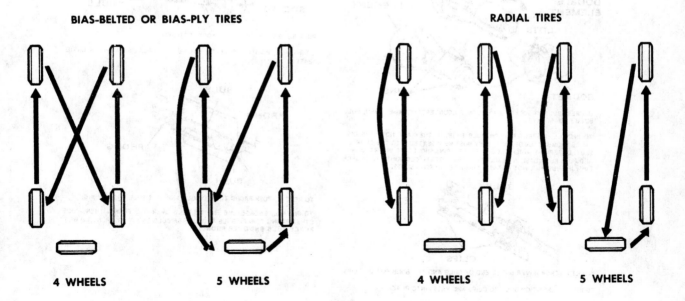

BIAS-BELTED OR BIAS-PLY TIRES   **RADIAL TIRES**

4 WHEELS   **5 WHEELS**   **4 WHEELS**   **5 WHEELS**

Tire rotation diagram to equalize tread wear. Note the different rotation for radial tires.

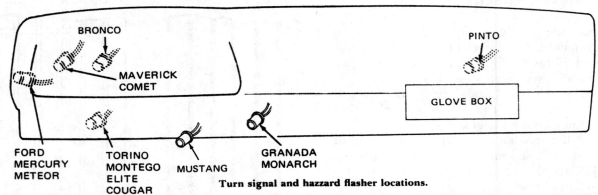

Turn signal and hazzard flasher locations.

BODY

INSPECTING THE BODY DRAIN HOLES

Make sure that the drain holes in the doors, rocker panels, and quarter panels are free from obstruction. A small screwdriver can be used to open plugged or partially plugged drain holes, but it must not be used on rubber dust valves. Visually check the dust valves for proper sealing and draining operation.

LUBRICATING BODY FRICTION POINTS

To eliminate binding conditions on pivot and friction points, spray lubricant on the luggage compartment hinge pivots, fuel filler door hinges, and station wagon and runabout tailgate or rear door support hinges.

Lubricate the lock cylinders, including the ignition lock, by applying lubricant sparingly in the key slot and working the key in the lock.

Spray polyethylene grease on hood and door hinges and hinge checks, and on the auxiliary hood catch.

Work all pivot points several times to be certain the lubricant has been worked in thoroughly.

LIGHTING AND ACCESSORIES

CHECKING THE LIGHTS

Check for proper operation of switches and the brightness of lights, including operation of the oil pressure and alternator warning lights.

Check the detent action and return of the turn signal lever by making full left and right turns during the road test. Check the operation of the hazard warning flasher system.

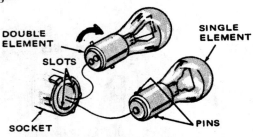

DEPRESS BULB IN SOCKET AND ROTATE COUNTERCLOCKWISE. THEN, PULL BULB FROM SOCKET.

TO INSTALL, INSPECT PINS ON BULB BASE. IF THEY ARE NOT SAME DISTANCE FROM BOTTOM OF BASE, THEY MUST BE INSERTED INTO THE CORRECT SLOT. DETERMINE WHICH SLOT IN SOCKET PINS SHOULD BE INSERTED INTO AND PUSH BULB BASE INTO SOCKET. THEN, ROTATE CLOCKWISE TO ENGAGE PINS. IF BULB WILL NOT ROTATE, PINS ARE IN WRONG SLOTS.

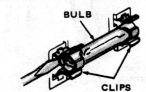

INSERT A SCREWDRIVER UNDER END OF BULB AND PRY BULB OUT OF CLIPS.

TO INSTALL, POSITION BULB TO CLIPS AND PRESS INTO PLACE.

PULL BULB STRAIGHT OUT OF SOCKET TO REMOVE.

TO INSTALL, POSITION BULB TO SOCKET AND PUSH STRAIGHT IN UNTIL SEATED.

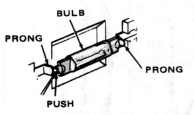

TO REMOVE, PUSH PRONG TOWARD BULB AND LIFT BULB FROM PRONG.

TO INSTALL, ENGAGE ONE END OF BULB OVER ONE PRONG. THEN, PUSH OTHER PRONG TOWARD BULB AND ENGAGE BULB END OVER PRONG. DO NOT FORCE BULB END OVER PRONG.

Replacing an interior light bulb.

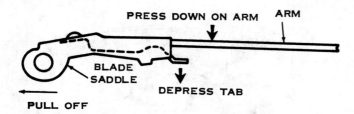

Trico bayonet-type blade removal.

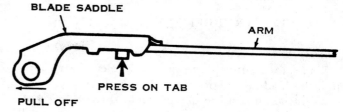

Anco bayonet-type blade removal.

CHECKING THE HORNS

Check the rim-blow and pad-blow horns to be sure the horn(s) blow at all rim or pad contact positions.

CHECKING THE WINDSHIELD WASHER AND WIPERS

Check for proper operation, including wiper sweep and park. Adjust if required. Check washer operation and adjust as required.

Fill with water and solvent meeting specifications. Use as directed on the container. Check the screen-type filter on the pick-up tube. Clean as necessary.

REPLACING WINDSHIELD WIPER BLADES

Wiper blade replacement intervals will vary with the amount of use, type of weather, chemical reaction from road tars or salts, and the age of the blades. Be sure that the windshield glass surface is not contaminated with oil, tree sap, or other substance which cannot be easily rubbed off.

Generally, if the wiper pattern across the glass is uneven and streaks over clean glass, the blades should be replaced.

SADDLE-PIN TYPE BLADE

To remove a pin type (Trico) blade, insert an appropriate tool into the spring release opening of the blade saddle, depress the spring clip, and pull the blade from the arm.

To install, push the blade saddle onto the pin so that the spring clip engages the pin.

BAYONET-TYPE BLADE

To remove a Trico blade, press down on the arm to unlatch the top stud. Depress the tab on the saddle, and then pull the blade from the arm.

To remove an Anco blade, press inward on the tab, and then pull the blade from the arm.

To install a new blade, slip the blade connector over the end of the wiper arm so that the locking stud snaps into place.

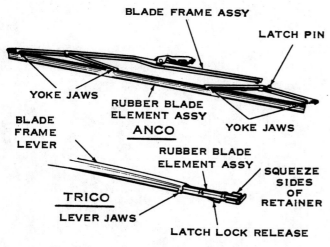

Replacing the windshield wiper blade.

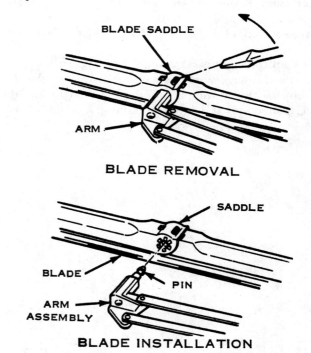

Trico or Anco pin-type wiper blade removal. The left side procedure is shown, which is similar for the right side.

REPLACING A RUBBER BLADE ELEMENT

TRICO

To remove, squeeze the latch lock release, and then pull the blade element out of the lever jaws.

To install, insert the new element through each of the lever jaws. Be sure the element is engaged in all lever jaws.

ANCO

To remove, depress the latch pin, and then slide the element out of the yoke jaws.

To install, slide the element through the yoke jaws, and then insert the blade frame assembly into the slots of the yoke jaws. **CAUTION: If the arm or blade assembly is bent or distorted, replace the complete blade assembly.**

CHECKING THE HEATER AND AIR CONDITIONER

Check for the following items: leaks, sufficient heat (approximately 140 degrees F at 32 degrees outside temperature and 50 percent relative humidity), blower operation, temperature control operation, operation of open air ducts and vents, operation of air conditioner controls and air conditioning temperatures (approximately 68 degrees F at 100 degrees outside temperature and 50 percent relative humidity). Adjust as necessary.

CHECKING THE AIR CONDITIONER SIGHT GLASS

Clean the sight glass before checking for a proper charge of refrigerant. Then, observe the sight glass for bubbles with the engine running at 1500 rpm and the A/C controls set at maximum cooling. A continuous or

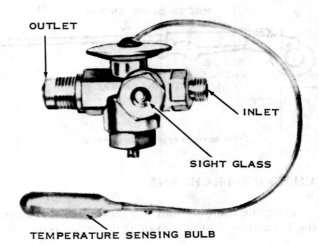

Air conditioner sight glass.

large amount of bubbles in the sight glass indicates an undercharge of refrigerant.

If an undercharge is found, check the system for leaks. Repair any leaks, evacuate the system with a vacuum pump, and charge the system with the proper amount of Refrigerant 12.

No bubbles in the sight glass indicates either too much refrigerant or a complete loss of regrigerant. While observing the sight glass, cycle the magnetic clutch off and on, with the engine running at 1500 rpm. If refrigerant is in the system, bubbles will appear while the clutch is engaged and disappear when the clutch is disengaged.

If no bubbles appear during the on and off cycle of the magnetic clutch, there is no refrigerant in the system, and it will be necessary to test for leaks and repair as required. Then, recharge the system. *NOTE: Under conditions of extremely high temperatures, occasional foam or bubbles may appear in the sight glass.*

4/engine tune-up

You must make repairs and adjustments to the ignition and fuel systems and it is considered good trade practice to do these jobs in the order which follows: (1) check the mechanical condition of the engine, (2) make repairs to the ignition system, and (3) adjust the carburetor. True, late-model engines, with their emission-control systems, present problems in that you must take into consideration the emission level of the exhaust, therefore, a separate section on tuning emission-controlled engines follows. Use both sections to obtain the most efficient-running engine possible.

MECHANICAL CONDITIONS

Before doing any work on the ignition system, it is good practice to tighten the cylinder head nuts, carburetor flange, and intake manifold bolts to the specified torque. If your engine has adjustable valves, make the adjustment according to the instructions in the accompanying illustration. The compression will be tested after removing the spark plugs.

TESTING THE COMPRESSION

A compression test is performed on an engine to

DO NOT SUCK IN TOO MUCH ELECTROLYTE

FLOAT MUST BE FREE

One of the first tune-up checks is to see that the battery is fully charged. Do this by using a hydrometer. A reading of 1,300 indicates a fully charged battery, while one of 1,150 means that the battery is discharged. Such a battery will make starting the engine difficult.

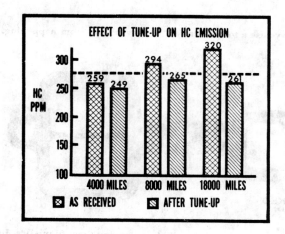

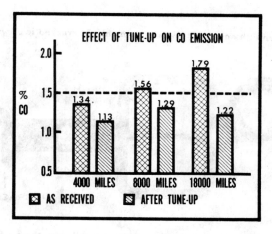

Improved engine performance, better gas mileage, and reduced exhaust emissions result from periodic tune-ups.

This manifold heat control valve was stuck, and the mechanic broke the casting while hammering on the shaft to free it up.

Uneven tightening of this exhaust manifold cracked it. Always use a torque wrench to prevent this from happening.

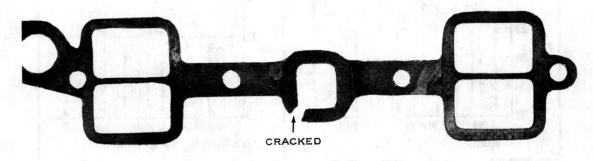

CRACKED

An intake manifold gasket with a section out will lean the air-fuel mixture to two cylinders, causing them to misfire. In addition to upsetting the air-fuel mixture, it causes the engine to idle roughly. Be sure to tighten all manifold gaskets, and the carburetor flange gasket nuts, to avoid air leaks which would upset carburetion.

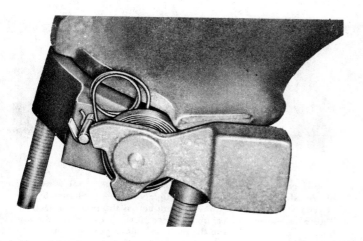

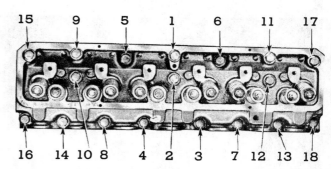

Typical cylinder head tightening diagram. Note that the center bolts are tightened first, and then the others are tightened alternately, working evenly from the center out to each end.

Check the exhaust manifold heat-control valve to be sure that it is free. A stuck valve can affect engine warm-up and waste gasoline as well as destroy engine performance during cold-driveaway. **CAUTION: Always use a graphite-type lubricant; otherwise, it carbonizes up from the heat and gums up the valve.**

determine the mechanical condition of the piston rings and valves. With both valves closed, a pressure of approximately 170 psi should be developed if the piston rings and valves are in good condition.

A low compression reading is caused by either a blown cylinder head gasket, worn piston rings, or valves that are not sealing properly. Worn piston rings will usually show up by a low reading on the gauge with a gradual build-up of pressure as the engine is cranked. A blown head gasket is indicated when two adjacent cylinders have low readings with the other cylinders normal. Valves not seating correctly will be indicated by consistently low readings with little or no compression build-up.

PERFORMING THE TEST

Warm the engine to its normal operating temperature, and then stop it. Remove the spark plug wires from the spark plugs by grasping the boot over the spark plug and twisting it slightly to break its grip on the spark plug. **CAUTION: Failure to remove the spark plug wires correctly from the plugs could break the linen filaments inside the secondary wires and cause misfiring after the engine is started.**

Adjusting the hydraulic valve lifter in a Chevrolet in-line, six-cylinder engine (left) and a V-8 engine. In each case, the rocker arm adjusting nut is turned down until there is zero lash, which you can determine when you can't turn the push rod easily. Then turn the nut down one additional turn to position the lifter in the center of its travel.

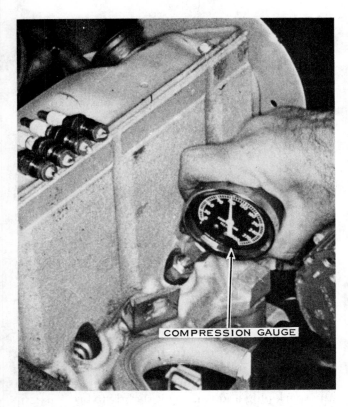

COMPRESSION GAUGE

Testing the compression in a Vega engine. Note how the spark plugs are laid out in order of removal so that the firing ends can be read.

Top Tuner Tip

Use a spark plug socket with a suitable ratchet or hinge handle to loosen the spark plugs. It is good practice to loosen all of the spark plugs two or three turns, and then crank the engine several revolutions to

This corroded battery cable connector caused all kinds of electrical problems due to the high voltage developed by the alternator in trying to force current across the poor connection. The alternator and regulator were destroyed, the headlamps burned out regularly, and the ignition contact points were quickly ruined.

blow away any dirt that is around the plugs. This will prevent it from falling into the combustion chamber when the plugs are removed. **CAUTION: It is important to be sure that the spark plug socket is seated on the spark plug and that sideways pressure is not exerted as the plugs are loosened because it is easy to crack the insulator or to break the spark plug.** Remove the spark plugs from the engine.

Block the throttle wide open to allow the engine to draw in enough air to obtain a true compression reading. *NOTE: Failure to block the throttle wide open will result in low readings which will not indicate the true condition of the engine.* **CAUTION: Be sure the emergency brake is firmly applied and the transmission is in NEUTRAL or PARK for safety reasons.** Insert the compression tester into #1 spark plug hole and have a helper crank the engine with the starter at least four turns. Note the reading on the compression

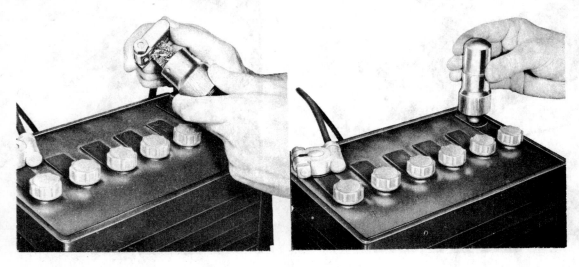

One of the greatest difficulties in the electrical system is the maintenance of the correct operating voltage and this, in turn, is dependent on minimizing resistance between the connections in the charging circuits. One of the most important service procedures is cleaning the battery terminals posts and cable connections of all corrosion. Scrape them until you can see bright metal. A pen knife will do the job if you don't have the illustrated tools.

gauge and record it. Test the next cylinder and record the reading. When all cylinders have been checked, compare the readings. Pay particular attention to the variation between the cylinders. There should be little variation between the readings on a normal engine.

Most manufacturers specify a 10-15% allowable variation between cylinders before remedial mechanical work is required. So if you have seven cylinders on your V-8 with readings of 160 psi and one cylinder with 140 psi, the low cylinder has a valve or ring problem that must be corrected.

A further check to isolate the condition should be made of a low-reading cylinder by putting a tablespoon of engine oil through the spark plug hole and performing the compression test again. A normal reading now indicates the oil has sealed worn piston rings. A continued low reading means the valves are not sealing.

Sometimes two adjacent cylinders will have low readings and this usually means that the head gasket is defective between the two cylinders.

Any abnormal condition that is found during the compression test must be corrected before proceeding with the tune-up, as it will be impossible to tune such an engine to top efficiency. See Chapter 5 for making repairs to the engine.

IGNITION SYSTEM

The ignition system consists of a distributor, ignition coil, and spark plugs. Of course, we need a battery to supply the energy for starting and to keep the engine running when the alternator is not charging. Three things must be done to the distributor to restore it to a good operating condition. You should replace the contact points, space them properly, and adjust the ignition timing. In addition, you should clean or replace the spark plugs and clean the battery terminals of all corrosion. Generally, the other parts of the ignition system require little attention.

SERVICING THE IGNITION SYSTEM

INSPECTING THE IGNITION POINTS

Remove the distributor cap. Some distributor caps are held to the distributor by two screws that must be turned a quarter turn to release them and other caps are retained by two spring clips. Carefully pull up on the rotor to remove it from the distributor shaft.

Separate the distributor points with your finger or a soft object to prevent damage in order to look at the mating surfaces of the points. The surfaces should have a light gray textured appearance and not have

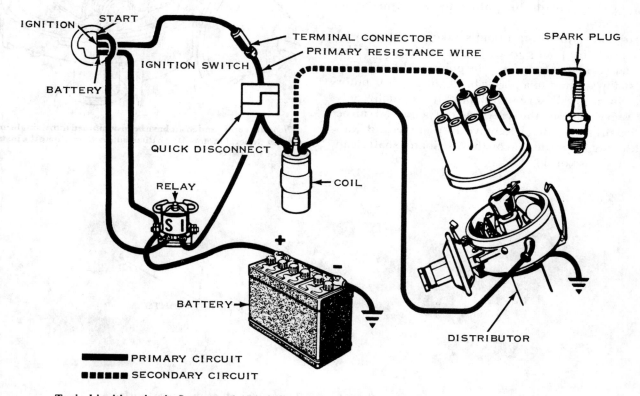

Typical ignition circuit. Some cars have a ballast resistor in place of the primary resistance wire shown.

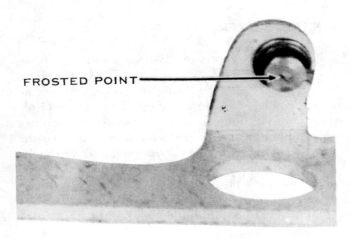

A good contact point has a frosted look. This point set does not need to be replaced.

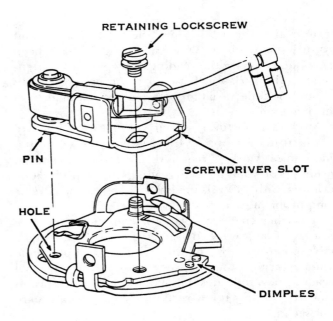

Contact point mounting details. Note the screwdriver slot in the point plate and the dimples in the plate support for adjusting the contact point gap.

any pits or protrusions in either side. If the points are excessively pitted or burned, they must be replaced.

INSTALLING IGNITION POINTS AND CONDENSER

Some ignition points are secured to the point plate with one retaining screw and others have two screws. All point sets have a pin extending from the bottom side that allows the points to pivot on the point plate to enable the gap of the points to be adjusted to specifications.

To remove the contact points, take out the screw(s) that hold the points to the plate. Disconnect the primary lead that runs from the points to the coil. This is usually secured to a plastic block on the distributor case by a small screw and nut. It is usually only necessary to loosen the screw and the point lead can be pulled off the terminal. Remove the point set and, with a clean rag, wipe the cam on the distributor shaft clean of any grease or oil.

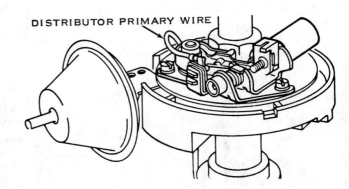

The points and condenser have been combined into a single unit on many General Motors Delco distributors to facilitate the installation of the parts.

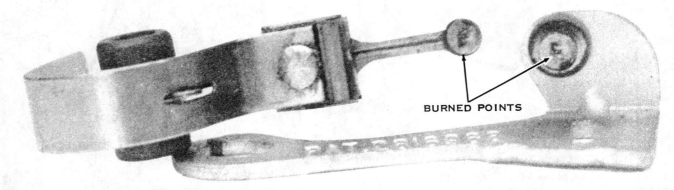

Details of a burned set of contact points, possibly caused by getting oil on the contact surfaces.

After installing a new set of contact points, make sure that they are aligned properly by bending the fixed contact support. CAUTION: Never bend the breaker arm.

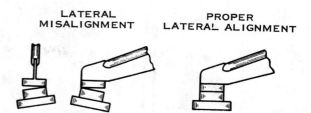

LATERAL MISALIGNMENT   PROPER LATERAL ALIGNMENT

Contact points must be aligned before adjusting the point gap. Always correct misaligned points by bending the fixed point support. If you bend the movable point, you will be causing misalignment between the rubbing block and the cam.

Top Tuner Tip

It is good practice to replace the condenser at the time the points are replaced as there is no way to predict how long a condenser will operate and a sudden failure could leave you stranded in some out-of-the-way place. While there are sometimes two condensers on a distributor, only the one that is connected to the point set is important to the operation of the ignition system. The other condenser is installed to prevent static in the car radio. The point condenser is usually inside of the distributor and secured to the point plate by a small screw. Remove the screw and lift out the condenser.

Install the new points on the point plate, being sure that the pivot pin of the point set fits properly into the hole on the point plate. The screw securing the point set should be installed, but not fully tightened at this time to allow the point gap to be adjusted. Install a new condenser, and then tighten the screw. Attach the point and condenser leads to the terminal on the distributor, and then tighten this connection. **CAUT-**

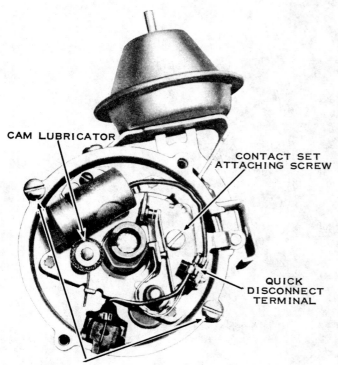

CAM LUBRICATOR

CONTACT SET ATTACHING SCREW

QUICK DISCONNECT TERMINAL

BREAKER PLATE ATTACHING SCREW

Details of the contact point set used in a six-cylinder engine distributor. The cam lubricator should be turned 180 degrees every 12,000 miles and replaced every 24,000 miles. Don't use engine oil on the cam lubricator, or it may get on the contact points and cause burning. Breaker point tension should be 19-23 ozs, and it can be adjusted by bending the spring.

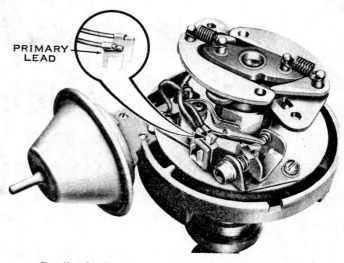

PRIMARY LEAD

Details of a distributor used on G.M. V-8 engines.

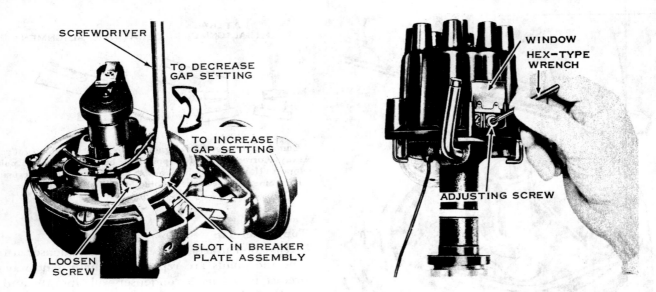

Adjusting the contact point gap in a G.M. distributor for a six-cylinder engine (left). The G.M. V-8 engine distributor (right) has a window in the distributor cap through which the contact point gap can be adjusted. CAUTION: Always close the window securely after having made the adjustment to keep out moisture and dust.

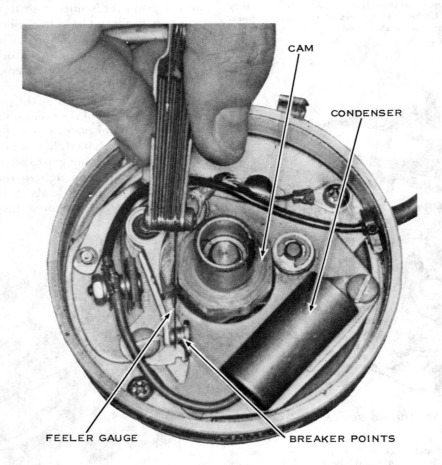

Spacing the contact points on a Chrysler six-cylinder engine distributor. CAUTION: Always use a cleaned feeler gauge to avoid depositing a film of oil on the contact points, which will oxidize and cause operating difficulties.

ION: If either lead touches the distributor body when tightened, the engine will not start due to the primary circuit being grounded.

ADJUSTING THE POINT GAP

Use a cleaned feeler gauge of the correct thickness (usually 0.019" for a four- or six-cylinder engine, or 0.016" for a V-8 engine) and slip it between the contact points. Move the stationary arm of the distributor until the feeler gauge has a slight drag as it is pulled through the point set. Tighten the hold-down screw(s) and recheck the point gap with the feeler gauge.

DWELL OR CAM ANGLE

These high-sounding words mean the angle of distributor cam rotation during which the contact points are closed. If you do have a dwell meter, you can set the point dwell rather than measuring the spacing with a feeler gauge, as discussed above. If you do, then set the dwell after the distributor is back in place and the engine running. Adjust the dwell to 28° for an eight-cylinder engine, or to 33° for a four- or six-cylinder unit.

Technicians will tell you that you cannot set the contact point gap accurately with feeler gauges, and that you must have a dwell meter to do this job properly. But all engine manufacturers allow a variation from specifications, usually ±3°, and this means that setting the contact point gap carefully with a feeler gauge can be done just as accurately as with the most expensive tune-up equipment.

Top Tuner Tips

If the point spacing specification is given as a range of setting, 0.014" to 0.019" for example, use the higher specification (0.019") as the setting for new breaker points. Setting to the high side of the specification will keep the point adjustment within the recommended

range as the rubbing block wears over many miles of service. Conversely, if you set it to the low side of the specification (0.014"), the gap will be affected adversely as rubbing block wear occurs.

When setting breaker point spacing with the use of a dwell meter, you will generally find dwell specifications given in the range of degrees, 28° to 32°, for example. In this situation, it is recommended that you set the point dwell to 28°. This will keep breaker point spacing within the recommended range over a longer period of time, even though wear of the rubbing block results in increased dwell up to 32°. Remember, points set too close will burn, while points set too wide will reduce coil output, especially at high engine speeds.

Engine performance can be keyed directly to distributor cam lubricant or, rather, to the lack of lubricant. Any undue friction between the breaker point rubbing block (or cam follower) and the distributor shaft cam will serve to increase point dwell and retard ignition timing.

For example, if the manufacturer's specifications call for a point dwell of 30°, it takes very little wear of the cam follower to increase the dwell to 31° and retard the ignition timing 2°. Point dwell, remember, is the length of time the points remain closed. As point gap is reduced, dwell angle is increased; therefore, as the cam follower wears, the point gap becomes less and the dwell angle increases. There is a direct relationship between dwell angle and ignition timing. For instance, when point dwell is changed one degree (through wear of the cam follower), ignition timing will change two degrees because the distributor rotates at half crankshaft speed.

It is not unusual to find ignition timing retarded several degrees after 5,000 to 10,000 miles of engine operation, even with a well-lubricated distributor cam. A dry cam accelerates this figure considerably.

Most specifications call for lubricating the distributor cam to prevent rapid wearing of the cam

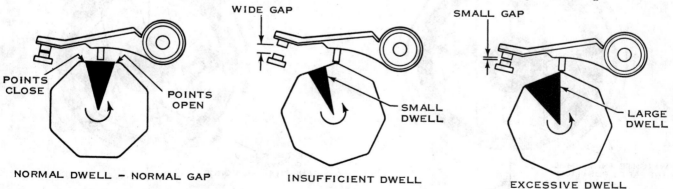

Point dwell is the length of time that the contact points remain together. The right drawings show the effect of wide and narrow gaps on the dwell angle.

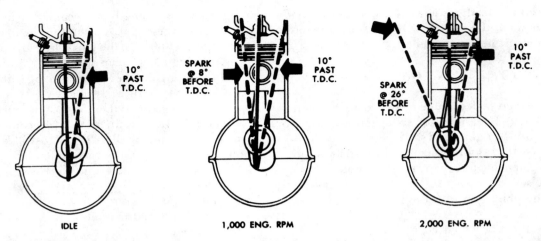

IDLE

1,000 ENG. RPM

2,000 ENG. RPM

The mechanical advance mechanism is designed to advance ignition timing as engine speed increases. At idle speed (left), the spark must occur at TDC for the burning fuel to develop its maximum pressure by 10° ATDC. At 1,000 rpm, it is necessary to advance the ignition timing by about 8° for maximum pressure to be developed by 10° ATDC because of the time it takes for combustion to develop. At 2,000 rpm, the spark must occur at approximately 26° BTDC for maximum pressure to develop by 10° ATDC (right).

follower (breaker point rubbing block). Unfortunately, the specifications never say how much lubricant should be applied. The usual is a "light film," and the caution is "not too much." The correct amount of lubricant, in all cases, is the amount which would equal the size of a kitchen match head. **CAUTION: The lubricant should be deposited behind the rubbing block as a reservoir, never placed on the cam where it can be thrown onto the contact points.**

It has been determined that greater amounts of lubricant will lead to "splattering" and contamination of the breaker points, and lesser amounts will not lubricate the cam-to-rubbing block contact surfaces sufficiently to minimize wear. **CAUTION: Some G.M. engines have distributors with an oil wick bearing against the cam for this kind of lubrication. Such a wick should be replaced periodically, usually during each tune-up, and it must never be oiled.**

Install the rotor on the distributor shaft. Inspect the distributor cap for cracks inside and out and for eroded terminals. Install the cap on the distributor and fasten the retaining clips.

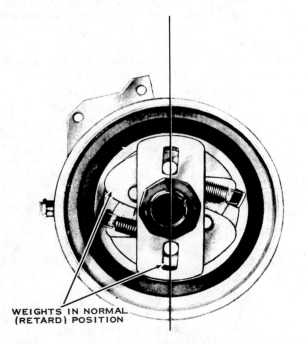

WEIGHTS IN NORMAL (RETARD) POSITION

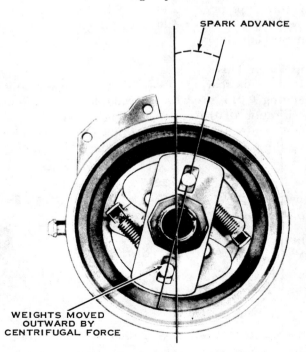

SPARK ADVANCE

WEIGHTS MOVED OUTWARD BY CENTRIFUGAL FORCE

Mechanical advance is accomplished by centrifugal force throwing out two rotating weights, the action of which causes the cam to move in the advanced direction (right).

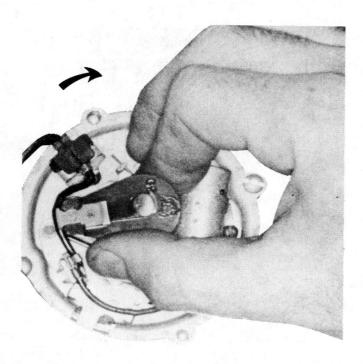

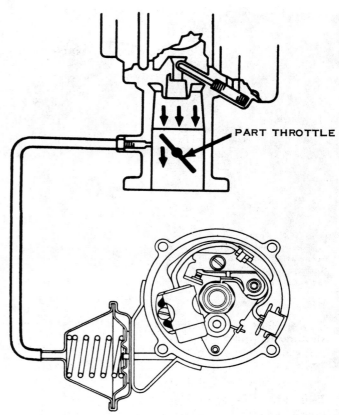

PART THROTTLE

Check the mechanical advance mechanism by turning the rotor. It must feel springy in the normal direction of rotation.

The vacuum-advance mechanism consists of a diaphragm unit which receives its vacuum supply from the intake manifold side of the throttle valve. Generally, this tap is above the throttle blade so that there is no vacuum to the advance mechanism when the engine is idling. This is especially true on emission-controlled engines.

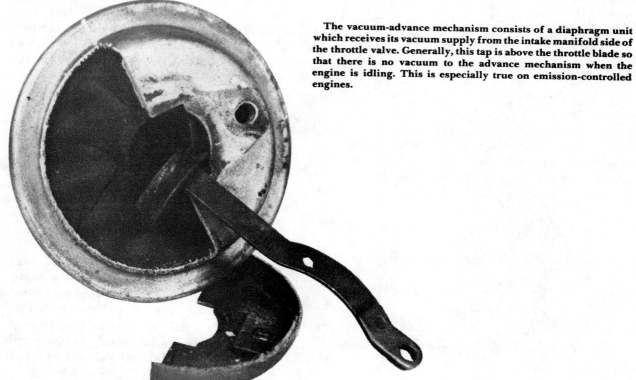

A leaking vacuum-advance actuator will cause a loss of vacuum advance and result in poor throttle response during light-throttle operation.

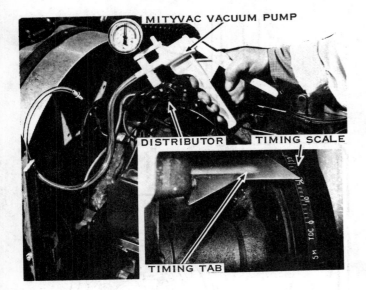

The distributor vacuum-advance unit can be tested by pumping up vacuum to the distributor while the engine is idling. If the unit is functioning properly, the ignition timing will advance as shown with a timing light.

SPARK PLUGS

The spark plug ignites the compressed air-fuel mixture to start combustion. The resulting heat drives the piston down to power the vehicle. The spark plug must do its work under extremely difficult conditions of heat and pressure, delivering a voltage surge across the electrodes high enough to fire the mixture every time.

The combustion temperatures are in the neighborhood of 4,000°F, the spark plug insulator's temperature is about 800°F, and the air-fuel mixture is compressed about 10 times, making the initial working pressures within the combustion chambers about 180

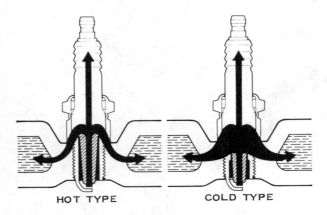

The heat range of a spark plug is determined by the length of the path from the insulator tip to the coolant.

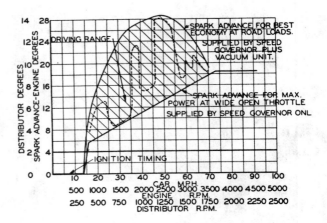

In operation, the ignition timing can be at any point in the shaded section of this graph due to the action of the centrifugal-advance mechanism, modified by the action of the vacuum-advance unit.

psi. In addition, each spark plug must fire every charge for the engine to develop maximum horsepower for efficient operation and good gas mileage.

With a six-cylinder engine operating at 3,000 rpm, at freeway driving speed, **each spark plug** of a six-cylinder engine must ignite a compressed air-fuel charge 250 times per minute. If any of the spark plugs fail, even once, the engine misfires, and that charge of fuel is pumped out of the combustion chamber to the muffler, doing absolutely no work in the process. On a vehicle with a catalytic converter the unburned fuel overloads the converter and can cause it to burn up. No wonder, then, we consider continuously firing spark plugs so important in the chain of events that leads to good engine performance and economical operation.

Your car's manufacturer installed a spark plug suitable for normal or average service. But, these plugs may not operate satisfactorily if you drive at sustained high speeds, or with unusually heavy loads, or if you do a lot of continual stop-and-go city driving. Also, as your spark plugs get older, their performance deteriorates.

When you match your spark plugs heat range to your engine needs and the type of driving you do, you'll get the optimum power and performance from your engine and the longest spark plug life.

Generally speaking, if you're a city stop-and-go driver, you might need a spark plug one step higher in heat range than the one recommended for your engine. This hotter spark plug will run at a higher operating temperature, and will resist gas and oil fouling that would normally result from stop-and-go driving. However, if you do a lot of high-speed free-

Note the dirty insulator, which should be cleaned with a solvent-soaked rag to prevent flash-over. This causes hard starting in wet weather.

Note the rounded wear on the ground electrode. This spark plug has run well over 15,000 miles and must be replaced to restore good engine performance.

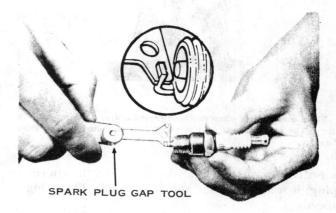

SPARK PLUG GAP TOOL

Bend the side electrode to adjust the gap, never the center one, or you will crack the insulator.

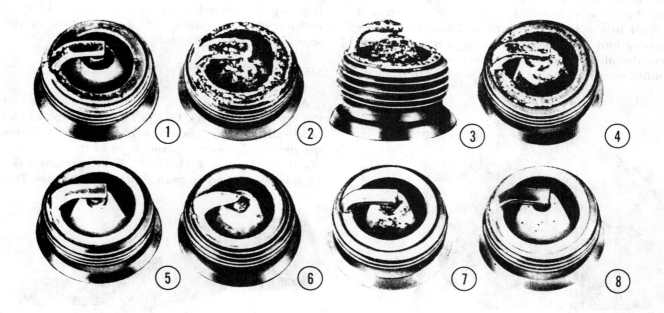

Spark plug identification guide. (1) Black, dry fluffy deposits, (2) wet deposits, (3) build-up closing the gap. (4) yellow or tan deposits, (5) light tan or gray deposits, (6) eroded electrodes, (7) melted or spotty deposits, (8) white or very light gray insulator, with bluish-burnt electrodes.

Flash-over occurs when you accelerate hard, and the insulator is dirty. The spark jumps over the insulator and the cylinder misfires.

A flat feeler gauge will give an erroneous setting (top) when there is electrode wear. Note how a round gap gauge compensates for this type of wear to give an accurate reading. However, a spark plug that is worn this much should be replaced.

way driving, you might need a step colder than normal plug; it will run cooler and have longer life at high speeds.

CLEANING AND GAPPING THE SPARK PLUGS

If the spark plugs you took out are in good condition, they can be installed after being cleaned and gapped to the manufacturer's specifications. When cleaning and gapping spark plugs, it is advisable to have the plugs sand-blasted in a plug cleaner. The ground electrode should be bent up first to facilitate

cleaning. The electrodes should be filed flat to remove the oxidized surfaces in order to decrease the voltage necessary to fire the plugs. They should then be gapped to the correct specifications. The plug threads should be cleaned and lightly oiled to facilitate installation and removal the next time. Install new gaskets and thread all the plugs into their holes fingertight; then tighten them an additional 1/2 turn with a wrench or to the specified torque. Connect the secondary wires to the spark plugs.

SETTING THE IGNITION TIMING

Adjust the engine idle speed to the rpm specified on the tuning decal. **CAUTION: The contact point gap (or dwell) must have been set first, because it affects the timing. Connect a timing light to an adapter for No. 1 spark plug. CAUTION: Don't puncture the high-tension wire, or you will damage the core.** Dis-

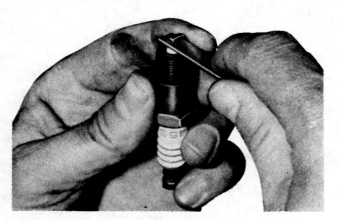

Filing the electrodes square will do more to restore spark plug performance than any other service if the plug insulator is not shorted out. Be sure to use a file to get the electrodes square. Don't use emery cloth, because this will round off the electrodes.

Check the condition of the high-tension wiring to make sure that it is not old and brittle, which will cause engine misfiring and hard starting, especially when wet.

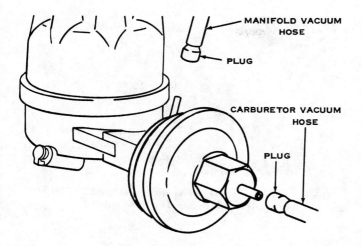

MANIFOLD VACUUM HOSE

PLUG

CARBURETOR VACUUM HOSE

PLUG

Before setting the ignition timing, it is essential that both vacuum hoses are disconnected and the ends plugged.

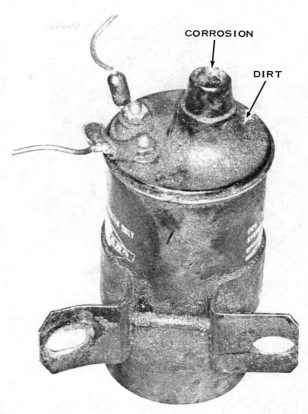

CORROSION

DIRT

Dirt and grime on the surface of the ignition coil can cause high-tension leakage, which will result in misfiring and hard starting.

connect the vacuum line(s) to the distributor and plug the source(s). Point the timing light toward the timing indicator. The specified timing mark on the timing decal should line up with the pointer. If it doesn't, loosen the distributor hold-down bolt and rotate the distributor until the mark lines up with the pointer. Tighten the hold-down bolt and recheck the timing. Connect the distributor vacuum line(s). Now, accelerate the engine to see if the centrifugal advance mechanism is operating. The position of the mark should advance on the pulley if the unit is in good condition.

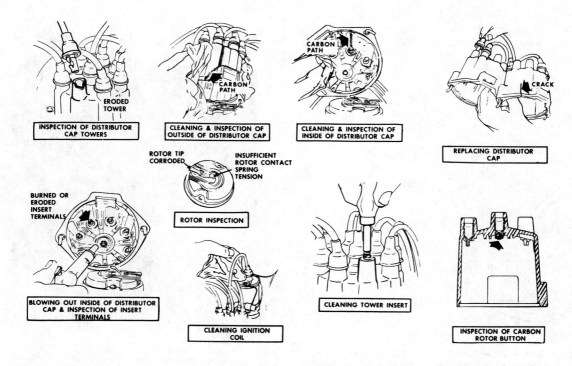

INSPECTION OF DISTRIBUTOR CAP TOWERS

ERODED TOWER

CLEANING & INSPECTION OF OUTSIDE OF DISTRIBUTOR CAP

CARBON PATH

CLEANING & INSPECTION OF INSIDE OF DISTRIBUTOR CAP

CARBON PATH

REPLACING DISTRIBUTOR CAP

CRACK

ROTOR TIP CORRODED

INSUFFICIENT ROTOR CONTACT SPRING TENSION

ROTOR INSPECTION

BURNED OR ERODED INSERT TERMINALS

BLOWING OUT INSIDE OF DISTRIBUTOR CAP & INSPECTION OF INSERT TERMINALS

CLEANING IGNITION COIL

CLEANING TOWER INSERT

INSPECTION OF CARBON ROTOR BUTTON

Cleaning and inspecting the distributor cap.

Check the inside of the distributor cap for a crack between terminals, which will cause engine misfiring, loss of power, and poor gas mileage.

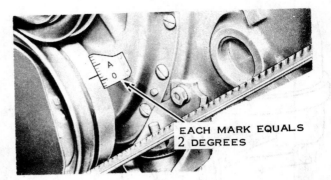

Timing indicator plate, with each mark equaling 2°. "O" is TDC and "A" means advanced (Before Top Dead Center).

POWER-TIMING THE ENGINE

Purists, especially those with elaborate tune-up equipment, will shake their heads in wonder at this one, but it is quite possible to adjust the ignition timing for optimum results with a vacuum gauge and a road test. They will point to the tuning decal and say that the specifications are, for example, exactly 5° BTDC (Before Top Dead Center), but the manufacturer always gives a leeway of plus or minus 2 or 2½° from that exact figure, which means that the engine in question can be timed anywhere from 7½° BTDC to 2½° BTDC and still be within specifications, this applies to all modern emission-controlled engines, as well.

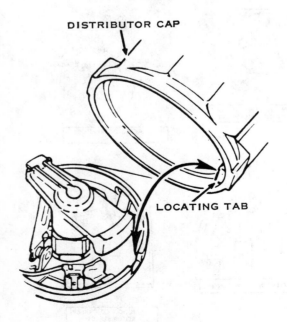

Align the locating tab and be sure it is fully seated before installing the cap. CAUTION: Failure to seat this locating tab will cause the tip of the rotor to strike one segment of the cap and crack it.

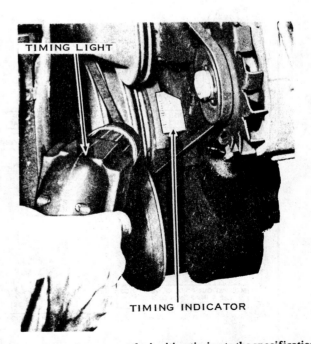

Use a timing lamp to set the ignition timing to the specifications on the tuning decal, as discussed in the text.

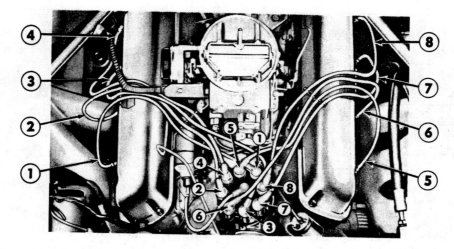

Typical high-tension wiring. Note the clips used to keep the wires separated so that cross-firing does not occur.

To prove that the above is true, the following is a quote from Chrysler Technical Service Bulletin No. 08-09-74D, which is entitled, *A method of reducing hydrocarbon emissions.* "The basic ignition timing of California passenger car models with 360-4 Bbl. standard-performance and 360-4 Bbl. high-performance engines has been changed from 2.5° BTDC to 5° BTDC." By advancing the ignition timing from that specified on the tuning decal, hydrocarbon emissions were reduced and, most important to our readers, the performance and gas mileage of this engine were increased significantly.

To power-time an engine, connect a vacuum gauge to any tap on the intake manifold, start the engine, and then open the throttle enough to engage the fast-idle cam to achieve a fast-idle speed of about 2,000 rpm. *NOTE: The exact speed is not important.* Now, turn the

A spark plug that is exposed to preignition will have a blistered porcelain.

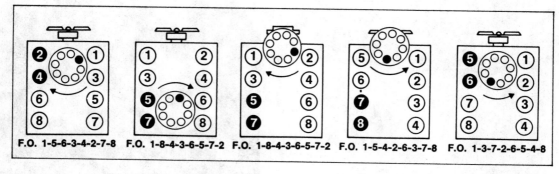

F.O. 1-5-6-3-4-2-7-8   F.O. 1-8-4-3-6-5-7-2   F.O. 1-8-4-3-6-5-7-2   F.O. 1-5-4-2-6-3-7-8   F.O. 1-3-7-2-6-5-4-8

Ignition cross-firing is a condition in which a spark plug fires out of time through a process called induction. This can cause engine roughness, backfiring, detonation, and serious engine damage. An electrical field develops around a spark plug wire when high voltage travels through it on the way to the spark plug. There is sufficient energy in this field to induce voltage in an adjacent wire if: (1) the adjacent wire is close enough and runs parallel to it, and (2) the wire runs to an adjacent cylinder which is next in the firing order. The result is that both fire, but one is advanced. To avoid this, spark plug wires must be installed in their original order. Above all, never tape the wires together in a neat bundle as this will aggravate this condition. These diagrams illustrate the firing orders (F.O.) of most V-8 engines. The cylinders in black are the critical ones and must be kept well separated to prevent cross-firing.

| *Ignited by hot deposit..* | *..regular ignition spark..* | *..ignites remaining fuel..* | *..flame fronts collide.* |

Preignition is premature ignition of the fuel charge, and this can be caused by advanced ignition timing or any hot spot within the combustion chamber capable of initiating ignition of the remaining fuel charge.

distributor body slowly to obtain the highest vacuum reading on the gauge, and then back it off slowly until the needle dips slightly from the maximum reading. The exact amount of backing off needed must be determined by the engine itself. If there is a lot of carbon in the combustion chambers or you are using low-test gasoline, you will have to retard the timing more than for a clean engine running on leaded fuel. *NOTE: The more advanced you can run the ignition timing, the better power and gas mileage you will obtain.*

Now, road-test the car to determine if the engine pings. If it does, retard the timing a small amount and repeat the road test. Do this until you lose all traces of ping. Now your engine is timed to the most efficient running position for its condition.

FUEL SYSTEM SERVICE

Carburetor adjustments must be made only after having serviced the distributor and adjusted the ignition timing, because these adjustments affect carburetion to a large extent. Before attempting to adjust the carburetor, it is good practice to clean or replace the air cleaner element and fuel filter. A partially clogged air filter element lowers your gas mileage to a considerable degree, depending on the amount of accumulated dirt. The fuel filter should be changed every 10,000 miles to keep small particles from passing into the fuel bowl, which can sometimes hold the carburetor needle valve off its seat and cause flooding; this will reduce gas mileage. These small service jobs

Preignition can cause the top of the piston to melt.

This illustration shows the high-tension wiring on a late-model Ford engine, with a firing order of 1-5-4-2-6-3-7-8. Cylinders 7 and 8 fire one after the other. Note how Ford engineers have arranged the wires so that they're well separated to prevent cross-firing.

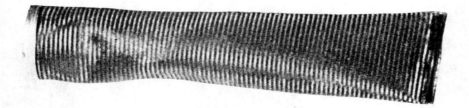

If you do have water in the gas tank, then you will find this type of strainer at the end of the intake pipe, inside of the gas tank, plugged enough to cause operating difficulties. The remedy is to remove the gas tank, drain and flush it, and then replace the filter.

Water damage inside of the fuel pump. This same condition occurs inside of the carburetor.

can be performed by anyone, and they sometimes significantly reduce your operating costs, usually way above the purchase price of the filters. And, too, they give you more trouble-free mileage.

AIR FILTERS

For every gallon of gasoline passing through the carburetor, it requires as much as 9,000 gallons of air for a combustible mixture. All the air must pass through the filter element in the air cleaner and, in 10,000 miles of operation, the filter will start to plug up with dirt; in 24,000 miles it can be costing about $46.00 a year in lost gas mileage. In addition, the rich fuel mixture will be destroying the cylinder wall

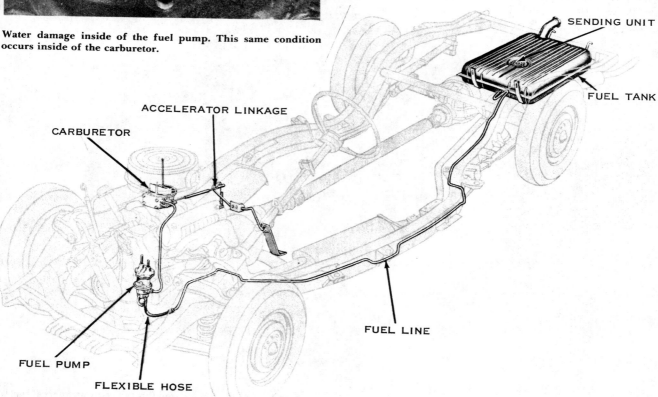

Typical fuel system.

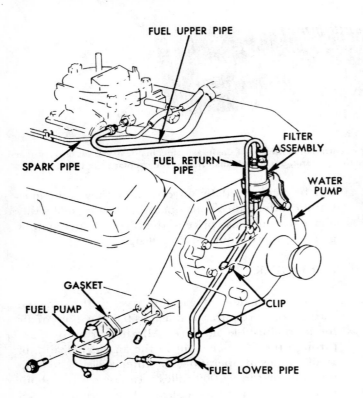

An in-line fuel filter should be changed every 12,000 miles.

The fuel filter element in the carburetor float bowl should be changed every 12,000 miles.

lubrication to cause excessive engine wear, and it will be raising your HC and CO emissions above legal limits.

The answer is to clean or replace the filter element

Defective fuel pump diaphragm shows how the constant flexing causes the diaphragm to crack, and this can cause an internal fuel leak into the crankcase, which will lower your gas mileage considerably. If the diaphragm is cracked, you will be able to smell gasoline on the oil dipstick. The remedy, of course, is to replace the fuel pump.

OILY DEPOSIT

A clogged air filter will enrich the air-fuel mixture and lower your gas mileage proportionally.

periodically. This is one of those simple service operations that anyone can perform, and you're home cost-free in addition.

THERMOSTATICALLY-CONTROLLED AIR CLEANER

This system provides heated air to the carburetor induction system. A sheet metal stove is attached to the exhaust manifold where underhood air is heated as it passes over the hot exhaust manifold. The heated air is conducted from the heat stove to the air cleaner through a flexible duct. The air cleaner is designed to control the inducted air temperature at approximately 100°F.

The use of a heated-air system does not materially affect the inducted air temperature during warm weather, but it does quickly raise the intake air

Compare this new air filter with the previous one.

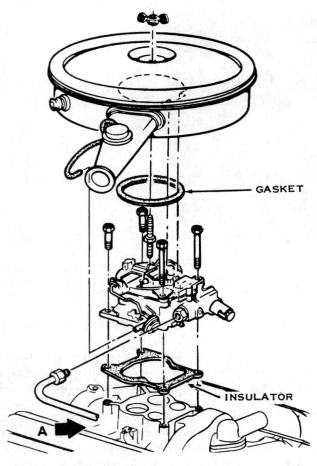

GASKET

INSULATOR

A

Surface scratches on a set of piston rings show how the dust in unfiltered air damages the moving parts of an engine.

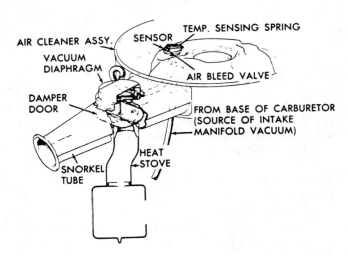

AIR CLEANER ASSY.
VACUUM DIAPHRAGM
TEMP. SENSING SPRING
SENSOR
AIR BLEED VALVE
DAMPER DOOR
FROM BASE OF CARBURETOR (SOURCE OF INTAKE MANIFOLD VACUUM)
SNORKEL TUBE
HEAT STOVE

When replacing the carburetor always tighten the hold-down bolts evenly to compress the insulator properly for avoiding an air leak. CAUTION: Uneven tightening can crack off one of the carburetor ears. CAUTION: Always replace the gasket between the air cleaner and the carburetor to make sure that no unfiltered air enters the engine to cause damage to the moving parts.

Modern emission-controlled engines have thermostatically controlled air cleaners. The damper door must be open (heat-off) without the engine running, and must close immediately (heat-on) when the engine starts.

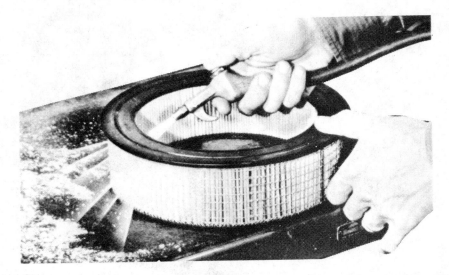

A dry filter element can be cleaned by directing low-pressure air through the element in a reverse direction. Hold the filter up to the light to be sure that there are no holes to admit unfiltered air.

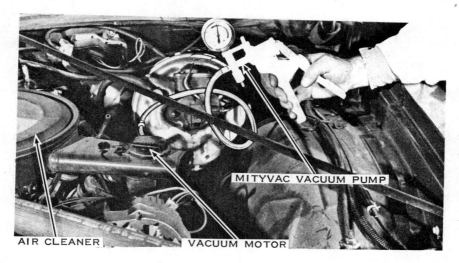

AIR CLEANER   VACUUM MOTOR   MITYVAC VACUUM PUMP

The Mityvac® vacuum pump can be used for testing the efficiency of the air cleaner vacuum motor. Pumping up vacuum should cause the heat-on door to move down, closing the fresh air vent. The vacuum gauge needle must retain the vacuum; otherwise, the diaphragm is leaking, and the motor must be replaced.

temperature in cold weather. A decreased spread in the temperature range permits the use of leaner air-fuel mixtures with satisfactory driveability.

SERVICE PROCEDURES

Check to see that the cold-air door is open before the engine is started, and that it closes immediately after starting as vacuum is built up. Then the door should open again gradually as the engine warms to operating temperature. A thermometer can be used to check the temperature of the thermostat accurately, and this should begin to control the vacuum motor for starting to close the heated-air door at about 105°F.

CARBURETORS

The carburetor furnishes a correctly proportioned air-fuel mixture to be burned in the combustion chambers. Dirt and gum restrict the flow of fuel, causing a lean operating condition; hesitation on acceleration results. Gum and carbon form in the automatic choke mechanism, resulting in the choke being applied for a longer than normal time, lowering the gasoline mileage proportionally. Wear occurs in the linkage, changing the timing of the mixture, which results in poor operation and lowered fuel mileage. The remedy, of course, is to repair the carburetor and

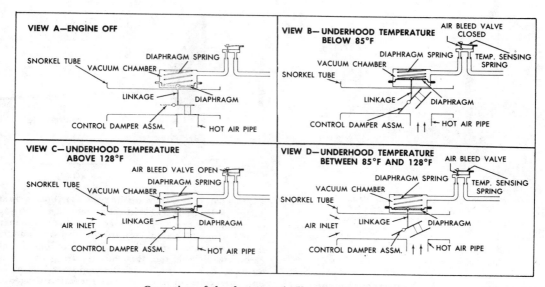

Operation of the thermostatically controlled air cleaner.

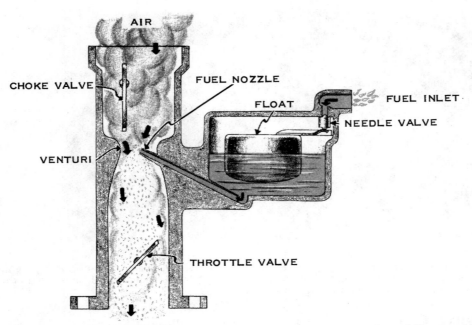

Sectioned view of a carburetor showing the passage of air and fuel. The throttle valve is partially opened in this drawing indicating that the engine is running at a normal road speed.

to make the adjustments which will restore it to its former operating efficiency.

Money Saving Tips

If you have some mechanical ability, you can service your carburetor yourself. However, if repairs are in-dicated because your mileage and engine performance has dropped significantly and you don't feel equal to the task, then you can remove the carburetor yourself and bring it to a carburetor speciality shop, where an expert will restore it to good operating condition. Many mechanics send their carburetor repairs out to the same type of shops. You can save the mechanic's mark-up of 15-40% if you remove and replace the carburetor yourself.

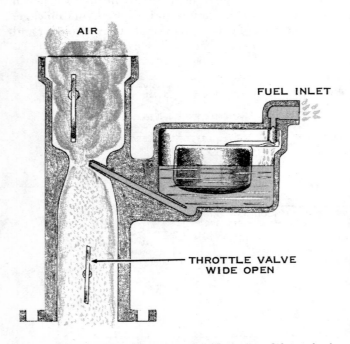

In this diagram, the throttle valve is wide open, and the engine is running at top speed.

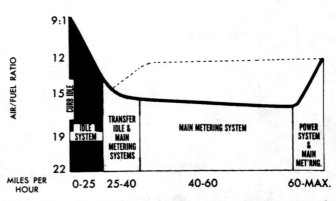

Typical flow curve, showing the systems in operation as compared with vehicle speed. The dotted line represents wide-open throttle operation. Note that the transfer from idle to the main metering system drops off sharply toward the lean side, and this is one of the improvements made in modern emission-controlled engine carburetors. Note, too, that the mixture goes rich again above 60 mph, and this is to cool the engine as well as to provide a power mixture to overcome the increased drag of high-speed operation.

WORN SECTION

A metering rod moves up and down each time the throttle is advanced and retarded. As the rod rubs against the main metering jet wall, wear occurs in both parts, and the air-fuel mixture becomes gradually richer. This is the reason why you must replace all wearing parts of the carburetor periodically.

SERVICE PROCEDURES

Because of the great number of carburetor types, it would be impossible in this kind of book to provide overhaul instructions for all of them. Instead this section will include a number of hints for replacing worn carburetor parts and for making adjustments that will restore your carburetor's efficiency.

CARBURETOR KITS

Generally, a kit of parts is purchased for a carburetor overhaul, or it can be a "Zip Kit" which contains a minimum of parts. These kits contains all of the jets and gaskets and a set of instructions covering the specifications and bench adjustments for the particular carburetor model you are working on. However, the usefulness of such kits is rather limited in restoring carburetor effectiveness, because most of the parts are not needed and some of them that are needed are not there. For example, most kits contain all of the jets used in the carburetor, but jets never wear and so don't need to be replaced unless drilled out. In fact, it would cause a great deal of damage, if an incorrect jet had been packaged and used in a carburetor. It would be far better to use the old jet than to replace it with an incorrect one.

On the other hand, wearing parts of the carburetor are not always included with kits. To be most effective,

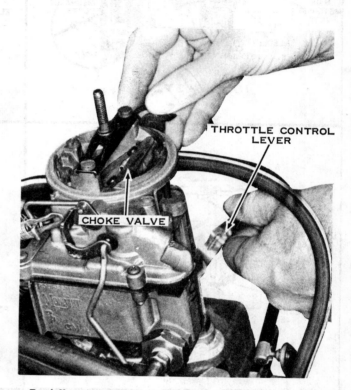

THROTTLE CONTROL LEVER

CHOKE VALVE

Partially restricting the air flowing into the carburetor with the engine running at about 2,000 rpm is a good way to determine the condition of the air-fuel mixture without elaborate equipment. If the engine speeds up as you partially restrict the air flow, then the mixture is on the lean side. If it slows down, without any speed increase, then the mixture is on the rich side and carburetor repairs are called for.

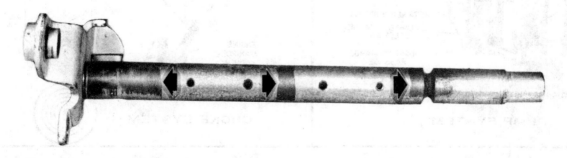

A worn throttle shaft (arrows) shows that all moving parts of this carburetor have worn. Cleaning (Boiling out) the carburetor and replacing the jets will not correct the problems of wear.

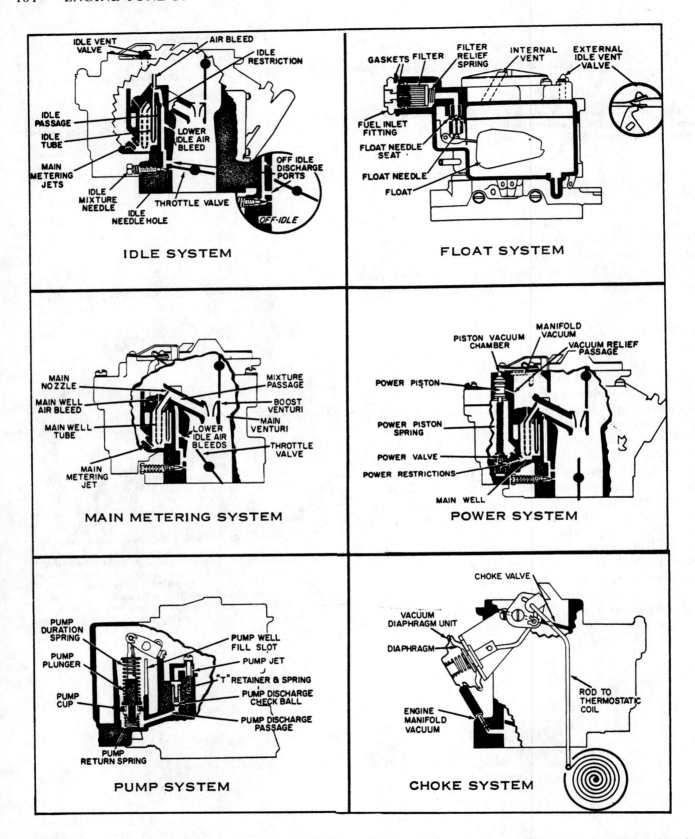

Operating circuits of a Rochester 2GC carburetor. Each of these circuits is discussed in the text so that you can see where the actual part is positioned. Other carburetor models have similar circuits.

a kit of carburetor parts should always include a set of gaskets and a new needle valve-and-seat assembly, because this is the most wearing part. Also the kit should include all diaphragms, the power jet, and main metering rods and jets, because they move which causes wear. Most carburetors have external linkages which move everytime the accelerator pedal is advanced or retarded, and these wearing parts must be replaced during an overhaul to "time" the operation of the various carburetor circuits precisely. These links are seldom packaged with the kits.

CARBURETOR CIRCUITS

FLOAT SYSTEM

Replace the carburetor fuel inlet filter element every 12,000 miles to minimize the passage of small dust particles past the needle valve-and-seat assembly. Dirt under the needle valve can hold it off the seat and cause flooding, with a resulting loss of gas mileage.

The needle valve-and-seat assembly are a matched set and must always be replaced everytime the carburetor is taken apart; otherwise, leaking will result. This will cause the float level to rise above specifications, resulting in a richer-than-normal air-fuel mixture for all ranges of carburetor operation.

Always adjust the float level to specifications. A higher-than-normal fuel level will cause a rich mixture, just as would a leaking needle valve-and-seat assembly.

IDLE SYSTEM

Make sure that the idle mixture adjusting needle is not damaged, or you will not be able to make an accurate adjustment. Because the idle mixture affects the other circuits up through 35 mph, it is essential that the mixture be adjusted accurately, as discussed in the section on engine tuning.

The needle and seat are the most wearing parts of the carburetor and must be replaced during each overhaul. As mileage accumulates, the ridge gets wider to provide a platform for the dirt particles to rest on, and this is what raises the fuel level in the float bowl, as discussed in the text. Always replace the needle valve and seat each time the carburetor is taken apart.

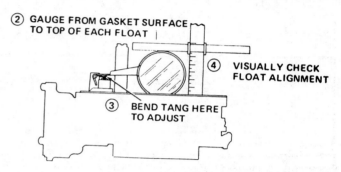

This drawing shows how to make the float level adjustment on most carburetors. The specifications will be included in the kit of parts you buy.

Note the bent-over end of this idle mixture adjusting needle, which will prevent you from making an accurate mixture adjustment. It was caused by turning in the needle tightly against the edge of the closed throttle valve.

A lean air-fuel mixture will cause higher burning temperatures, and the spark plug will provide this indication.

A soot-covered spark plug insulator indicates a rich air-fuel mixture. The combustion chamber temperature was not high enough to burn off the deposits. This carburetor requires an overhaul.

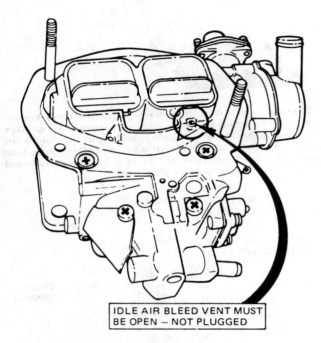

IDLE AIR BLEED VENT MUST
BE OPEN – NOT PLUGGED

On some Holley carburetors used on Pinto, Vega, Mustang, and Bobcat, this idle air bleed plugs up after long mileage, and this reduces gas mileage considerably. This is shown as an indication of how small air bleed holes in a carburetor must be cleaned periodically to restore operating efficiency and gas mileage.

If the carburetor has 50,000 miles of operation on it, chances are that the idle air bleed at the top of the carburetor is restricted in size by carbon accumulation. Any reduced air bleed enriches the air-fuel mixture and drops the gas mileage. Cleaning the parts in carburetor cleaner is the answer to this problem. Or you can replace the air bleed with a new one.

Main Metering System

Main metering jets never wear unless they have a metering rod moving up and down in them. In this case, always replace the metering jet and metering rod to restore the air-fuel mixture.

The Holley carburetor economizer valve contains a diaphragm which eventually leaks due to the constant flexing that occurs. This enriches the idle mixture to the point where it is impossible to make an idle mixture adjustment properly.

Power System

Sometimes the power jet fails to seat properly, and this causes an enriched mixture which lowers the gas mileage at least 15%. That's wasting $7.50 per month. On some carburetor models, the power jet is vacuum-operated, and this means that it has a diaphragm, which becomes porous from constant flexing. In these cases, it is well worthwhile to replace the power jet whenever you take the carburetor apart.

Some power jet openings are "timed" to throttle opening, and this is accomplished by linkage between the throttle valve and power piston actuating lever. If this linkage wears, then the timing is off. Always replace such worn linkage.

Most power jets are actuated by intake manifold vacuum. In this way, they are sensitive to engine load. When the engine is accelerated hard, the vacuum drops and, when it reaches about 8"Hg, the vacuum piston return spring forces the piston down to open the power jet. In a number of cases, the incorrect carburetor flange gasket was furnished in the kit of parts. If the gasket blocks the vacuum source to the power jet, then the mixture will be enriched through-

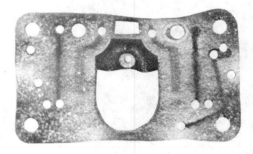

New gasket (left) compared with one removed from the bowl of a Holley carburetor shows why you should always use new gaskets when rebuilding a carburetor.

The Holley carburetor carburetor accelerator pump diaphragm eventually leaks due to the constant flexing. The diaphragm should be replaced everytime the carburetor is disassembled for service.

Corroded automatic choke thermostatic coil is evidence of a defective heat tube leaking exhaust gas into the choke mechanism.

out the driving range, resulting in a 15% reduction in economy, for a cost of $90.00 per year. Take the time to trace out this vital passageway to make sure that the flange gasket has the proper hole and that you're installing it so that the hole matches the vacuum passageways in the intake manifold flange and in the carburetor casting.

ACCELERATING SYSTEM

The accelerator pump forces a stream of gasoline into the air stream everytime the throttle is advanced to accelerate. Dirt can cause the two check valves to stick, and this will result in a "flat spot" during acceleration, which affects performance to a considerable degree. Clean or replace the check valves at each overhaul.

The pump leather dries out after long use in gasoline, therefore, the plunger should be replaced everytime the carburetor is taken apart for service. Also, the linkage connecting the accelerator pump plunger with the throttle valve wears, and this linkage must be replaced at the same time. When making the bench adjustments, the position of the piston is always measured with regard to the throttle, and this

LEATHER WORN THROUGH

The accelerator pump leather wears through like this in some models due to the constant movement of the pump plunger everytime the throttle is moved. Naturally, such worn parts must be replaced.

When the inside of the choke housing is carbonized in this manner, the operating mechanism is sticking and improper choke action will occur. Such a condition is caused by a leaking heat intake pipe; exhaust fumes are getting into the choke housing to cause these deposits. Gas mileage on this engine will be very low.

A vacuum gauge is handy for adjusting the idle mixture screws. Make the adjustments to obtain the highest reading on the vacuum gauge. CAUTION: Most manufacturers require that you have the air cleaner in place during this adjustment.

measurement affects the stroke of the piston and, therefore, the performance of the engine.

Some carburetors have provision for changing the piston stroke length for summer and winter driving. If you are interested in saving money, especially in city driving, and are willing to sacrifice some performance in the winter months, you can move the pump stroke adjustment to the shortest one. Make a few tests to determine whether the fuel saving is worthwhile.

AUTOMATIC CHOKE

The thermostatic coil within the choke is heated by the exhaust, and this can cause the formation of gum, which will result in a sticking choke. Depending on how bad the situation is, you can be losing 100-200 dollars per year in this sticky situation. Cleaning the choke mechanism is the only solution to restore choke performance.

The setting of the automatic choke is always made to ensure good driveability with a cold engine. It is possible to save some bucks if you are willing to sacrifice some of the warm-up driveability, especially in the winter months. Try loosening the choke cover screws and turning the choke cover one notch to the lean setting. You may like the savings.

CARBURETOR ADJUSTMENTS

The only adjustments on modern carburetors are those that can be made at idle speed. However, carburetor design is such that the effects of these adjustments have a definite influence on the air-fuel mixture delivered to the engine up to 35 mph, and this can affect your gas mileage to a considerable degree, especially if you drive in the city a great deal.

EMISSION-CONTROLLED ENGINES

All emission testing by highway patrols or official smog stations is done at idle speed so it is important that you follow these instructions precisely if you don't want to run afoul of the law. Really, it's no big deal to get your emissions within legal limits, **without expensive tune-up equipment.** All you need is our familiar and inexpensive vacuum gauge and a tachometer to adjust the carburetor mixture using the "lean-drop method" described below. An expensive HC/CO analyzer is not needed.

Lean-Drop Method

First check the tuning decal for the idle speed specifications, which is always given as two figures, such as 650-750. This means that you have 100 rpm leeway in making the idle speed adjustment. The engine can be running between 650 and 750 rpm and still be within the specified limits. Hook up your vacuum gauge to a tap on the intake manifold and the tachometer to the primary distributor terminal of the ignition coil. Now start the engine and warm it to operating temperature. Disconnect the hose leading to the evaporative emission-control system charcoal

GM 101-1 140 Cu. In. Federal	Transmission	
	Automatic	**Manual**
Exhaust Emission Control System	CCS−EGR	CCS−EGR
Timing (°BTC @ RPM)	12° @ 750	10° @ 700
Lean Drop Idle Mixture (RPM)	800-750	800-700
GM 101-1 140 Cu. In. NB−2		
Exhaust Emission Control System	CCS−EGR	CCS−EGR
Timing (°BTC @ RPM)	8° @ 750	8° @ 700
Lean Drop Idle Mixture (RPM)	800-750	800-700
GM 101-2 140 Cu. In. — Nationwide —		
Exhaust Emission Control System	CCS−EGR	CCS−EGR
Timing (°BTC @ RPM)	12° @ 750	10° @ 700
Lean Drop Idle Mixture (RPM)	800-750	800-700

Example of three emission-control decals. Note that the Lean-Drop Idle Mixture Specification is a spread of two idle speeds, as discussed in the text.

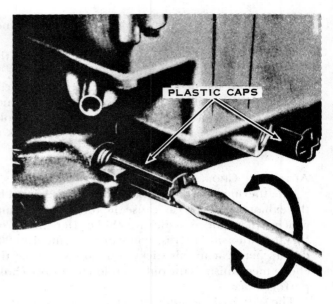

This illustration shows how the plastic limiter caps prevent making an overrich mixture adjustment.

Making the idle speed adjustment on a Vega carburetor.

canister to avoid having gasoline-laden vapors entering the induction system and affecting your carburetor adjustments. Or you can remove the gas tank cap to avoid pressurizing the system which will minimize the flow of vapors from the canister.

Turn the idle speed adjusting (throttle stop) screw to obtain the higher of the speeds shown on the tuning decal which, in the case above, is 750 rpm. Now adjust the idle mixture screw to obtain the highest vacuum reading (or the best running engine if you are not

The rpm gain with artificial enrichment would be equivalent to the curb-idle speed increase above specifications for using the "lean-drop" method discussed above.

VEHICLE EMISSION CONTROL INFORMATION

ENGINE FAMILY 2.3 CATALYST EGR/AIR (1CEF)				MAKE ALL ADJUSTMENTS WITH ENGINE AT NORMAL OPERATING TEMPERATURES. A/C AND HEADLIGHTS OFF
ENGINE DISPLACEMENT CID 140 CID				
SPARK PLUG AGRF-52 GAP .032-.036				CURB IDLE—ADJUST WITH THROTTLE SOLENOID POSITIONER ENERGIZED, THERMACTOR AIR ON, ALL VACUUM HOSES CONNECTED AND AIR CLEANER IN POSITION. WHENEVER CURB IDLE IS RESET, CHECK AND ADJUST THE DECEL VALVE ACCORDING TO THE SERVICE MANUAL
DISTRIBUTOR—BREAKERLESS				
CHOKE HOUSING	MAN/TRANS 1 LEAN			
NOTCH SETTING	AUTO/TRANS 1 LEAN			
TRANSMISSION	AUTO NEUTRAL	AUTO DRIVE	MANUAL NEUTRAL	IDLE MIXTURE—PRESET AT THE FACTORY. DO NOT REMOVE THE LIMITER CAP(S). CONSULT THE SERVICE MANUAL FOR DESCRIPTION OF ARTIFICIAL ENRICHMENT METHOD OF IDLE MIXTURE ADJUSTMENT TO BE USED ONLY DURING TUNE-UPS AND MAJOR CARBURETOR REPAIRS; IDLE MIXTURE MUST BE MEASURED WITH THERMACTOR AIR OFF
IGNITION TIMING	10° BTDC		6° BTDC	
TIMING RPM	550		550	
CURB IDLE	A/C		750	900
RPM	NO A/C		750	900
IDLE MIXTURE—ARTIFICIAL ENRICHMENT				INITIAL TIMING—ADJUST WITH HOSES DISCONNECTED AND PLUGGED AT THE DISTRIBUTOR
RPM GAIN		20-60	20-60	
RPM RESET		40	40	REFERENCE TO A/C, THROTTLE SOLENOID, THERMACTOR AIR AND DECEL VALVE APPLICABLE ONLY IF THE ENGINE IS SO EQUIPPED. CONSULT SERVICE PUBLICATIONS FOR FURTHER INSTRUCTIONS ON TIMING AND IDLE SET
THIS VEHICLE REQUIRES MAINTENANCE SCHEDULE "B"				

THIS VEHICLE CONFORMS TO U.S.EPA. REGULATIONS APPLICABLE TO 1975 MODEL YEAR NEW MOTOR VEHICLES. THIS VEHICLE ALSO CONFORMS TO THE STATE OF CALIFORNIA CERTIFICATION STANDARDS APPLICABLE TO 1975 MODEL YEAR NEW MOTOR VEHICLES.

FORD MOTOR COMPANY   D52E-9C485-DA

The Ford emission-control decal calls for articicial enrichment, the gain in speed is equal to the lean-drop speed on the previous decal.

using a vacuum gauge). With a two- or four-barrel carburetor, you must adjust both mixture adjusting screws the same amount. *NOTE: If you are tuning a modern emission-controlled engine, it will be necessary to break off the tab on the plastic cap covering the mixture adjusting screw to make the adjustment.* If engine speed changes from our initial setting of 750 rpm, it is essential to adjust the idle speed screw again to return engine speed to the previous figure of 750 rpm.

To make the final mixture and speed adjustments so your emissions are within legal limits, turn the idle mixture adjusting screw(s) clockwise (lean) to lower your idle speed to the lower of the two figures specified on the tuning decal, which in this case would be 650 rpm for a 100-rpm reduction. **CAUTION: Don't touch the idle speed screw.** Make this engine speed reduction by leaning the mixture with the mixture adjusting screw to keep your hydrocarbon emissions within legal limits.

Replace the plastic limit caps with new ones that are sold for service so that the job is done legally. In most cases, the manufacturer supplies the idle speed specifications with the proper spread so that the "lean-drop method" can be used to obtain legal emission limits without an expensive CO meter.

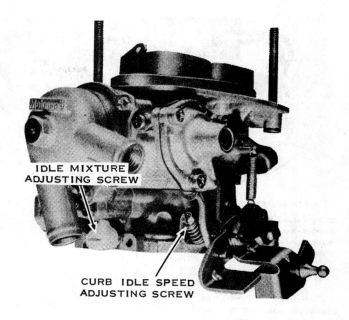

IDLE MIXTURE ADJUSTING SCREW

CURB IDLE SPEED ADJUSTING SCREW

The idle mixture and speed adjustments for the 2V carburetor used on the Vega, Pinto, Bobcat, Mustang II, and Capri II.

IDLE DECEL CONNECTION

MECHANICAL FUEL BOWL VENT VALVE

ACCELERATOR PUMP LEVER

TURN TO ADJUST CURB-IDLE SPEED WITH SOLENOID ENERGIZED

SOLENOID QUICK-DISCONNECT

SOLENOID DASHPOT THROTTLE POSITIONER

SOLENOID OFF (TSP OFF) SLOW-IDLE SPEED ADJUSTING SCREW (THROTTLE-STOP SCREW)

Idle mixture and curb-idle speed adjusting screws on the Ford 2150-2V carburetor used on V6 and V8 engines since 1975.

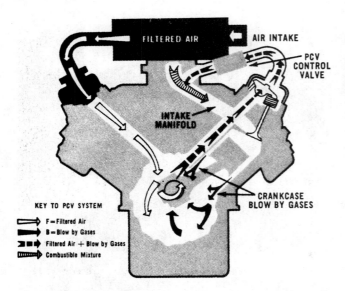

KEY TO PCV SYSTEM

⇨ F = Filtered Air
➡ B = Blow by Gases
▶▶➡ Filtered Air + Blow by Gases
▭▭▭▭ Combustible Mixture

This diagram shows how the air and blow-by gases from the crankcase pass through the PCV valve and into the combustion chamber for burning.

EMISSION-CONTROL SYSTEMS

Crankcase, exhaust, and evaporative emission-control systems are an inherent part of modern engines, and some of these systems can be gas gulpers, especially if they are not functioning properly. This section will be for the mechanically handy person who wants to check out the functioning of the systems on his car to isolate a recent gas mileage drop to determine whether the trouble is due to a malfunction in an emission-control system, or to some ignition/fuel system problems.

In all cases, some quick tests are provided for you to check the efficiency of the system. If you find that your engine emission-control system does not pass this quick test, then you should return the vehicle to your dealership for more detailed testing to determine the exact part that has failed. This will restore your gas mileage as well as make your vehicle conform to legal emission limits.

CRANKCASE EMISSION-CONTROL SYSTEMS

All of these systems depend on an air bleed into the intake manifold connected to a sealed-type crankcase. Its purpose is to draw the blow-by gases from the crankcase into the intake manifold so that they can be consumed in the combustion process. Some systems use a calibrated bleed hole, but most of them have a PCV (Positive Crankcase Ventilation) valve in the circuit.

If the PCV valve or the calibrated bleed hole in the intake manifold clogs, then the designed amount of air

A quick test of the efficiency of the PCV system is to clamp off the hose running to the PCV valve. Engine speed should drop about 60 rpm if the system is functioning properly.

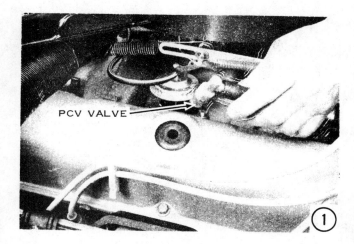

will be shut off from the intake manifold, and your gas mileage will decrease at least 10%; this is going to cost you about $5.00 per month in added fuel costs.

System Quick Test

With the engine running at about 1,000 rpm, use a pair of pliers to clamp off the hose running from the PCV valve to the intake manifold. Engine speed should drop about 60 rpm if the system is functioning properly. Another quick test is to remove the oil filler cap with the engine idling; engine speed should increase at least 60 rpm to indicate the fact that you are allowing extra air to enter the system and relieve some of the vacuum designed into it. The added air flow leans the air-fuel mixture, and the engine should run slightly faster. If the **System Quick Test** indicates trouble, then make the detailed tests which follow to isolate it.

SERVICE PROCEDURES

①Remove the PCV valve from the rocker arm cover and shake it. You should hear a clicking noise if the valve is free. If not, replace the valve. **CAUTION: Don't attempt to clean the valve. Also, make sure that**

you replace it with one having the correct part number, as each has a different calibration.

②Start the engine and a hissing noise should be heard as air passes through the valve. A strong vacuum should be felt when you place your finger over the valve inlet.

③Reinstall the valve, and then remove the oil filler cap. Start the engine and hold a piece of cardboard over the opening in the rocker arm cover. If the system is functioning properly, the cardboard will be sucked against the opening with a noticeable force. If the cardboard is not sucked against the opening with a new PCV valve, it is necessary to clean the hoses, vent tube, and passageway in the lower part of the carburetor.

EXHAUST EMISSION-CONTROL SYSTEMS

There are three basic systems: (1) Transmission-Controlled Spark (TCS), (2) Spark-Delay System (SDS), and (3) Exhaust-Gas Recirculation (EGR). There are other exhaust emission-control systems

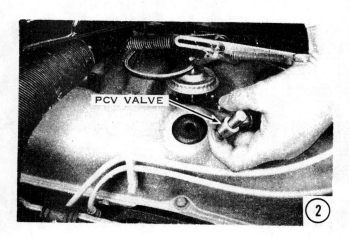

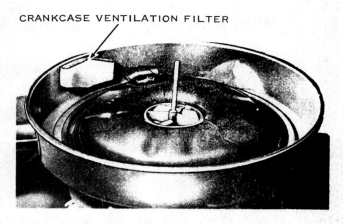

If the crankcase ventilation system has a filter element in the air cleaner shell, it must be cleaned or replaced every 12,000 miles.

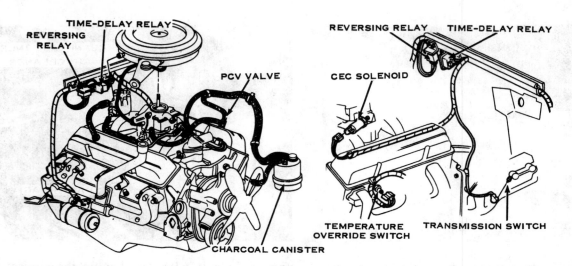

Layout of the various control units making up the TCS system used on a Chevrolet V-8 engine. Other models have the same parts, but placed in different positions.

(and evaporative emission-control systems), but they have more effect on emissions than mileage; therefore, we will not discuss them in this book.

TRANSMISSION-CONTROLLED SPARK

The TCS system, also known as the NOx system on Chrysler engines, Transmission-Regulated Spark (TRS) on Ford products, or Speed-Controlled Spark (SCS) on others, is designed to deny vacuum to the distributor vacuum-advance actuator during certain engine-operating modes. Generally, vacuum is denied until the transmission is shifted into high gear (TCS) or until it reaches a designed vehicle speed of about 35 mph (SCS). If this system is not functioning properly, you can be losing as much as 25° vacuum advance, and this can be costing you about 40% efficiency in average-speed, high-gear operation, where the TCS

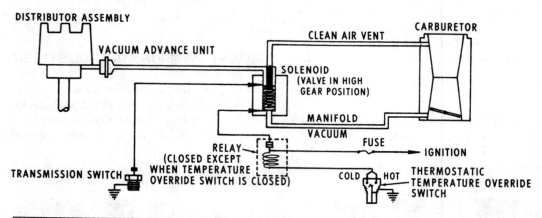

	TRANSMISSION GEAR						
TRANS	PARK	NEUTRAL	REVERSE	1ST	2ND	3RD	4TH
3 SPD						V.A.	—
4 SPD (PASS)						V.A.	—
4 SPD (TRUCK)							V.A.
TORQUE DR					V.A.		
POWERGLIDE					V.A.	—	
H/M			V.A.			V.A.	

(V.A.—VACUUM ADVANCE)

Circuit diagram of the Transmission-Controlled Spark (TCS) system used on a Chevrolet engine. This same system is used on most G.M. produced cars, as discussed in the text. If there should be a malfunction in the system, you may not be getting vacuum to the distributor vacuum-advance diaphragm, and this would lower your gas mileage and power considerably.

system should not function. A defective TCS system can cost you almost $250.00 per year in added fuel costs.

System Basic Tests

Disconnect the vacuum hose leading to the vacuum-advance actuator on the distributor and connect it to a vacuum gauge that can be viewed from the driver's seat. (This needs a long hose.) If you already have the suggested vacuum driving gauge mounted on the dash, it is relatively easy to connect a jumper hose from the distributor hose to the existing hose leading to your dash-mounted gauge.

Now drive the vehicle until it is thoroughly warmed. With the ambient air temperature above 68°F, and the engine running over 1,500 rpm, you should get full vacuum to the gauge only after shifting into HIGH or DRIVE (or get above 35 mph with an SCS system). **CAUTION: You may have to wait for almost 60 seconds for full vacuum to appear on some of the later engines with a time-delay relay.** The vacuum gauge must drop to zero when you shift into NEUTRAL. The same test can be made in the garage by jacking up the rear axle and supporting the car on safety stands during the test. **CUATION: Make sure**

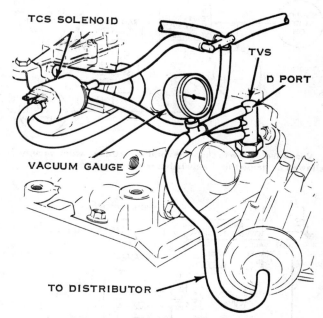

To check the TCS system, hook a vacuum gauge into the hose leading to the distributor vacuum-advance unit. You should obtain vacuum in high gear with a manual transmission, or in reverse gear with an automatic transmission. If you don't get vacuum, then you're running on a retarded spark timing, and this is costing you lost engine performance.

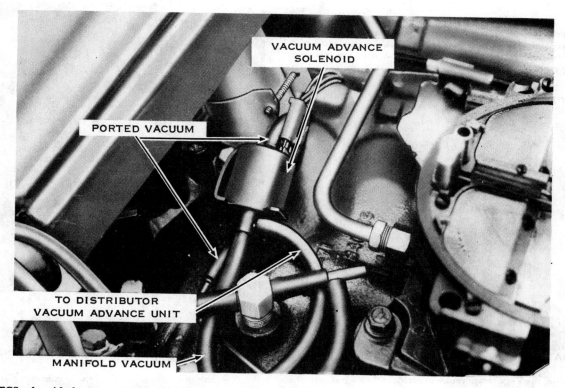

Typical TCS solenoid placement and the position of the hoses that supply vacuum to the distributor. In many cases, it is only necessary to pull the connector from the TCS solenoid to obtain vacuum for testing purposes, as discussed in the text.

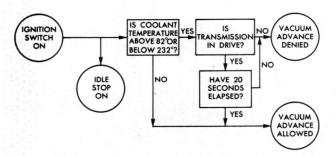

Vacuum diagram to show the conditions under which vacuum is allowed or denied to the distributor vacuum-advance unit.

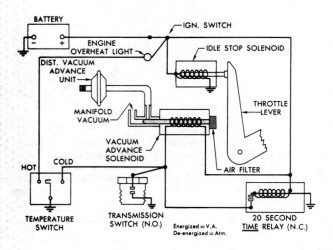

Circuit diagram of the TCS system used on a Chevrolet V-8 engine in the low-gear operating mode. Note that the temperature switch, transmission switch, and time-delay relay are open circuited to deprive the distributor of vacuum in the low-gear operating mode.

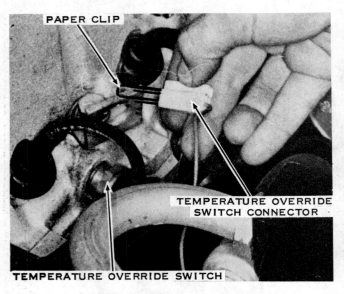

Grounding the Vega temperature override switch wires restores vacuum to the distributor vacuum-advance unit for testing purposes.

the parking brake is firmly applied and the front wheels blocked for safety reasons.

If the system passes these two checks, no further testing is needed.

System Isolation Test

To isolate trouble between the ignition/fuel systems and the TCS system, it is often desirable to disconnect the TCS system and test-drive the vehicle without it in operation to determine whether the problem is resolved. **CAUTION: After making the following tests, be sure to reconnect the system properly so that the vehicle conforms to legal emission standards.**

On most early G.M. TCS systems, the solenoid was energized to provide vacuum advance and, on later models, it is de-energized to provide vacuum advance; therefore, it is necessary to determine which system you are working on for the proper procedure.

All Ford, Chrysler, and American Motors systems provide vacuum advance when the solenoid is de-energized. On these systems, it is only necessary to disconnect the feed wire to the solenoid and drive the vehicle without the system in operation. This also works on all 1970-71 General Motors cars, except Chevrolet, in which case, it is easiest to disconnect the wires at the heat sensor in the cylinder head and ground them with a jumper wire to provide full

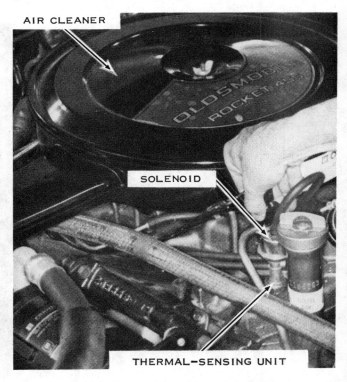

You can pull off the TCS solenoid connector on many G.M. engines to restore vacuum to the distributor for testing purposes.

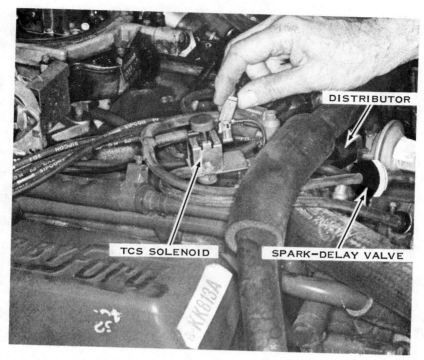

On Ford engines, you can disconnect either wire leading to the TCS solenoid to disarm the system for testing purposes.

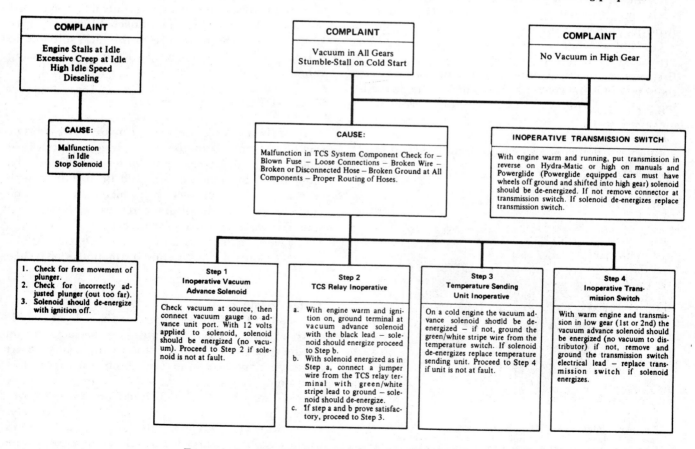

Transmission-Controlled Spark (TCS) system troubleshooting guide.

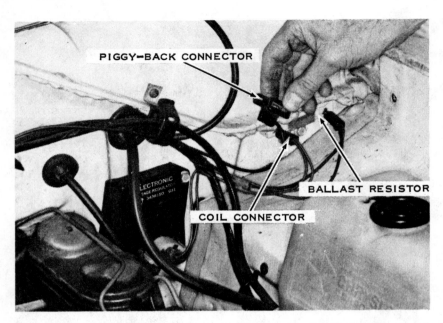

The Chrysler NOx system can be disarmed for testing purposes by disconnecting the piggyback connector on the ballast resistor, and then reconnecting the wires to the terminal.

vacuum advance for testing purposes. After testing, reconnect the wires to restore the TCS system's functions for reducing exhaust emissions.

On engines where the solenoid must be energized o provide full vacuum advance for testing purposes, it is first necessary to determine which of the two wires to the solenoid is the feed wire and which is the grounding one; otherwise, you could ground the wrong wire and blow a fuse to complicate the testing procedure. Check both wires to the solenoid with a test lamp or voltmeter to determine which one is the feed wire, and

The Spark-Delay Valve (SDV) should always have the black side connected to the source of vacuum. This sintered metal valve must be replaced every 10,000 miles or engine performance will be adversely affected.

then use a jumper wire to ground the other solenoid terminal to provide full vacuum advance for testing purposes. After testing, disconnect the jumper wire and reconnect the feed wire to the TCS solenoid to restore the TCS system's functions for reducing exhaust emissions.

SPARK-DELAY SYSTEMS (SDS)

All of these systems delay vacuum to the distributor vacuum-advance actuator for a designed period of time, which can be as long as 60 seconds. Generally, these valves are made of sintered bronze discs, with very small pores for vacuum to bleed through. The more discs stacked inside of the SDS valve, the longer it takes for vacuum to pass through it.

Chrysler calls its delay system Orifice Spark Advance Control (OSAC), and it functions exactly like the SDS.

System Basic Test

Disconnect the vacuum hose at the side of the SD valve which leads to the vacuum-advance actuator on the distributor and connect it to a vacuum gauge. Start the engine and accelerate it to about 1,500 rpm. The vacuum gauge should show no reading for a few seconds and then it should build up slowly to over 15"Hg, **provided you keep the throttle steady.** Everytime you accelerate the engine, the vacuum reading will drop and it will take time to reach the normal level again **if you hold the throttle steady.**

The Ford Spark-Delay System (SDS) can be tested with a vacuum gauge as discussed in the text.

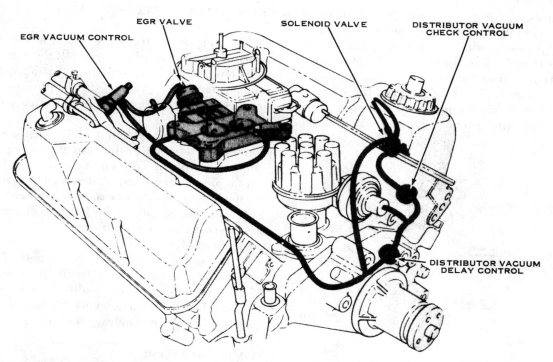

Typical Spark-Delay Valve (SDV) system as used on many late-model Ford engines. Note that this system is used in conjunction with an EGR valve, which is controlled by a Thermal Vacuum-Switching valve. EGR is limited to operating conditions when the engine has reached normal operating temperature.

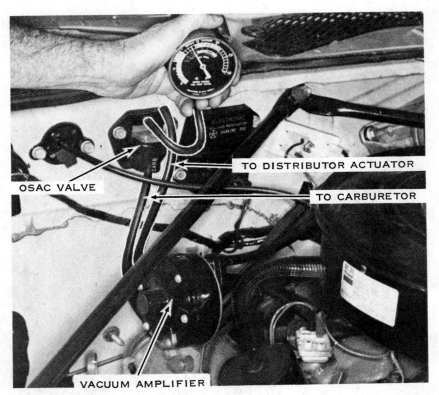

Testing the Chrysler Orifice Spark Advance Control (OSAC) valve with a vacuum gauge. This test is similar to that for the SDV system discussed in the text.

SERVICE PROCEDURES

These valves are subject to blockage by particles of dust that build up as air, influenced by throttle action, continuously moves both ways through the valve. After about 10,000 miles, the valve will be obstructed enough to reduce your vacuum advance, and this can lower your gas mileage as much as 40% for a loss of about 35 gallons of gas per month. Replacing the SDS valve every 10,000 miles is good insurance against this happening.

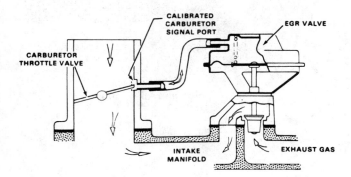

The EGR system allows calibrated amounts of exhaust gas to enter the intake manifold for reducing the temperature of combustion to minimize the formation of NOx. If this valve does not seat properly, the engine will idle roughly.

EXHAUST-GAS RECIRCULATION (EGR)

The purpose of the EGR system is to control the emissions of oxides of nitrogen (NOx). It does this by returning a small amount of exhaust gas into the intake manifold to reduce the combustion chamber temperature below a critical level so that less NOx is formed.

Because the introduction of exhaust gas reduces combustion efficiency, the system is designed to be inoperative during cold engine starts and low-speed operation in order to restore driveability. It introduces the maximum amount of exhaust gas when the engine is heavily loaded, as during hard acceleration when combustion chamber temperatures reach higher-than-normal levels.

If the control system is defective and allows EGR while the engine is cold, it will be difficult to start. If the EGR valve leaks, idling quality will be seriously affected. In any case, a defective EGR valve or control system will lower gas mileage accordingly.

System Quick Tests

To test the EGR valve, open the throttle of a thoroughly warmed engine and observe the EGR valve shaft, which should move up and down as the throttle is moved back and forth. If it doesn't, the EGR valve or the control system is defective.

To test the EGR control system, start the engine, clamp off the vacuum supply hose to the EGR valve, and then raise engine speed to about 1,500 rpm. Release the clamping hose pressure, and engine speed should drop about 150 rpm to reflect the passage of exhaust gas into the intake manifold as the EGR system becomes effective. If it doesn't, the control system is defective.

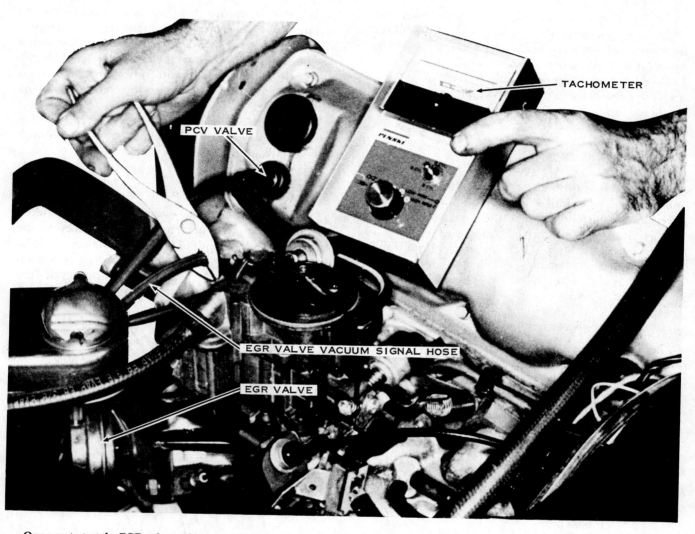

One way to test the EGR valve and its control circuit is to clamp shut the EGR vacuum signal hose with a pair of pliers, and then run the engine speed up to about 2,000 rpm. Note the tachometer reading, and then release the clamping hose pressure. Engine speed should drop at least 100 rpm to indicate the passage of exhaust gas into the intake manifold as the EGR system becomes effective.

5/engine service

In this chapter, we will cover some of the simple repair jobs that anyone can do with a minimum of skill and tools. These are jobs that frequently need to be done on a maintenance or yearly basis. This section is followed by some reconditioning jobs on six-cylinder and V-8 engines, both General Motors and Ford. The final section will cover some simple service procedures on your engine's electrical system.

MONEY SAVING TIPS

While you may think that you can't do some of these jobs because of lack of skill and equipment, you can save money by doing most of the work yourself with the assistance of the clear text and the many illustrations in this book. There are many photographs of worn parts so that the unskilled reader will recognize such wear when he sees it. These pictures take the place of years of experience.

You can take your cylinder head, piston-and-rod assemblies, or electrical equipment from the engine, and have it serviced by a parts house that includes a machine shop. In this way, the difficult part of the job that requires special skills and equipment will be done for you to avoid the customary mechanic's markup, which runs 25-40%.

Where such advice is needed, it will be provided in the section where it applies, and be labeled Money Saving Tips, or just MST in many cases.

ENGINE THEORY

Most engines used in passenger cars operate on the four-stroke cycle principle. During this cycle, the piston travels the length of its stroke four times. As the piston travels up or down, the crankshaft is rotated halfway (180 degrees). To accomplish one cycle, the crankshaft rotates two complete turns; the camshaft,

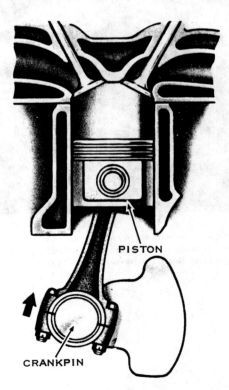

On the intake stroke of a four-stroke cycle internal-combustion engine, the piston moves down while the intake valve is open to draw in a combustible air-fuel mixture.

On the compression stroke, both valves are closed as the piston moves up to compress the air-fuel mixture.

which controls the valves, is driven by the crankshaft at half crankshaft speed. Valve action, intake and exhaust, occurs once in each four-stroke cycle, and the piston acts as an air pump during the two remaining strokes.

INTAKE STROKE

The intake valve is opened as the piston moves down the cylinder, and this creates an area of pressure lower than that of the surrounding atmosphere. Atmospheric pressure will cause air to flow into this low-pressure area. By directing the air flow through the carburetor, a measured amount of vaporized fuel is added. When the piston reaches the bottom of the intake stroke, the cylinder is filled with air and vaporized fuel. The exhaust valve is closed during the intake stroke.

COMPRESSION STROKE

When the piston starts to move upward, the compression stroke begins. The intake valve closes, trapping the air-fuel mixture in the cylinder. The upward movement of the piston compresses the mixture to a fraction of its original volume; exact pressure depends principally on the compression ratio of the engine.

POWER STROKE

The power stroke is produced by igniting the compressed air-fuel mixture. When the spark plug arcs, the mixture ignites and burns very rapidly during the power stroke. The resulting high temperature expands the gases, creating very high pressure on top of the piston, which drives the piston down. This downward motion of the piston is transmitted through the connecting rod and is converted into rotary motion by the crankshaft. Both the intake and exhaust valves are closed during the power stroke.

EXHAUST STROKE

The exhaust valve opens just before the piston completes the power stroke. Pressure in the cylinder at this time causes the exhaust gas to rush into the exhaust manifold (blowdown). The upward movement of the piston on its exhaust stroke expels most of the remaining exhaust gas.

As the piston pauses momentarily at the top of the exhaust stroke, the inertia of the exhausting gas tends to remove any remaining gas in the combustion chamber; however, a small amount always remains to dilute the incoming mixture. This unexpelled gas is captured in the clearance area between the piston and the cylinder head.

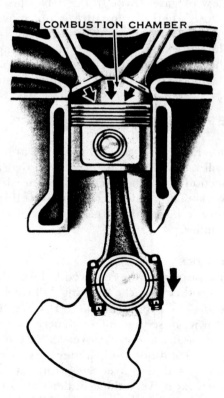

On the power stroke, the tightly compressed combustible mixture is ignited by the spark plug and the resulting burning of the fuel pushes the piston down the cylinder.

On the exhaust stroke, the exhaust valve is open, while the piston moves up to force the burned gases from the cylinder.

COMBUSTION

The power delivered from the piston to the crankshaft is the result of a pressure increase in the gas mixture above the piston. This pressure increase occurs as the mixture is heated, first by compression, and then (on the down stroke) by burning. The burning fuel supplies heat that raises temperature and, at the same time, raises pressure. Actually, about 75 percent of the mixture in the cylinder is composed of nitrogen gas that does not burn but expands when heated by the burning of the combustible elements, and it is this expanding nitrogen that supplies most of the pressure on the piston.

The fuel and oxygen must burn smoothly within the combustion chamber to take full advantage of this heating effect. Maximum power would not be delivered to the piston if an explosion took place, because the entire force would be spent in one sharp hammer-like blow, occurring too fast for the piston to follow.

Instead, burning takes place evenly as the flame moves across the combustion chamber. Burning must be completed by the time the piston is about half-way down so that maximum pressure will be developed in the cylinder at the time the piston applies its greatest force to the crankshaft. This will be when the mechanical advantage of the connecting rod and crankshaft is at a maximum.

At the beginning of the power stroke (as the piston is driven down by the pressure), the volume above the piston increases, which would normally allow the

pressure in the cylinder to drop. However, combustion is still in progress, and this continues to raise the temperature of the gases, expanding them and maintaining a continuous pressure on the piston as it travels downward. This provides a smooth application of power throughout the effective part of the power stroke to make the most efficient use of the energy released by the burning fuel.

VALVE TIMING

On the power stroke, the exhaust valve opens before bottom dead center in order to get the exhaust gases started out of the combustion chamber under the remaining pressure (blowdown). On the exhaust stroke, the intake valve opens before top dead center in order to start the air-fuel mixture moving into the combustion chamber. These processes are functions of camshaft design and valve timing.

Valves always open and close at the same time in the cycle; the timing is not variable with speed and load as is ignition timing. There is, however, one particular speed for each given engine at which the air-fuel mixture will pack itself into the combustion chambers most effectively. This is the speed at which the engine puts out its peak torque. At low engine speeds, compression is somewhat suppressed due to the slight reverse flow of gases through the valves just as they open or close when the mixture is not moving fast enough to take advantage of the time lag. At high speeds, the valve timing does not allow enough time during the valve opening and closing periods for effective packing of the air-fuel mixture into the cylinders.

SERVICE PROCEDURES

The general service procedures that apply to all engines will be discussed in the section that follows, and this section should be referred to before doing any engine work. This general section is followed by specific service instructions that apply to each of the engine families.

CYLINDER BLOCK

The ring ridge must be removed before taking out the pistons; otherwise, the top ring will catch on the ledge and break a piston ring land. Inspect the cylinder walls for wear, scores, and evidence of scuffing. If the cylinder walls are worn over 0.012″, it will be necessary to recondition the cylinder bores to the next oversize and install new oversize pistons. If the bores are not worn excessively, the cylinder walls should be honed to remove the glaze, which could prevent the new piston rings from seating quickly.

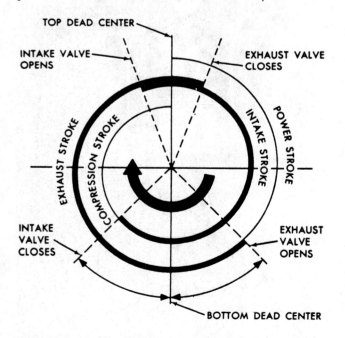

Typical valve timing diagram. Note that this represents two complete turns of the crankshaft (720°).

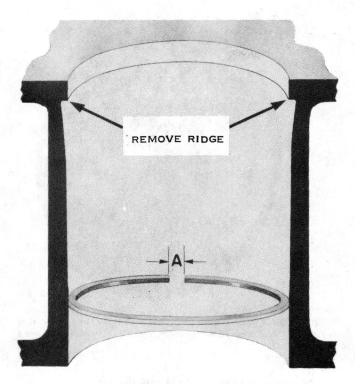

A ridge remover is needed to cut the ridge from the top of the cylinder walls. The stop under the blade keeps you from cutting into the walls too deeply. Don't cut more than 1/32″ below the bottom of the ridge.

It is necessary to remove the ring ridge before taking the pistons out; otherwise, you will break the piston when a ring jams under the ledge. When measuring the piston ring end gap, it is essential to position the piston ring near the bottom of the cylinder in the unworn area, so that there will be sufficient clearance at all times.

CYLINDER HEADS AND MANIFOLDS

Scrape all gasket materials from the manifolds and heads. Remove the deposits in the combustion

The cylinder walls wear the greatest amount at the top, due to the borderline lubrication conditions that exist. All measurements must be made in the worn area. This cylinder bore has been surfaced with a fine hone to remove the glaze for better piston ring seating.

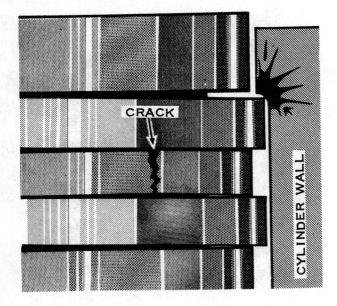

The ring ridge must be removed before the piston is pushed out of the top of the bore; otherwise, the top ring will strike it and break the piston ring land.

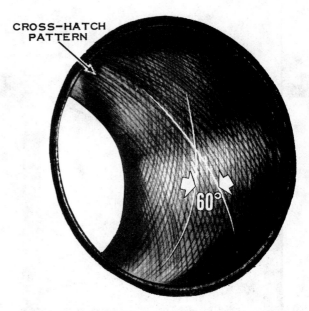

The cylinder walls should be honed to remove the glaze so that the new piston rings will seat quickly. The ideal crosshatch pattern is 60°.

chambers with a wire brush and scraper. **CAUTION: Be careful not to damage the gasket surfaces.** Clean the valve guides with a guide-cleaning brush. Apply some lacquer thinner to the revolving brush in order to dissolve the gum inside of the valve guides.

Check the gasket surface of the cylinder head for burrs and scratches, which could prevent the gasket from sealing properly. Check the flatness of the gasket surface with a straightedge and a feeler gauge. Surface irregularity must not exceed 0.003″ in any six-inch space, and the total must not exceed 0.007″ for the entire length of the head. If necessary, the cylinder head gasket surface can be machined. **CAUTION: Do not remove more than 0.010″ of stock.**

Measuring the cylinder wall taper and wear with a dial indicator.

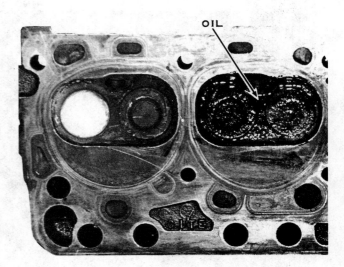

Always study the cylinder head when it is removed. The coloring of the valves tells a graphic story of the condition of the engine. In this case, the cylinder at the left was firing normally, as evidenced by the white (heated) exhaust valve. The cylinder at the right was pumping oil, possibly due to a scored cylinder wall or broken piston ring.

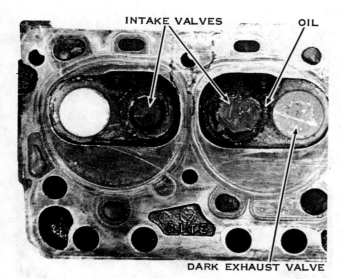

Note the relatively darker coloring of the exhaust valve in the right combustion chamber and the oil around the intake valve. This means that the compression in the right cylinder is lower than the compression in the left cylinder and that the intake valve guide and seal are defective and were allowing oil to leak into the combustion chamber.

CRANKSHAFT

Clean the crankshaft with solvent and wipe the journals dry with a lint-free cloth. **CAUTION: Handle the shaft carefully to avoid damaging the highly finished journal surfaces.** Blow out all oil passages

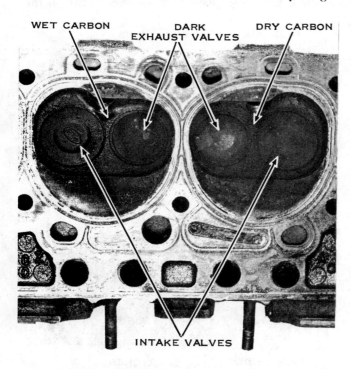

The sooty black appearance of these combustion chambers indicates an excessively rich air-fuel mixture. Note the wet carbon in the left combustion chamber which indicates that piston ring trouble is starting there.

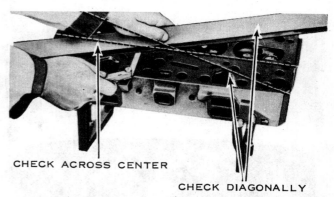

Check the cylinder head gasket surface for uneven spots. Surface irregularities must not exceed 0.003″ in any six-inch space.

with compressed air. **CAUTION: Oil passageways lead from the rod to the main bearing journal. Be careful not to blow the dirt into the main bearing journal bore.**

Scored crankshaft journals indicate the need for reconditioning. New inserts would soon be destroyed by this rough shaft.

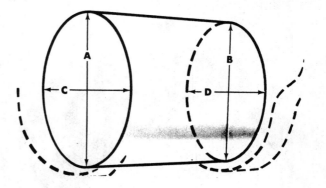

A VS B = VERTICAL TAPER
C VS D = HORIZONTAL TAPER
A VS C AND B VS D = OUT OF ROUND
CHECK FOR OUT-OF-ROUND AT EACH END OF JOURNAL

Measure the diameter of each journal at four places to determine the wear, taper, and out-of-roundness that exists.

The coloring of the old bearing inserts tells a story. Note the light gray coloring of the upper bearing insert, which indicates that the bearing was operating with the proper clearance. The dark coloring of the lower insert indicates excessive bearing clearance.

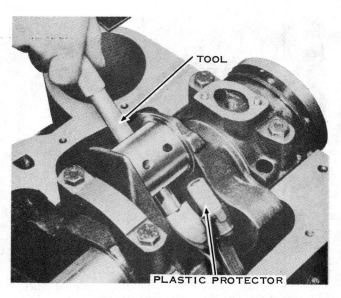

Always use a piece of rubber hose to cover the rod bolt threads when removing the piston and rod assembly; otherwise, you may damage the bearing surface by scraping the threads over it.

Measure the diameter of each journal at four places to determine the out-of-round, taper, and wear. The out-of-round limit is 0.001″; the taper must not exceed 0.001″; and the wear limit is 0.0025″. If any of these limits is exceeded, the crankshaft must be reground to an undersize, and undersized bearing inserts must be installed.

removal tool into the oil hole in the crankshaft, and then rotate the shaft in the direction of engine rotation to force the insert out of the block.

Clean the journal with solvent, and then wipe it dry with a lint-free cloth. If a new upper insert is to be installed, place the plain end over the shaft on the

Main Bearings

Mark each bearing cap and the block so that the cap can be replaced in its proper position. Remove the main bearing cap and inspect the insert. If the upper half of the insert is to be removed, insert a bearing

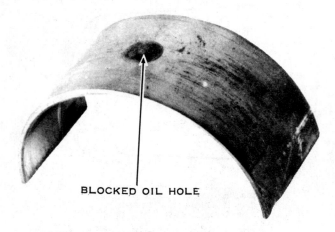

BLOCKED OIL HOLE

It is difficult to install a main bearing insert properly without removing the crankshaft because you can't see what you are doing. Be careful to check for oil holes and locking recesses before installing a new insert. A blocked oil hole will cause rapid destruction of the engine.

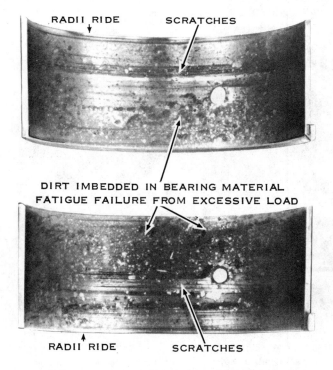

RADII RIDE   SCRATCHES

DIRT IMBEDDED IN BEARING MATERIAL
FATIGUE FAILURE FROM EXCESSIVE LOAD

RADII RIDE   SCRATCHES

Bearing defects caused by improper installation. Carefully wipe each insert before installing it and make sure that your hands are reasonably clean.

This shows how a piece of Plastigage is placed on the crankpin to measure the clearance. Then the cap is torqued to specifications.

This shows how the squeezed-out Plastigage strip looks after being compressed by the cap. Note the use of a scale on the side of the package to compare. New bearing insert clearance should be 0.001-0.003".

locking tang side and partially install it so that the inserting tool can be placed in the oil hole. Rotate the crankshaft in the direction opposite to engine rotation until the bearing is seated. Remove the tool.

MEASURING THE OIL CLEARANCE

The clearance between the shaft and insert can be measured by using Plastigage. To check the clearance, support the crankshaft with a jack so that its weight will not compress the Plastigage and thereby provide an erroneous reading. Position the jack so that it bears against the counterweight adjoining the bearing to be checked.

Clean the journal thoroughly of all traces of oil, and then place a piece of Plastigage on the bearing surface, the full width of the cap. Install the cap and torque the retaining bolts to specifications. **CAUTION: Don't turn the crankshaft with the Plastigage in place or you will distort it.** Remove the cap. To determine the clearance, use the scale on the package to check the width of the squeezed-out piece in the bearing insert. If the squeezed-out plastic strip is tapered, the journal is tapered. Measuring at the widest and narrowest points will determine the minimum and maximum clearances. If the clearance exceeds 0.0025", a new insert should be installed. If installing a new insert does not return the clearance to specifications, then an undersized insert should be used.

PRY CRANKSHAFT FORWARD   PRY CAP BACKWARDS   TIGHTEN CAP

Before tightening the thrust bearing, it is essential to align it properly. This is done by prying the crankshaft forward and prying the main bearing cap backward, and then torquing the bolts to specifications.

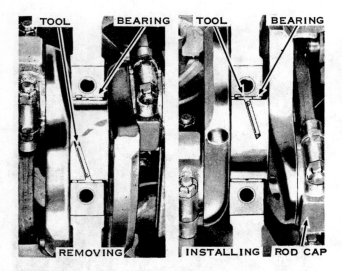

This illustration shows how to remove and install an upper main bearing insert. The round body of the tool is inserted in the oil hole in the main bearing journal, and then the crankshaft is rotated in a direction to unlock the retaining lip. The same tool can be used to install a new insert as shown at the right. Clean the insert and the shaft carefully to avoid getting dirt behind the insert.

CONNECTING RODS

Remove the inserts from the rod and cap. Identify

To measure the wear on a piston pin, it should be miked on an unworn section (center), and then on both ends for a comparative measurement.

the inserts if they are to be used again. Clean the parts in solvent and blow dry.

Check the rod bolts and nuts for defects in the threads. Inspect the inside of the rod bearing bore for evidence of galling, which indicates that the insert is loose enough to move around. Check the parting cheeks to be sure that the cap or rod has not been filed. Replace any defective rods.

Whenever servicing the piston and rod assembly, it is generally advisable to install new piston pins, especially if the mileage is over 50,000. Loose piston pins, coupled with tight piston assemblies because of new piston rings, will cause piston pin noises, which may disappear as the engine loosens but this is difficult to explain to a customer who has just paid the bill. Most mechanics have this work done by automotive

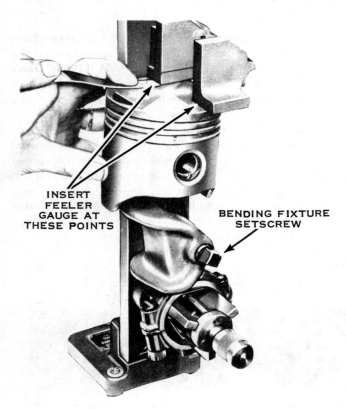

Showing the method of testing for, and correcting, a bent connecting rod.

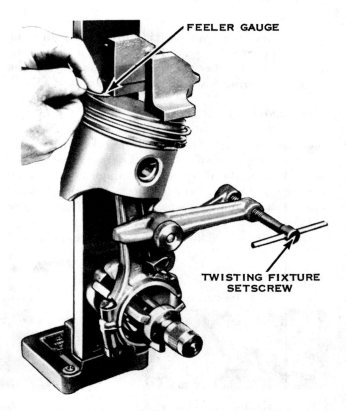

To check a connecting rod for twist, turn the piston as far as possible on its wrist pin, and then measure the clearance, as shown. The twisting jig can be used to straighten the rod.

machine shops, which have the neccessary equipment for a precision job. At the same time, the connecting rods will be aligned so that the pistons and rings will run true with the cylinder walls.

You can measure the connecting rod bearing clearance in the manner described in the previous section on main bearings.

PISTONS

Remove deposits from the piston crown with a scraper. Clean the piston in solvent and blow dry. **CAUTION: Don't soak the pistons in a caustic solu-**

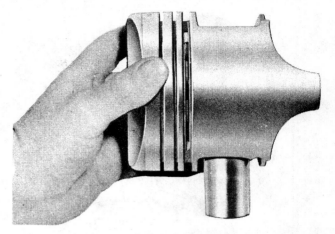

A properly fitted pin should support its own weight in either pin boss when coated with light engine oil at room temperature.

tion because it will corrode the aluminim. **CAU-TION: Don't buff the pistons on a wire brush because it will deform the soft metal.** Clean the ring grooves with a ring groove cleaner or a piece of broken ring. **CAUTION: Don't scrape or nick the sides of the grooves, or you will damage the sealing surfaces.**

Inspect the piston for scuffed surfaces, cracks, and wear. Install a new compression ring in the top groove, and then insert a 0.006″ feeler gauge to check for ring groove wear. If you can insert the feeler gauge over halfway into the top ring groove, it is worn, and the

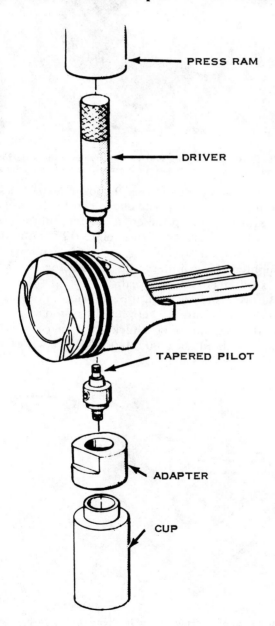

PRESS RAM

DRIVER

TAPERED PILOT

ADAPTER

CUP

Details of the tool being used to press out a piston pin.

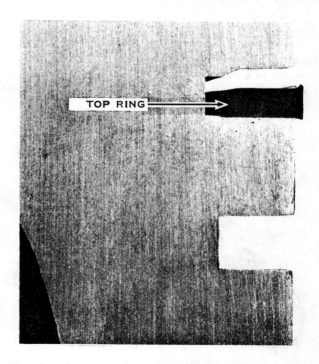

TOP RING

Top ring groove wear is commonplace, and this one requires that the groove be turned oversize and a steel spacer installed above the piston ring to restore production clearances.

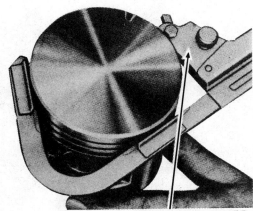

Always clean the ring grooves so that the new rings can seat properly. Be careful not to nick the sealing surfaces, or the ring will leak compression.

piston must be reconditioned by cutting the groove wide enough to accept a steel spacer.

Check the piston skirt-to-cylinder bore clearance by inserting the cleaned piston into the cylinder bore. If the cylinder walls have worn enough to form a ring ledge, the piston will be excessively loose. Generally, when installing new piston rings, it is considered good practice to have the pistons expanded in an automotive machine shop in order to compensate for this wear. The pistons can be expanded at the same time that the piston pins are fitted and the rods aligned.

RINGS

Always install a new set of piston rings when overhauling an engine. Order the ring set according to the amount of cylinder wall wear. If the wear is less than 0.005″, a standard set of piston rings can be used. If the

Check the piston ring end gap by pushing the ring into the cylinder bore. The end gap must not exceed specifications.

cylinder wall wear is between 0.006″ and 0.012″, a set of piston rings with a special oil ring and expanders will be required to keep the engine from pumping oil. If the cylinder bore is worn over 0.012″, it should be reconditioned by boring or honing in order to straighten the cylinder walls so that the new piston rings will make a better seal.

Before installing a set of piston rings, the end gaps and the side clearance between the piston ring groove and the ring must be checked. The correct side clearance should be 0.002″-0.004″, with a wear limit of

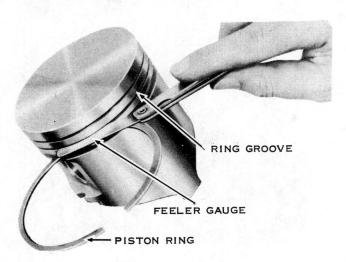

Measure the piston ring side clearance, which must not exceed 0.004″.

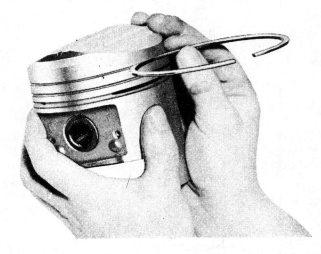

Roll each piston ring around its groove in this fashion to make sure that the groove is not nicked, which would keep the ring from "breathing" properly.

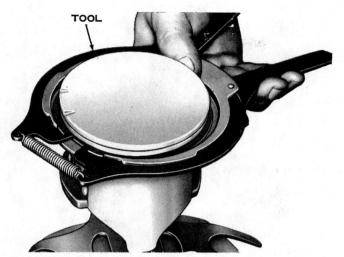

Always use a piston ring expanding tool to install the new piston rings. This tool avoids distorting a ring which could cause it to bind in the ring groove.

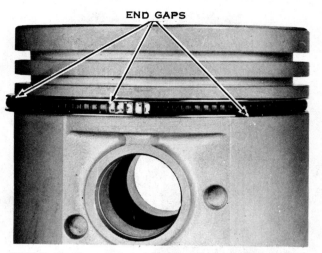

This picture shows how to space the rail gaps and the spacer gap on a compound oil ring.

0.002″. Generally, the side clearance of a new ring is not excessive unless the ring groove is worn. But a burr in the soft piston metal may cause the ring to bind.

Rotate the back of each piston ring around the groove to make sure that it doesn't bind in any spot.

The end gaps must be checked by inserting each piston ring into its cylinder bore at the bottom, where very little wear exists, and then squaring up the ring by inserting the piston upside down. Measure the end gap, which generally must be 0.010″-0.020″, except for steel rails of the oil rings, which must be 0.015″-0.030″ unless specified differently in a specific engine family.

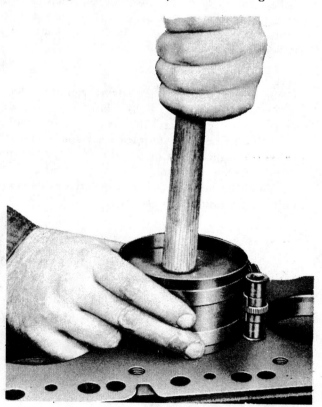

Oil the piston and rings, and then install the assembly with a compressor tool. Use the hammer handle to push the piston into the cylinder. Do not force it, because the edge of a ring may be caught on the top of the block. CAUTION: The side of the piston with the cast depression in the crown must be facing the front of the engine.

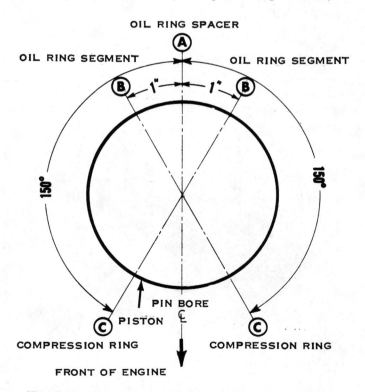

This diagram shows how to position the piston ring gaps for most efficient operation.

Localized heat areas on the valve face cause it to crack. Note how the small crack in the upper valve compares with the wider one in the lower valve face. This destructive process starts with a localized hot spot, possibly a piece of white-hot carbon on the seat.

This exhaust valve face is severely burned. Note the gum on the neck of the valve stem, indicating that it was sticking in the guide. Be sure to clean the valve guide of all gum and carbon.

If the end gap is too small, the ends of the ring can be filed to increase the gap.

When installing the rings on the piston, check the compression and scraper rings for the proper method of installation. Some rings have the word TOP stamped on the side that must face up. A compression ring with a groove in its outer face must be installed with this groove facing down. If the groove is cut into the rear face of the ring, the groove must face up when installed. If a steel spacer is used in conjunction with a top compression ring in order to compensate for machine work on the groove, the steel spacer must be installed above the cast iron ring.

VALVE MECHANISM

Clean the valves, springs, spring retainers, locks, and sleeves in solvent, and the blow the parts dry. Inspect the valve face and the head for pits, grooves, and scores. Inspect the stem for wear and the end for grooves. The face must be trued on a valve grinding machine, which will remove minor pits and grooves Valves with serious defects, or those having heads with a knife edge, must be replaced.

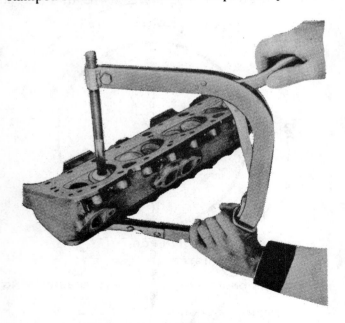

Use the illustrated tool to compress the valve spring, which will release the tapered keepers.

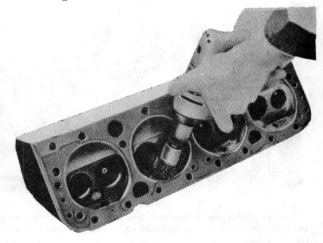

Use a wire brush to clean all carbon from the cylinder head.

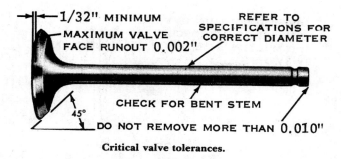

1/32" MINIMUM
MAXIMUM VALVE FACE RUNOUT 0.002"
REFER TO SPECIFICATIONS FOR CORRECT DIAMETER
CHECK FOR BENT STEM
45°
DO NOT REMOVE MORE THAN 0.010"

Critical valve tolerances.

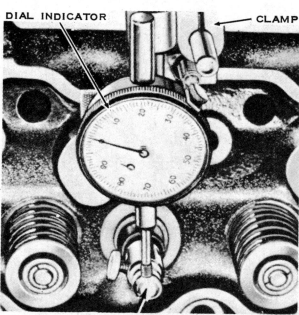

Checking the valve stem clearance with a dial indicator. Total indicator reading with a new valve installed must not exceed 0.0025" for an in.take valve or 00035" for an exhaust.

VALVE GUIDES

Clean the inside of the valve guides with a wire brush and lacquer thinner to remove all gum and carbon deposits, since such deposits could prevent the valve from closing properly.

If the valve guide is worn excessively, it can be reamed to an oversize for new valves with oversize stems of 0.015", and 0.030". When going from a standard size to an oversize, always use the reamers in sequence. After reaming a valve guide, always break the sharp ID corner at the top of the guide to prevent galling the valve stem. **CAUTION: Always reface the valve seat after reaming a valve guide in order to true it up with the new guide hole.**

To check the valve stem-to-guide clearance, insert the valve and measure its sideways movement with a dial indicator. The clearance must not exceed 0.0025". If the play is excessive, repeat the measurement with a new valve to determine whether the wear is in the valve guide or on the valve stem.

VALVE SPRINGS

Check the valve spring for the correct tension

Loose intake valve guides, or defective oil seals, can cause an oil leak onto the top of the intake valve.

Clean the valve guides with a brush. Add some lacquer thinner to remove the gum that causes valve sticking. Worn valve guides can be reamed oversize and valves with oversize stems used to restore production clearances.

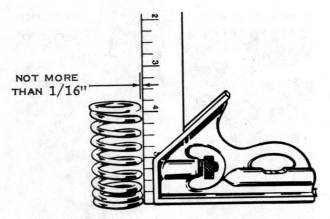

NOT MORE THAN 1/16"

For a rough check on a valve spring, determine whether or not it is square with the end coils.

against specifications. A quick check can be made by laying all of the springs on a flat surface and comparing the heights, which must be even. Also, the ends must be square or the spring will tend to cock the valve stem. Weak valve springs cause poor engine performance; therefore, if any spring is weak or out of square more than 1/16", replace it.

VALVES

Grind a 45° valve face to a 44° angle, and a 30° valve face to 29° for a 1° interference angle. Remove only enough stock to correct runout or to dress off the pits and grooves. If the edge of the valve head is less than 1/32" after grinding, replace the valve as it will run too hot in the engine. **CAUTION: Don't lap the valves together with grinding compound, or you will remove the interference angle.**

VALVE SEATS

The valve seat must be reground so that the pits and grooves are removed. Grind the seats to a 45° or 30°

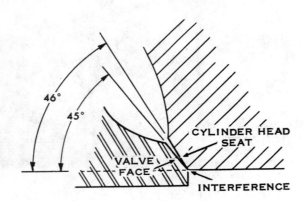

An interference angle of 1° should be ground into the valve or seat so that the seal is at the outer edge. This prevents carbon from being blown into the seating surfaces.

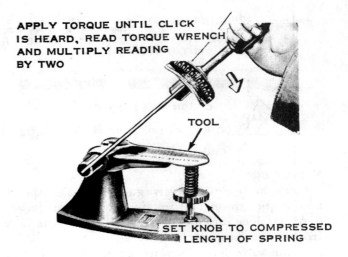

APPLY TORQUE UNTIL CLICK IS HEARD, READ TORQUE WRENCH AND MULTIPLY READING BY TWO

TOOL

SET KNOB TO COMPRESSED LENGTH OF SPRING

Accurate equipment is available to measure spring pressure, as shown.

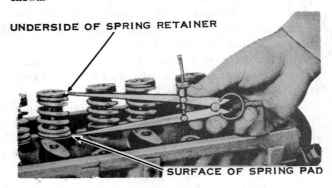

UNDERSIDE OF SPRING RETAINER

SURFACE OF SPRING PAD

Always measure the valve spring height and compare it with specifications. This measurement must be made from the underside of the retainer to the machined surface of the head. Spacers are available for adjusting the compressed height.

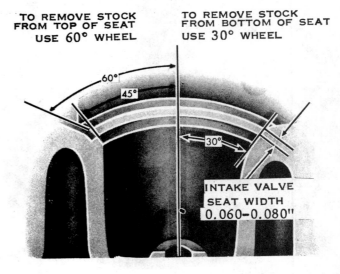

TO REMOVE STOCK FROM TOP OF SEAT USE 60° WHEEL

TO REMOVE STOCK FROM BOTTOM OF SEAT USE 30° WHEEL

60°

45°

30°

INTAKE VALVE SEAT WIDTH 0.060-0.080"

If it is necessary to narrow the valve seat, use a 60° grinding wheel to remove stock from the top.

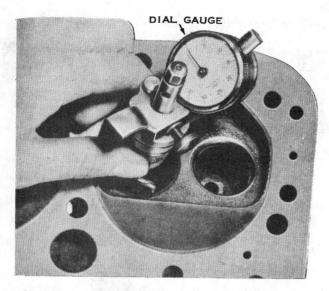

Use a dial gauge to see that the reground seat is concentric with the guide. The runout should not exceed 0.002".

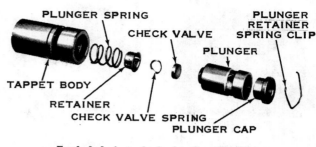

Exploded view of a hydraulic valve lifter.

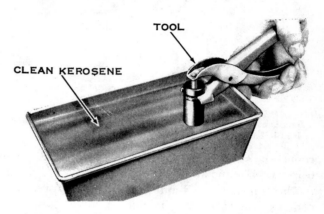

Testing a hydraulic tappet with a pair of special pliers. A good tappet will have considerable resistance to movement of the parts.

angle. Remove only enough stock to clean up the pits and grooves and to correct any runout of the seat and guide.

Measure the valve seat widths, which should be 3/64-1/16" for the intake and 5/64-3/32" for the exhaust or as specified. The seats can be narrowed by

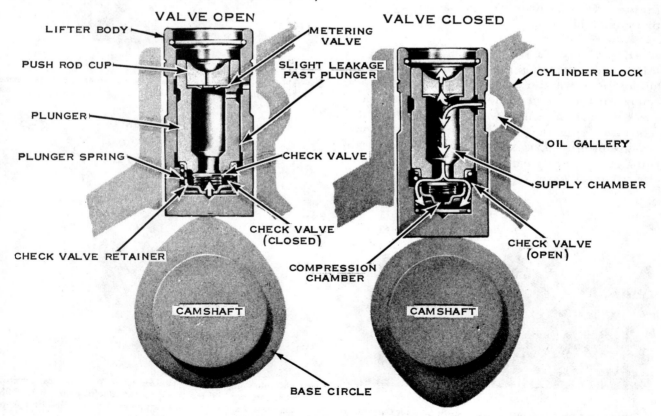

Operation of the hydraulic valve lifter.

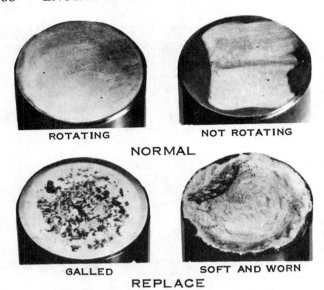

NORMAL

REPLACE

Details of the wear pattern to expect on the base of a tappet or hydraulic lifter.

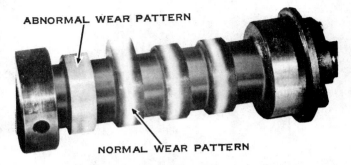

Typical wear patterns on the cam lobes of a camshaft.

removing stock from the top and bottom edges by using a 30° stone and a 60° stone.

The finished seat should contact the approximate center of the valve face. To determine the position of the seat on the valve face, coat the seat with Prussian blue, and then rotate the valve in place with light pressure. The blue pattern on the valve face will show the position of the seat.

HYDRAULIC VALVE LIFTERS

Dirt, deposits of gum, and air bubbles in the lubricating oil can cause the hydraulic lifters to wear enough to cause failure. The dirt and gum can keep a check valve from seating, which will cause the oil to return to the reservoir during the time that the push rod is being lifted. Excessive movement of the parts of the lifter causes wear, which soon destroys its effectiveness.

The backlash between the timing gear teeth should be between 0.004-0.006".

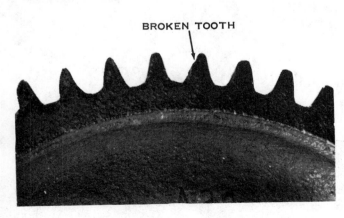

Timing gear wear is spotty. Note that the teeth at the right are fairly well formed, while those on the left are badly worn.

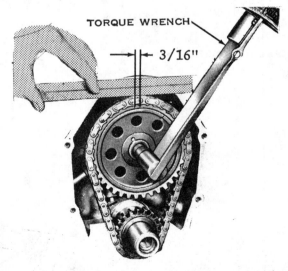

Measuring the timing chain stretch. With the crankshaft kept from rotating, tighten the sprocket attaching bolt to 15 ft-lbs of torque, and apply the same torque in a reverse direction. Replace the timing chain if its movement exceeds 3/16".

Timing sprocket wear caused by the teeth of the chain. This type of wear causes noise from the front of the engine.

With the timing chain properly installed, the timing marks on the crankshaft and camshaft sprockets must be in alignment, as shown.

The valve lifter assemblies must be kept in the proper sequence so that they can be re-installed in their original position. Clean, inspect, and test each lifter separately so as not to intermix the internal parts. If any one part of a lifter needs to be replaced, replace the entire assembly.

To test a cleaned lifter, assemble the parts dry, and then quickly depress the plunger with your finger. The trapped air should partially return the plunger if the lifter is operating properly. If the lifter is worn, or if the check valve is not seating, the plunger will not return.

Install the assembled lifters in the engine dry. They will bleed to their correct operating position quicker than if you filled them with lubricating oil before installing.

MEASURING TIMING GEAR OR SPROCKET AND CHAIN WEAR

Place a scale next to the timing chain so any movement of the chain may be measured. Place a torque wrench and socket over the camshaft sprocket attaching bolt and apply torque in the direction of crankshaft rotation to take up the slack; 30 ft-lbs with the cylinder heads installed or 15 ft-lbs with the cylinder heads removed. With torque applied to the camshaft sprocket bolt, the crankshaft must not be permitted to move. *NOTE: It may be necessary to block the crankshaft to prevent rotation.*

Holding a scale with the dimensional reading even with the edge of a chain link, apply the same torque in the reverse direction and note the amount of chain movement. Install a new timing chain if its movement exceeds 3/16".

If the chain is satisfactory, slide the crankshaft oil slinger over the shaft and up against the sprocket (flange away from the sprocket). If the chain is not satisfactory, remove the camshaft sprocket attaching bolt and remove the timing chain with the crankshaft and camshaft sprockets.

A worn timing chain can be bowed in this fashion, indicating wear in every link.

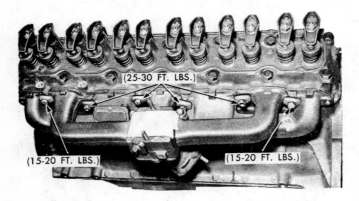

Installing the intake-and-exhaust manifold assembly. Tighten the center bolts to 25-30 ft-lbs and the end bolts to 15-20 ft-lbs of torque.

A broken heat-control valve housing is caused by someone hammering on it to free up the valve. Note that one crack was an old one, as shown by the darker coloring (arrow).

SIX-CYLINDER ENGINE SERVICE PROCEDURES

In this section we are going to show you how to disassemble and assemble a Chevrolet engine, which is also used in Buick, Oldsmobile, and Pontiac, so that a person with some mechanical ability can do a valve and piston ring job. In the event that you don't have adequate skills and equipment, you can employ **MST** by removing the parts and having them serviced by an automotive machine shop. You will still be saving the mechanic's markup of 25-40%. These same instructions apply to Chrysler and Ford six-cylinder engines, but the tool numbers and specifications will vary in most instances.

CYLINDER HEAD SERVICE

REMOVING

Remove the air cleaner. Disconnect the crankcase ventilation hoses at the rocker arm cover, air injection pipe, and EGR valve. Disconnect all wires from the rocker arm cover clips. Remove the rocker arm cover.

Drain the coolant, disconnect the radiator hoses and the spark plug wires. Remove the spark plugs, being careful not to tilt the spark plug socket, which

could crack the insulator. Remove the manifold assembly as previously discussed. Remove the rocker arm nuts, balls, rocker arms, and push rods. **CAUTION: Place all parts in a rack so that they can be reinstalled in the same way as removed.**

Disconnect the fuel and vacuum lines from the retaining clip at the water outlet, and then disconnect the wires from the temperature sending units. Disconnect the battery ground strap at the cylinder head, and the upper radiator hose at the water outlet housing. Remove the ignition coil. Loosen and remove the cylinder head bolts, take off the head, and discard the gasket.

CLEANING AND INSPECTING

Take off the valve rocker arm nuts, balls, and rocker arms. Keep all parts in their proper order for assembly purposes. Use a tool to compress the valve springs to remove the keys. Release the compressor, and then take off the spring caps, spring shields, springs, spring dampers, oil seals, and valve spring shims. Note the number of shims under each of the valve springs for assembly purposes. Remove the valves from the cylinder

A blown cylinder head gasket will cause a compression loss between cylinders.

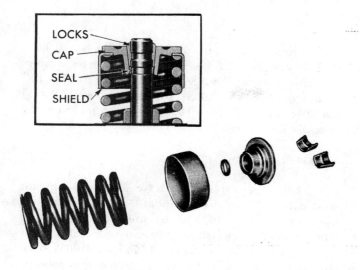

Details of the parts of the valve mechanism.

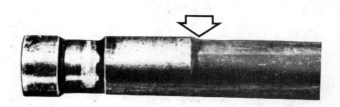

The valve stem wear can be measured with a micrometer. However, a good indication is a wear lip as shown by the arrow.

head and place them in a rack in their proper sequence so that they can be installed in their original positions.

Clean all carbon from the combustion chambers and valve ports. Thoroughly clean the valve guides using lacquer thinner to cut the gum which causes sticky valves. Clean all carbon and sludge from the push rods, rocker arms, and push rod guides. Clean the valve stems and heads on a buffing wheel. Clean

all carbon deposits from the head gasket mating surface.

Inspect the cylinder head for cracks in the exhaust ports, combustion chambers, or external cracks to the water chamber. Inspect the valves for burned heads, cracked faces, or damaged stems. **CAUTION: Excessive valve stem-to-bore clearance will increase oil consumption and may cause valve breakage.** Insufficient clearance will result in noisy and sticky valves and also disturb engine smoothness.

Measure the valve stem clearance with a dial indicator clamped on one side of the cylinder head. Locate the indicator so that movement of the valve stem will cause a direct movement of the indicator stem. The indicator stem must contact the side of the valve stem just above the valve guide. With a new valve and the

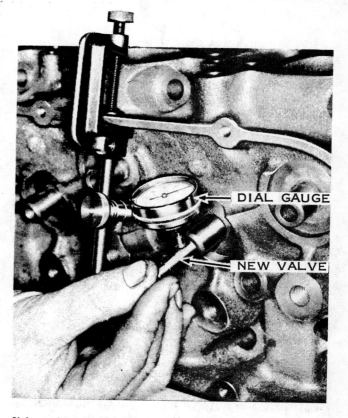

To remove the valve locks, compress the spring, and then take off the locks, caps, springs, dampers, and oil seal. Push out the valve and keep it in a rack in its proper sequence.

Valve guide wear can be measured by the deflection of a new valve stem. The wear limit is 0.001″ for intake guides and 0.002″ for exhaust guides.

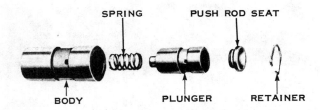

SPRING   PUSH ROD SEAT

BODY   PLUNGER   RETAINER

Exploded view of the hydraulic valve lifter.

head dropped about 1/16" off the valve seat, move the stem of the valve from side to side, using light pressure to obtain a clearance reading. If the clearance exceeds 0.001" for the intake or 0.002" for the exhaust, it will be necessary to ream the valve guides for oversize valve stems.

Valves with oversize stems are available for inlet and exhaust valves in the following sizes: 0.003", 0.015", and 0.030". Use the 3/8" diameter reamer sizes from Reamer Tool Set J-7049, which are: J-7049-7 Standard; J-7049-4, 0.003" oversize; J-7049-5, 0.015" oversize; and J-7049-6, 0.030" oversize to ream the bores for new valves.

ROCKER ARM STUDS

Rocker arm studs that have damaged threads should be replaced with standard studs. If the studs are loose in the head, oversize studs are available in 0.003" or 0.013" oversize. They can be installed after reaming the holes with Tool J-5715 for 0.003" oversize and Tool J-6036 for 0.013" oversize as follows: Remove the old stud by placing Tool J-5802 over the stud. Install the nut and flat washer and remove the stud by turning the nut. Ream the hole for an oversize stud, using Tool J-5715 for 0.003" oversize or Tool J-6036 for 0.013" oversize. Coat the press-fit area of the stud with hypoid axle lubricant. Install a

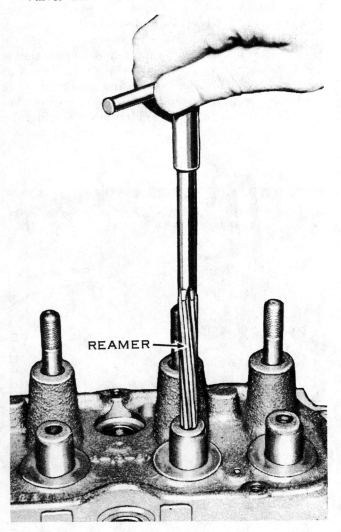

REAMER

Worn valve guides can be reamed oversize, and valves with oversize stems can be used to restore production clearances.

REMOVING TOOL

The pressed-in valve rocker arm studs can be pulled by using Tool No. J-5802.

Use hypoid axle lubricant on the parts, and then drive the new rocker arm stud into place with an installer tool, as shown.

new stud using Tool J-6880. The tool must bottom on the head.

VALVE SEATS

Reconditioning the valve seats is very important, because the seating of the valves must be perfect for the engine to deliver the power and performance

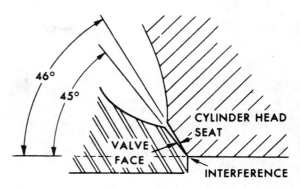

Valve seat angle for the in-line engine should be 46° to provide an interference angle of 1°.

built into it. Another important factor is the cooling of the valve heads. Good contact between each valve and its seat in the head is imperative to insure that the heat in the valve head will be properly carried away.

Regardless of what type of equipment is used, however, it is essential that valve guides be free from carbon, gum, or dirt to insure proper centering of the pilot in the guide. Use a 46° stone for the intake and exhaust valve seats. Narrow the seats to 1/32-1/16″ for the intake and to 1/16-3/32″ for the exhaust. Check the valve seat concentricity with a dial gauge, which should read within 0.002″ total indicator reading.

Details of the rocker arm studs and the push rod guides as the parts are to be assembled to the head.

Check the valve spring tension with an accurate tester.

Assembling the valves to the cylinder head, with all of the parts shown in their correct placement.

VALVES

Valves that are pitted should be refaced to a 45° angle. Valve heads that are warped or have a knife edge will cause pre-ignition and should be replaced. If the edge of the valve head is less than 1/32" thick, replace the valve.

ASSEMBLING THE CYLINDER HEAD

Starting with No. 1 cylinder, place the well-lubricated exhaust valve in the port and the valve spring and cap in position. **CAUTION: The spring end with the closed coil must be against the cylinder head.** Place spring and rotator on the exhaust valves. Then compress the spring and install the oil seal and valve keys. **CAUTION: See that the seal is flat and not twisted in the valve stem groove and also that the keys seat properly.**

Assemble the remaining valves, valve springs, rotators, spring caps, oil seals, and valve keys in the cylinder head. Check the seals by placing a vacuum cup over the valve stem and cap; squeeze the vacuum cup to make sure there are no leaks past the oil seal.

Measure the valve spring compressed height, which should be 1-21/32 to 1-23/32". If necessary, shims can be placed between the lower end of the spring and the spring recess in the cylinder head to obtain this dimension.

INSTALLING THE CYLINDER HEAD

The gasket surfaces on both the head and the block must be clean of any foreign matter and free of nicks or heavy scratches. Bolt threads in the block

Measure the valve seat run-out with a dial indicator; it must not exceed 0.002".

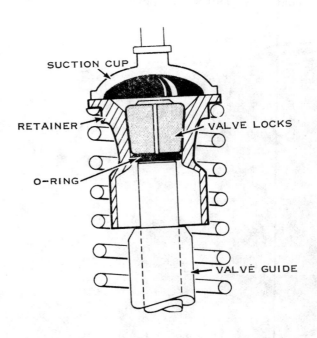

Use a suction cup to apply vacuum to the assembly to make sure that the O-ring seal is not leaking, or you will have an oil leak into the combustion chamber.

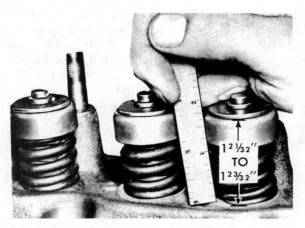

The installed valve spring height should be 1-21/32" to 1-23/32". If necessary, spring shims are available to correct if the measurement exceeds 1-23/32".

To make the valve lash adjustment, first loosen the rocker arm adjusting nut until the push rod can be turned easily. Now, turn down the adjusting nut slowly until you obtain zero lash, and then one additional turn to position the plunger in the center of the lifter travel.

and threads on the cylinder head bolts must be cleaned. (Dirt will affect bolt torque.) **CAUTION: Do not use gasket sealer on a composition steel-asbestos gasket.** Place the gasket in position over the dowel pins, with the bead up. Carefully guide the cylinder head into place over the dowel pins and gasket. Coat the threads of the cylinder head bolts with sealing compound and install them finger-tight. Tighten the cylinder head bolts a little at a time in the sequence shown until 95 ft-lbs of torque is reached. Install the push rods and rocker arms. Install the manifold assembly.

Install the coil, spark plugs, and high-tension wires. Connect the radiator upper hose and the engine ground strap. Connect the temperature sending unit wires and install the fuel and vacuum lines in the clip at the water outlet. Connect the vapor hoses at the canister. Fill the cooling system. Adjust the valve mechanism as discussed in the next paragraph. Install and torque the rocker arm cover to 45 in-lbs. Connect the air injection pipe, crankcase ventilation hoses, and EGR valve.

VALVE LASH

The valve lash can be made with the engine stationary or with it hot and idling. In either case, the adjustment is one turn down from the zero-lash position.

With the engine running, loosen the adjusting nut until the valve clatters, indicating a loose adjustment. Then, turn the push rod while you tighten the adjusting nut until all noise disappears and you feel

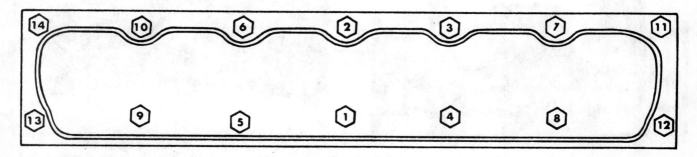

Cylinder head bolt tightening sequence for the six-cylinder engine.

resistance to turning the push rod. Now, turn the adjusting nut down exactly one complete turn to position the plunger in the center of its lifter travel. *NOTE: The engine may run rough until the lifter stabilizes itself, and then it should smooth out.* If it doesn't, replace the lifter, because it is sticky.

To make the valve lash with the engine not running, disconnect the spark plug wires, and then remove the spark plugs. Crank the engine until the distributor rotor points to number one cylinder position and the breaker points are open. The following valves can be adjusted with the engine in number one firing position:

Exhaust	Intake
1	1
3	2
5	4

Crank the engine until the distributor rotor points to number six position and the breaker points are open. The following valves can be adjusted with the engine in number six firing position:

Exhaust	Intake
2	3
4	5
6	6

PISTON AND RODS, R&R

REMOVING

With the oil pan, oil pump, and cylinder head off, use a ridge reamer to remove the ridge and deposits from the upper end of the cylinder bore. Before the ridge and/or deposits are removed, turn the crankshaft until the piston is at the bottom of its stroke and place a cloth on top of the piston to collect the cuttings. After the ridge is removed, turn the crankshaft until the piston is at the top of its stroke to remove the cloth and cuttings.

Scored crankshaft journals indicate the need for reconditioning. New inserts would soon be destroyed by this rough shaft.

Inspect the connecting rods and connecting rod caps for cylinder identification. If necessary, mark them. Remove the connecting rod cap nuts and install a thread-protecting tool on the studs. Push the connecting rod and piston assembly out of the top of the cylinder block. *NOTE: It will be necessary to turn the crankshaft slightly to disconnect some of the connecting rod and piston assemblies and push them out of the cylinders.*

CLEANING AND INSPECTING

CYLINDER BLOCK

Check the cylinder block for cracks in the cylinder walls, water jacket, and main bearing webs. Check the cylinder bores for taper, out-of-round, or excessive ridge wear at the top of the ring travel. This should be done with a dial indicator. Set the gauge so that the thrust pin is forced in about 1/4″ to enter the gauge in the cylinder bore. Center the gauge in the cylinder and turn the dial to "0". Carefully work the gauge up and down the cylinder to determine the amount of taper. Turn it to different points around the cylinder wall to determine the out-of-round condition. If the cylinders have more than 0.002″ out-of-round, boring will be necessary. If the cylinder bores are not worn excessively, use a 220-grit stone to remove the wall glaze so that the new rings will seat quickly. **CAUTION: Use a solution of soap and hot water to remove all traces of abrasives to prevent excessive engine wear.**

The coloring of the old bearing inserts tells a story. Note the light gray coloring of the upper bearing insert, which indicates that the bearing was operating with the proper clearance. The dark coloring of the lower insert indicates excessive bearing clearance.

To measure the wear on a piston pin, it should be miked on an unworn section (center), and then on both ends for a comparative measurement.

Press-in piston pins must be removed with an arbor press and a special tool, as shown.

PISTONS AND PINS

Wash the connecting rods in cleaning solvent and dry with compressed air. Check for twisted or bent rods and inspect for nicks or cracks. Replace any connecting rods that are damaged.

Clean varnish from the piston skirts and pins with a cleaning solvent. **CAUTION: Do not wire brush any part of the piston.** Clean the ring grooves with a groove cleaner and make sure the oil ring holes and slots are clean. Inspect the pistons for cracked ring lands, skirts, or pin bosses; wavy or worn ring lands; scuffed or damaged skirts; and eroded areas at the top of the pistons. Replace pistons that are damaged or show signs of excessive wear. Inspect the grooves for nicks or burrs that might cause the rings to hang up.

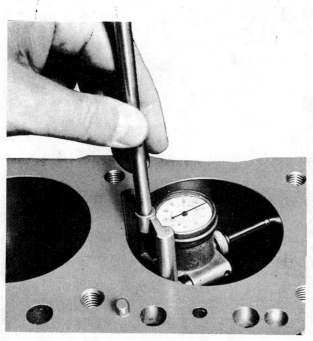

Measuring the cylinder wall taper and wear with a dial indicator.

Top ring groove wear is commonplace, and this one requires that the groove be turned oversize and a steel spacer installed above the piston ring to restore production clearances.

Measure the piston skirt (across the center line of the piston pin) and check the clearance, which should not exceed 0.0025".

Inspect the piston pin bores and piston pins for wear. Piston pin bores and piston pins must be free of varnish or scuffing when being measured. The piston pin should be measured with a micrometer, and the piston pin bore should be measured with a dial bore gauge or an inside micrometer. If the clearance is in excess of 0.001", the piston and/or piston pin should be replaced.

Disassembling

Install the pilot of the piston pin removing and installing tool, J-6994, on the piston pin. Position the piston and rod assembly on a support and place the assembly in an arbor press as shown. Press the pin out of the connecting rod. Remove the assembly from the press, lift the piston pin from the support, and remove the tool from the piston and rod.

Assembling

Lubricate the piston pin holes in the piston and connecting rod to facilitate installation of the pin. Position the connecting rod in its respective piston so that the flange or heavy side of the rod at the bearing end will be toward the front of the piston (cast depression in the top of the piston head).

Install the piston pin on the installer and pilot spring and the pilot in the support. Install the piston and rod on the support, indexing the pilot through the piston and rod. Place the support on the arbor press, start the pin into the piston, and press on the installer until the pin pilot bottoms. Remove the installer-and-support assembly from the piston-and-connecting rod assembly. Check the piston pin for freedom of movement in the piston bores.

PISTON RINGS

Check the end gap of the two compression rings by inserting them into the proper cylinder bore and pushing them down with a piston held upside down. This squares the ring with the walls. Measure the end gaps, which should be between 0.010-0.020". The oil ring rail end gap should be 0.015-0.055".

Check the side clearance of each piston ring in its groove on the piston. The top ring side clearance is specified as 0.0012-0.0027", while that of the second ring is 0.0012-0.0032". The oil ring side clearance is 0.000-0.005".

All compression rings are marked on the upper side of the ring. When installing compression rings, make sure the marked side is toward the top of the piston. The top ring is chrome faced or treated with molybdenum for maximum life.

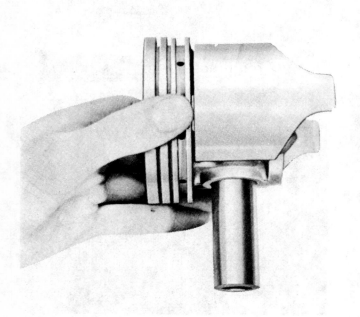

A correctly fitted and lightly oiled piston pin should just hold its own weight in either boss at room temperature.

Check the piston ring end gap with a feeler gauge, as shown.

This is the result of insufficient piston ring end gap. The ends of the rings butted at operating temperature and, having no place for expansion, broke and seized in the ring grooves.

Install the oil ring spacer in the groove with the gap in line with the piston pin hole. Hold the spacer ends butted, and then install the lower oil ring steel rail, with the gap located one inch to the left of the spacer gap. Install the upper oil ring steel rail, with the gap one inch to the right of the spacer gap. Install the second compression ring expander, and then the ring. Install the top compression ring. Adjust the location of the gaps of the two top rings so that each is 1/3 of the way around the piston and no gaps are aligned.

INSTALLING THE PISTON AND ROD ASSEMBLY

Lightly coat the piston, rings, and cylinder walls

250 CU. INCH

INSERT PISTONS WITH NOTCHES TOWARD FRONT OF ENGINES

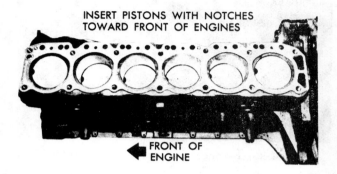

← FRONT OF ENGINE

Piston markings and installation diagram for the 250 CID engine.

Measure the ring side clearance of each ring in its groove, as shown.

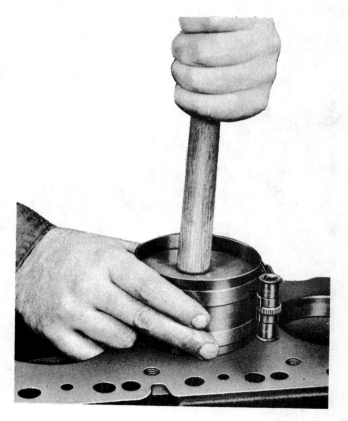

Install the well-lubricated piston and ring assembly into its proper cylinder. CAUTION: Don't hammer on the piston head, or you could break a piston ring that may have popped out of its groove.

The connecting rod side clearance must not exceed 0.014″.

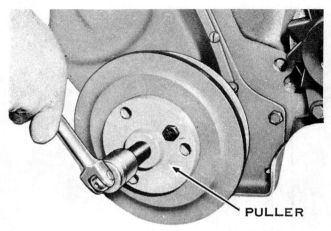

PULLER

Attach a puller to remove the harmonic (torsional) balancer.

with light engine oil. With the bearing cap removed, install Tool J-5239 on the bearing cap bolts. Install each piston in its respective bore. The side of the piston with the cast depression in the head should be to the front of the cylinder block, and the oil hole on the connecting rod should face the camshaft side of the engine. Guide the connecting rod bearing into place on the crankshaft journal. Install the bearing cap and check the bearing clearance.

Install the oil pan gaskets, seals, and oil pan as previously described. Install the cylinder head gasket and head as previously described. Refill the crankcase and cooling system and check for leaks.

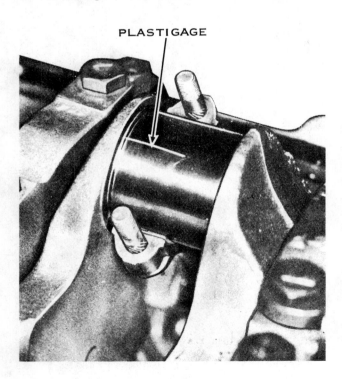

PLASTIGAGE

This shows a strip of Plastigage on the crankpin for measuring the oil clearance. CAUTION: Make sure there is no oil on the shaft, or the Plastigage will dissolve.

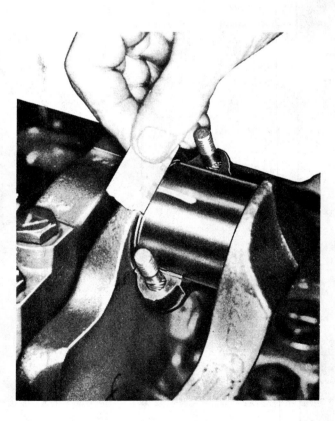

After tightening the connecting rod cap, the squeezed-out Plastigage can be compared with a scale on the side of the package to determine the clearance.

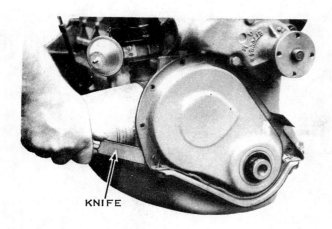

The ends of the oil pan gaskets must be cut with a knife to remove the crankcase front cover.

Sealer must be applied to these points (arrows) in order to prevent an oil leak, after having cut the gaskets.

CUT THIS PORTION FROM NEW SEAL

Oil pan front seal modifications, as discussed in the text.

CRANKCASE FRONT COVER, R&R

REMOVING

Remove the radiator and front grille. Pull off the torsional damper. Remove the two oil pan-to-front cover screws, and then take out the front cover-to-block attaching screws. Pull the cover slightly forward.

Using a sharp knife, cut the oil pan front seal flush with the cylinder block at both sides of the cover, as shown. Remove the front cover and attached portion of the oil pan front seal. Remove the front cover gasket.

A puller is required to take off the crankshaft gear.

A new oil seal should be driven into the cover to prevent an oil leak at this point.

APPLY SEALANT TO SHADED AREAS ONLY

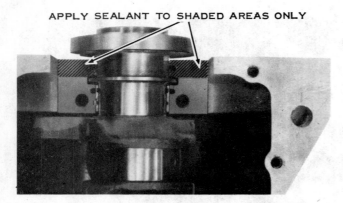

Apply sealer only to the shaded areas to prevent an oil leak at the rear main bearing.

INSTALLING

Clean the gasket surfaces on the block and crankcase front cover. Cut the tabs from the new oil pan front seal, as shown in the accompanying illustration. Use a sharp instrument to ensure a clean cut. Install the seal on the front cover, pressing the tips into the holes provided in the cover. Coat the gasket with sealer and place it in position on the cover. Apply a 1/8″ bead of RTV (Part No. 105-1435) Silicone Rubber Seal to the joint at the oil pan and cylinder block as shown.

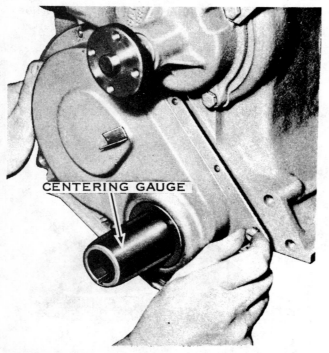

A centering gauge must be used to prevent an oil leak when installing the crankcase front cover.

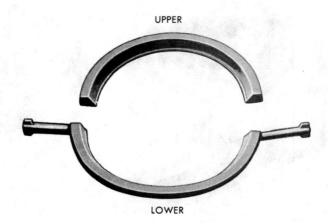

UPPER

LOWER

Details of the rear main bearing oil seal used on the in-line engine.

Install the centering tool J-23042 into the crankcase front cover seal. **CAUTION: It is important for a centering tool to be used to align the crankcase front cover, so that the torsional damper installation will not damage the seal, and that the seal will be positioned evenly around the balancer.** Install the crankcase front cover to the block. Install, and partially tighten, the two oil pan-to-front cover screws. Install the front cover-to-block attaching screws. Remove the centering tool. Torque all cover attaching screws to 80 in-lbs. Install the torsional damper, radiator, and front grille.

ENGINE SERVICE SPECIFICATIONS

CRANKSHAFT

The crankshaft main bearing journals measure 2.2983-2.2993″, with a taper and out-of-round wear limit of 0.001″. The main bearing oil clearance should be 0.0003-0.0029″, with a wear limit of 0.002″ for the front main bearing and 0.0035″ for all others. The crankshaft end play should be 0.002-0.006″, and this is measured at the rear main bearing.

The crankpins should measure 1.999-2.000″, with a taper and out-of-round wear limit of 0.001″. The rod bearing clearance should be 0.0007-0.0027″, with a wear limit of 0.0035″. The connecting rod side clearance should be 0.0009-0.0014″.

CAMSHAFT

The camshaft, with journal sizes of 1.8682-1.8692″, is supported in four bearings. Timing gear backlash should be 0.004-0.006″, and the camshaft gear runout must not exceed 0.0015″. The lifter is a hydraulic type, with an adjustment of one turn down from the zero-lash position. The rocker arm ratio is 1.75:1.0.

Mounting a dial gauge to measure the cam lift.

Timing gear backlash must not exceed 0.006″.

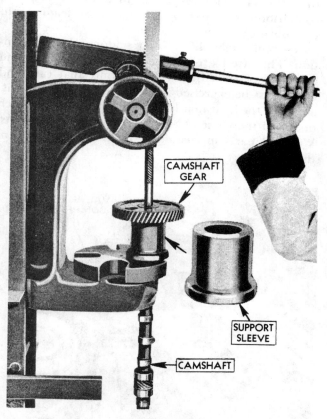

CAMSHAFT GEAR

SUPPORT SLEEVE

CAMSHAFT

The timing gear is a press-fit and must be removed in an arbor press.

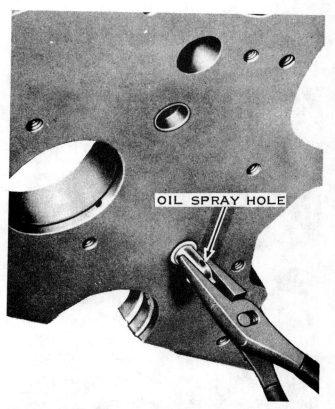

OIL SPRAY HOLE

The timing gear oil nozzle passageway must be clean and the nozzle aimed in this fashion to assure adequate lubrication for the timing gears.

V-8 ENGINE SERVICE PROCEDURES—FORD 302 CID

In this section we are going to show you how to disassemble and assemble a typical Ford V-8 engine so that a person with some mechanical ability can do a valve and piston ring job. In the event that you don't have adequate skills and equipment, you can employ **MST** by removing the parts and having them serviced by an automotive machine shop. You will still be saving the mechanic's markup of 25-40%. These same instructions apply to Chrysler and General Motors V-8 engines, but the tool numbers and specifications will vary in most instances.

CYLINDER HEAD SERVICE

The condition of the cylinder head and valve mechanism, more than anything else, determines the power, performance, and economy of an engine. Extreme care should be exercised when reconditioning the cylinder head and valves to maintain correct valve stem-to-guide clearance, correctly ground valves, valve seats of correct width, and correct valve adjustment.

REMOVING

Remove the intake manifold and carburetor as an assembly. Remove the rocker arm covers. Isolate and remove the air conditioner compressor. With power steering, disconnect the power steering pump bracket from the left cylinder head and remove the drive belt from the pump pulley. Position the power steering pump out of the way and in a position that will prevent the oil from draining out. Remove the alternator mounting bracket bolt and spacer. Remove the ignition coil and air cleaner inlet duct from the right cylinder head. Disconnect the exhaust manifolds from the muffler inlet pipes.

Loosen the rocker arm stud nuts so that the rocker arms can be rotated to one side. Remove the push rods in sequence so that they can be installed in their original positions. Remove the exhaust valve stem caps. Install the cylinder head holding fixtures.

Remove the cylinder head attaching bolts and lift the cylinder head off the block. Remove the exhaust manifolds to gain access to the lower attaching bolts. Remove and discard the cylinder head gasket.

CLEANING AND INSPECTING

Scrape and buff all carbon from the head, valve ports, valves, and the tops of the pistons. Clean the valve guides, using a brush and lacquer thinner to dissolve the gums that cause sticking valves. Inspect the cylinder heads for cracks in the exhaust ports, combustion chambers, or external cracks leading into the coolant chamber.

Hydraulic valve lifters very seldom require attention. The lifters are extremely simple in design and servicing of the lifters requires only that care and cleanliness be exercised in the handling of parts. Disassemble the hydraulic lifters one at a time, clean each one, and then assemble it to avoid mixing the parts. Wash all parts in cleaning solvent and dry them thoroughly.

MAGNET

Removing the valve lifters. Keep them in a rack so that they can be replaced correctly.

VALVE SPRING COMPRESSOR

Using a valve spring compressor to remove the valve collets.

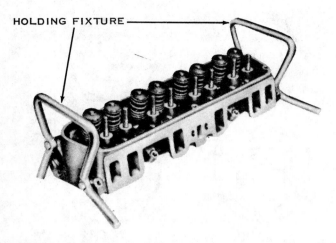

HOLDING FIXTURE

Mount the cylinder head in a holding fixture to keep from damaging the gasket surfaces.

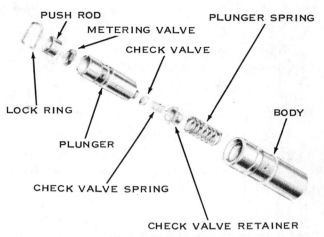

PUSH ROD   PLUNGER SPRING
METERING VALVE
CHECK VALVE
LOCK RING   BODY
PLUNGER
CHECK VALVE SPRING
CHECK VALVE RETAINER

Type I hydraulic valve lifter.

VALVES

Inspect the valves for burned heads, cracked faces, or worn stems. Check the fit of each valve stem in its respective guide. Excessive valve-to-guide clearance will cause lack of power, rough idling, excessive oil consumption, and noisy valve-operating mechanism. The clearance should not exceed 0.004″ for intake valves and 0.005″ for exhaust valves, or the valve must be replaced. Check the valve spring tension against specifications, the valve lifters for a free fit in the block, and the push rods for a bent condition. The intake valve springs should measure 190-210 lbs. at a compressed height of 1.31″ while the exhaust should measure 180-210 lbs. at the same height.

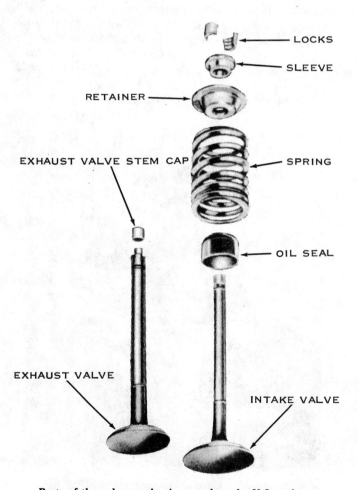

LOCKS
SLEEVE
RETAINER
EXHAUST VALVE STEM CAP
SPRING
OIL SEAL
EXHAUST VALVE
INTAKE VALVE

Parts of the valve mechanism used on the V-8 engine.

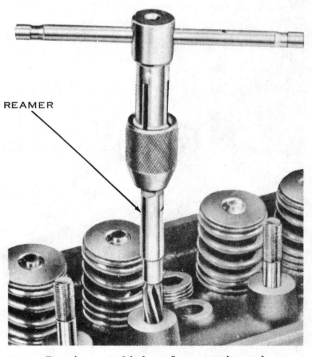

REAMER

Reaming a stud hole to fit an oversize stud.

VALVE FACES

Valves that are pitted can be refaced to the proper angle, insuring correct relation between the head and stem, on the valve-refacing machine. Dress the valve-refacing machine grinding wheel to make sure it is smooth and true. Set the chuck at the 44° mark for grinding all valve faces.

VALVE SEATS

Reconditioning the valve seats is very important, because the seating of the valves must be perfect for the engine to deliver the power built into it. Another important factor is the cooling of the valve heads. Good contact between each valve and its seat in the head is imperative to insure that the heat in the valve head will be properly carried away.

Use a 45° stone on the valve seats. Use a forming cutter of 30° and 60° at the top and bottom of the seat to narrow it to 0.030-0.060″ for an intake seat and 0.060-0.090″ for an exhaust seat. Check the valve seat with a dial indicator; it must be concentric within 0.002″ total indicator reading.

ROCKER ARM STUD REPLACEMENT

If it is necessary to remove a rocker arm stud, tool kit T62F-6A527-B is available which contains the following: a stud remover, a 0.006-inch oversize reamer, and a 0.015-inch oversize reamer. For 0.010-inch oversize studs, use reamer T66P-6A527-B. To press in replacement studs, use stud replacer T69P-6049-D.

Rocker arm studs that are broken or have damaged

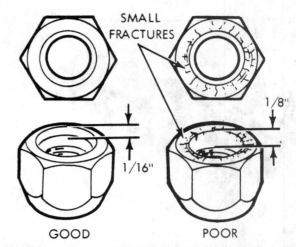

Inspect the rocker arm stud nut carefully for this kind of damage.

threads can be replaced with standard studs. Loose studs in the head may be replaced with 0.006, 0.010 or 0.015-inch oversize studs which are available for service. Standard and oversize studs can be identified by measuring the stud diameter within 1-1/8 inch from the pilot end of the stud. The stud diameters are:

Standard............	0.3714-0.3721″
0.006″ oversize....	0.3774-0.7781″
0.010″ oversize....	0.3814-0.3821″
0.015″ oversize....	0.3864-0.3871″

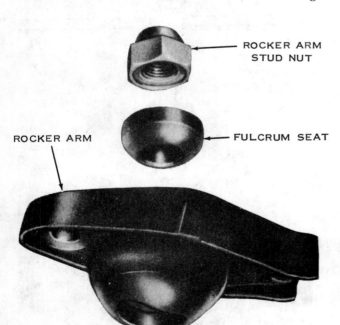

Details of the rocker arm.

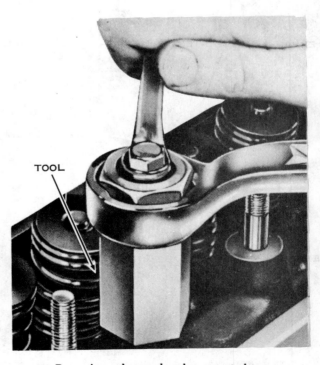

Removing a damaged rocker arm stud.

When going from a standard size rocker arm stud to a 0.010 or 0.015-inch oversize stud, always use the 0.006-inch oversize reamer before finish-reaming with the 0.010 or 0.015-inch oversize reamer.

To remove a broken stud, position the sleeve of the rocker arm stud remover (Tool T62F-6A527-B) over the stud with the bearing end down. When working on a 302 CID cylinder head, cut the threaded part of the stud off with a hacksaw. This is necessary due to the puller being designed for 3/8-inch studs and it will not grip the 5/16-inch thread on a 302 CID cylinder head stud. Thread the puller into the sleeve and over the stud until it is fully bottomed. Hold the sleeve with a wrench, then rotate the puller clockwise to remove the stud.

If a loose rocker arm stud is being replaced, ream the stud bore using the proper reamer (or reamers in sequence) for the selected oversize stud. **CAUTION: Make sure the metal particles do not enter the valve area.**

To install the new stud, coat the end with Lubriplate. Align the stud and installer T69P-6049-D with the stud bore, then tap the sliding driver until it bottoms. When the installer contacts the stud boss, the stud is installed to its correct height.

ASSEMBLING THE CYLINDER HEAD

All of the valves, valve stems, and valve guides should be lubricated with heavy SE engine oil. Apply Lubriplate to the valve tips before installation. Install

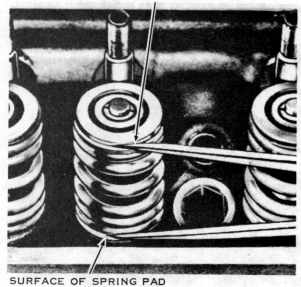

UNDERSIDE OF SPRING RETAINER

SURFACE OF SPRING PAD

Measure the valve spring installed height to be sure that it is within specifications of 1-43/64″ to 1-45/64″ for intake valve springs and 1-19/32″ to 1-34/64″ for exhaust valve springs.

each of the valves in the same port from which it was removed.

Install the valve stem seal and valve, and then replace the spring retainer. Compress the spring and install the sleeve and retainer locks.

Measure the assembled height of the valve spring from the surface of the cylinder head spring pad to the underside of the spring retainer.

If the assembled height is greater than specifications, install required 0.030″ spacers between the cylinder head spring pad and the valve spring to bring the assembled height to specifications. **CAUTION: Don't install the spacers unless necessary, or you will be overstressing the valve springs and putting an extra load on the camshaft lobes, which can lead to worn lobes and spring breakage.**

INSTALLING THE CYLINDER HEAD

Position the new cylinder head gasket over the cylinder dowels on the block. Position the cylinder head on the block and install the attaching bolts. Remove the holding fixtures. The cylinder head bolts are tightened in three progressive steps. Torque all the bolts in sequence to: (1) 50 ft-lbs., (2) 60 ft-lbs., and (3) 65-72 ft-lbs.

Install the exhaust manifolds and retorque the attaching bolts to 12-16 ft-lbs. Apply Lubriplate to both ends of the push rods. Install the push rods in their original positions. Apply Lubriplate or equivalent to the valve stem tips. Install the rocker arms. Perform a valve lash check as follows:

CHECKING THE VALVE LASH

Valve stem to valve rocker arm clearance should be within specifications with the hydraulic lifter completely collapsed. Repeated valve reconditioning operations (valve and/or valve seat refacing) will decrease the clearance to the point that, if not compensated for, the hydraulic valve lifter will cease to function and the valve will be held open.

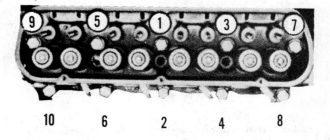

Cylinder head bolt tightening sequence.

To determine whether a shorter or a longer push rod is necessary, connect an auxiliary starter switch in the starting circuit. Crank the engine with the ignition switch OFF until No. 1 piston is on TDC after the compression stroke. Position the hydraulic lifter compressor tool on the rocker arm of each of the following valves:

No. 1 Intake, No. 1 Exhaust
No. 7 Intake, No. 5 Exhaust
No. 8 Intake, No. 4 Exhaust

Slowly apply pressure to bleed down the hydraulic lifter until the plunger is completely bottomed and check the available clearance between the rocker arm and the valve stem tip with a feeler gauge, which should be 0.090-0.190". **CAUTION: The feeler gauge width must not exceed 3/8-inch.** If the clearance is less than specifications, install a 0.060" shorter push rod. If the clearance is greater than specifications, install a 0.060" longer push rod.

Rotate the crankshaft 1/2 turn (180°) and check the following valves:

No. 5 Intake, No. 2 Exhaust
No. 4 Intake, No. 6 Exhaust

COMPLETING THE ASSEMBLY

Connect the exhaust manifolds at the muffler inlet pipes. Tighten the nuts to 12-16 ft-lbs. Install the alternator attaching bracket and air cleaner inlet duct on the right cylinder head assembly. Install the alternator. Adjust the drive belt tension.

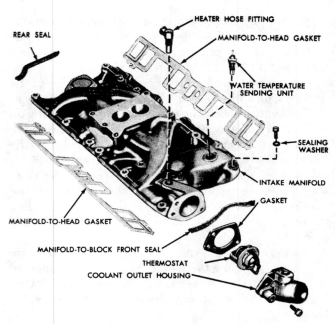

Details of the intake manifold assembly.

Clean the valve rocker arm covers. Position the valve rocker cover gasket in each cover, making sure that the tabs engage the notches in the cover. Install the valve rocker arm cover. The valve rocker cover is tightened in two steps. Tighten the bolts to 3-5 ft-lbs. Two minutes later retighten bolts to the same specifications.

Install the air conditioner compressor. Install the drive belt and power steering pump bracket. Install the bracket attaching bolts. Adjust the drive belt.

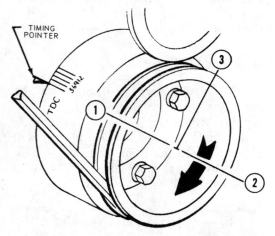

POSITION 1 — No. 1 at TDC at end of compression stroke.
POSITION 2 — Rotate the crankshaft 180 degrees (one half revolution) clockwise from POSITION 1.
POSITION 3 — Rotate the crankshaft 270 degrees (three quarter revolution) clockwise from POSITION 2.

Position of the crankshaft for checking the valve lash. With No. 1 piston at TDC at the end of the compression stroke, make a chalk mark at points No. 2 and No. 3, approximately 90° apart, as shown.

Checking the collapsed hydraulic lifter lash. Longer or shorter push rods are available to keep the clearance between 0.090-0.190".

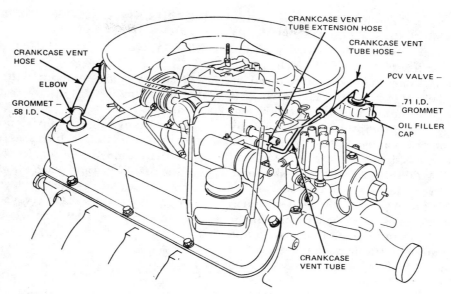

Details of the crankcase ventilation system.

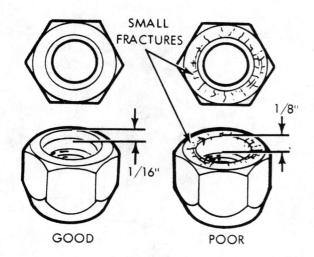

Inspect the rocker arm stud nut carefully for this kind of damage.

Clean the mating surfaces of the intake manifold, cylinder heads, and cylinder block. Use a solvent such as lacquer thinner, chlorothane, or trichlorethylene. Apply a 1/8 inch bead of silicone rubber sealer at the points shown. Position new seals on the cylinder block

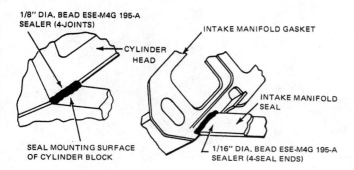

Intake manifold sealer application to minimize oil and air leaks.

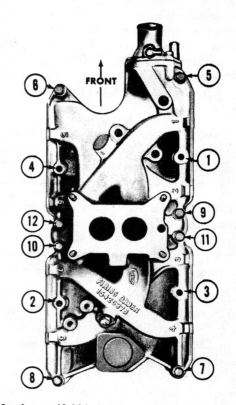

Intake manifold bolt tightening sequence.

and new gaskets on the cylinder heads, with the gaskets interlocked with the seal tabs. **CAUTION: Be sure the holes in the gaskets are aligned with the holes in the cylinder heads.** Apply a 1/16 inch bead of sealer to the outer end of each intake manifold seal for the full width of the seal (4 places). **CAUTION: This sealer sets up in 15 minutes, so it is important that assembly be completed promptly. Do not drip any sealer into the engine valley.** Carefully lower the intake manifold into position of the cylinder block and cylinder heads. **CAUTION: After the intake manifold is in place, run a finger around the seal area to make sure the seals are in place. If the seals are not in place, remove the intake manifold and reposition the seals.** Be sure the holes in the manifold gaskets and manifold are in alignment. Install the intake manifold attaching bolts and nuts. Torque the intake manifold bolts in sequence to 19-27 ft-lbs.

Install the water pump bypass hose on the coolant outlet housing. Slide the clamp into position and tighten the clamp. Connect the radiator upper hose. Install the heater hose against the automatic choke housing and connect the hose at the intake manifold. Install the carburetor fuel inlet line and the automatic choke heat tube, if so equipped.

Rotate the crankshaft damper until No. 1 piston is on TDC at the end of the compression stroke. Position the distributor in the block with the rotor at the No. 1 firing position and the points just open. Install the hold-down clamp. Install the distributor cap. Position the spark plug wires in the harness brackets on the valve rocker arm covers and connect the wires to the spark plugs.

Install the Thermactor bypass valve and the air-supply hoses. Connect the crankcase vent hose. Connect the high-tension lead and coil wires. Connect the accelerator rod or cable and retracting spring.

On a vehicle with an automatic transmission, connect the transmission vacuum line. On a vehicle equipped with vacuum-operated accessories, connect all vacuum lines to the intake manifold. Install the air conditioning compressor-to-intake manifold brackets.

Fill and bleed the cooling system. Start the engine and check and adjust the ignition timing. Connect the distributor vacuum hoses to the distributor. Operate the engine at a fast idle and check all hose connections and gaskets for leaks. When the engine temperatures have stabilized, adjust the engine idle speed and idle fuel mixture. Retorque the intake manifold bolts to 19-27 ft-lbs.

PISTONS, RINGS, AND RODS: R&R

REMOVING

Drain the cooling system and the crankcase. Remove the intake manifold, cylinder heads, oil pan, and oil pump.

Remove any ridges and/or deposits from the upper end of the cylinder bores as follows: Turn the crankshaft until the piston to be removed is at the bottom of its travel and place a cloth on the piston head to collect the cuttings. Remove the cylinder ridge with a ridge cutter. **CAUTION: Never cut the ring travel area in excess of 1/32 inch when removing ridges.**

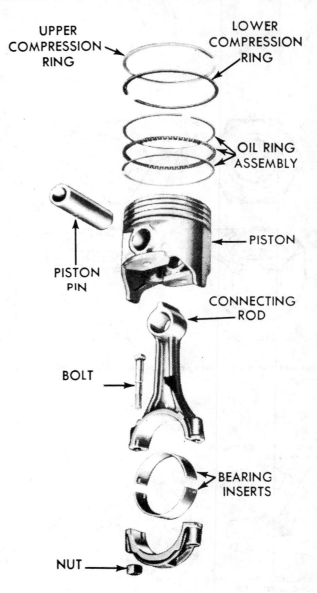

Piston, rod, and related parts for the V-8 engine.

Make sure all connecting rod caps are marked so that they can be installed in their original positions. Turn the crankshaft until the connecting rod being removed is down. Remove the connecting rod nuts and cap. Push the connecting rod-and-piston assembly out the top of the cylinder with the handle end of a hammer. **CAUTION: Avoid damage to the crankshaft journal or the cylinder wall when removing the piston and rod.**

Remove the bearing inserts from the connecting rod and cap. Install the cap on the connecting rod from which it was removed.

CLEANING AND INSPECTING

Cylinder Bores

If the cylinder bores are worn excessively, they must be bored to the next oversize. Piston and rings are available in 0.010″, 0.020″, 0.030″, and 0.040″ oversizes. If the cylinder bores are not worn too much, the glazed surfaces must be removed by honing with a 220-grit stone. **CAUTION: Clean all traces of abrasives with soap and hot water to prevent excessive wear after the engine is placed back in service.**

Piston Pins

The piston pins are locked in the rod by an interference fit, and the pins turn in the piston. New pins are available in 0.0015″, 0.003″, and 0.010″ oversizes. To remove a piston pin, install the illustrated tool, and then push the piston pin out. Remove the connecting rod from the piston.

To assemble a fitted piston pin to its rod, lubricate the piston pin holes in the piston and connecting rod to facilitate installation. Insert the connecting rod in the piston so that the illustrated connecting rod and piston marks will face the correct side of the engine, and then press in the piston pin, as shown.

Piston Rings

Compression rings in all engines are the deep-section twist type. This type of compression ring takes its name from its installed position which is cocked or twisted. It assumes and maintains this position for life because the upper edge of its diameter is chamfered, making the ring unbalanced in cross section. All compression rings are marked in the upper side of the ring. When installing compression rings, make sure the marked side faces the top of the piston.

The oil-control rings consist of two segments (rails) and a spacer. Piston rings are furnished in standard sizes as well as 0.020″, 0.030″, 0.040″ oversizes.

Check the space or gap between the ends of the compression rings with a feeler gauge, which should be 0.010-0.020″ for the two top rings. The oil ring rail gap should be 0.015-0.055″.

Slip the outer surface of each ring into the piston ring groove and roll the ring entirely around the groove to make sure that it is free and does not bind in the groove at any point. The compression rings side clearance should be 0.002″ to 0.004″. The assembled oil ring side clearance should be 0.0005-0.0065″.

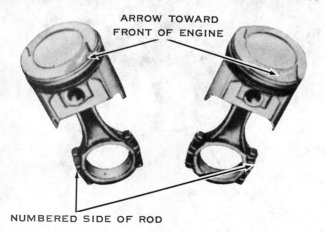

Correct positions of the pistons and rods for the V-8 engine.

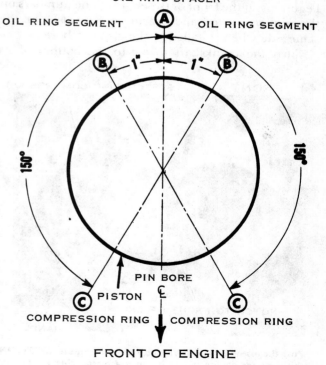

Piston ring spacing.

Install the oil ring spacer in the oil ring groove and position the gap in line with the piston pin hole. Hold the spacer ends butted, and then install a steel rail on the top side of the spacer. Position the gap at least 1" to the left of the spacer gap, and then install the second rail on the lower side of the spacer. Position the gap at least 1" to the right of the spacer gap. Flex the oil ring assembly in its groove to make sure the ring is free and does not bind in the groove at any point.

INSTALLING

If new piston rings are to be installed, remove the cylinder wall glaze. **CAUTION: Clean all traces of abrasives to prevent excessive wear.**

Oil the piston rings, pistons, and cylinder walls with light engine oil. Make sure the ring gaps are properly spaced around the circumference of the piston. Install a piston ring compressor on the piston and push the piston in with a hammer handle until it is slightly below the top of the cylinder. **CAUTION: Be sure to guide the connecting rods to avoid damaging the crankshaft journals. CAUTION: Install the piston with the indentation notch in the piston head toward the front of the engine. CAUTION: Be sure to install the pistons in the same cylinders from which they were removed or to which they were fitted.** The connecting rod and bearing caps are numbered from 1 to 4 in the right bank and from 5 to 8 in the left bank, beginning at the front of the engine. The numbers on the connecting rod and bearing cap must be on the same side when installed in the cylinder bore.

Turn the crankshaft throw to the bottom of its stroke. Push the piston all the way down until the connecting rod bearing seats on the crankshaft journal. Install the connecting rod cap. Tighten the nuts to 19-24 ft-lbs.

After all the piston-and-connecting rod assemblies have been installed, check the side clearance between the connecting rods on each crankshaft journal, which should be 0.010-0.020".

Disassemble, clean, and assemble the oil pump. Clean the oil pump inlet tube screen and the oil pan and block gasket surfaces.

Prime the oil pump by filling either the inlet port or outlet port with engine oil and rotating the pump shaft to distribute the oil within the housing. Install the oil pump and the oil pan.

Install the cylinder heads and intake manifold.

Fill and bleed the cooling system. Fill the crankcase with the proper grade and quantity of engine oil. Start the engine and check and adjust the ignition timing. Connect the distributor vacuum hoses at the carburetor.

Operate the engine at fast idle and check for oil and coolant leaks. When the engine temperature has stabilized adjust the engine idle speed and idle fuel mixture.

Install the air cleaner and intake duct assembly. Connect the automatic choke heat chamber air inlet hose.

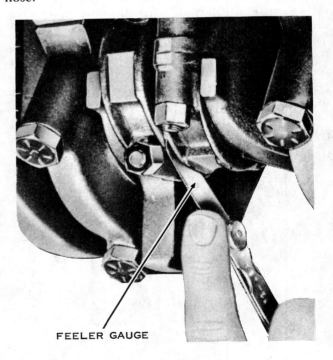

FRONT   PISTON RING COMPRESSOR

NOTCH TO FRONT OF ENGINE   HAMMER HANDLE

Push the piston into the bore with a hammer handle. **CAUTION: Don't hammer on the piston because a piston ring might have popped out of its groove.**

FEELER GAUGE

Measure the connecting rod side clearance, which should be 0.010-0.020".

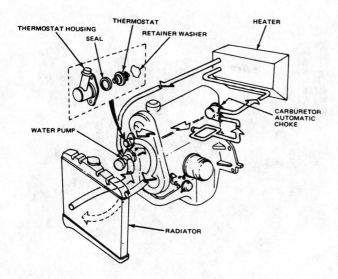

Ford 2,300cc engine cooling system, which is typical of most engines, except for the water-cooled choke. As long as the engine is cold, coolant passes only from the water pump through the engine intake manifold, automatic choke, and heater core, back to the water pump to ensure a warmup. When the coolant reaches 190°F, the thermostat opens and allows coolant to flow through the radiator.

COOLING SYSTEM SERVICE

OVERHEATING

Engine overheating is one of those conditions that is extremely vexsome, because it generally occurs during a hot summer day, when you're climbing a steep hill and there's no service station near. At the first signs of trouble, you can turn around for a downhill run to cool the engine until you can be back home to service the cooling system.

Engine overheating can be caused by a loose or broken fan belt, clogged radiator hoses, or the block and cylinder head clogged with rust and debris.

SERVICE PROCEDURES

FAN BELT

Check the condition of the fan belt by twisting it so that you can see the underside. **CAUTION: Make sure that the engine is not running before you reach for**

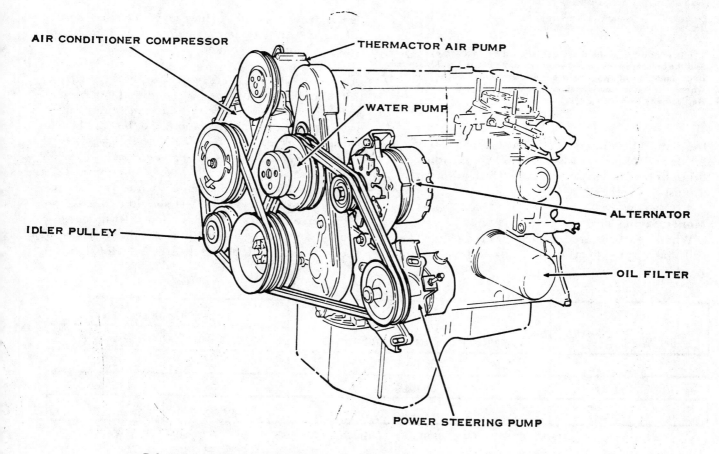

Belt arrangement on the Ford 2,300cc engine with all optional accessories installed.

The condition of the drive belt should be checked every year, and the belt replaced every two years, or 24,000 miles. This is very important in today's engines with emission-control systems, where the underhood heat is much greater than ever before. Replace any belt with a crack or tear.

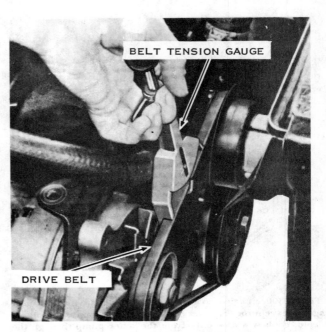

To check the belt tension, position a tension gauge as shown. The tension is correct when the indicator marks are lined up with the gauge body.

the belt. The undersurface must be firm, but not brittle and with no cracks or frayed ends. If the belt is brittle or has cracks running across the bottom surface, it must be replaced.

Money Saving Tip

When new belts are installed and the old belts are still usable, put them in the trunk to be used in an emergency. It is better to have an old belt than none at all, which can happen if a belt breaks in a small town where supplies are limited.

ADJUSTING THE BELT TENSION

If the drive belt is in good condition, but loose, it may slip and this will reduce fan and pump speed, causing poor coolant circulation, and this could be the cause of overheating. *NOTE: Frequently, a loose belt will make a squealing noise as the engine is accelerated.*

Check the tension of each drive belt by depressing it with your thumb in the center of the longest span between two pulleys. The belt should depress about ½" when a moderate force is applied. If it depresses more than this, the belt tension should be adjusted. If the belt does not depress at least ½", it is too tight and

Belt Width	Minimum Tension (for use at maintenance interval only) (Hot Engine)	Installation Tension	
		Used Belt ①	New Belt
1/4"	30 lbs.	60 lbs.	80 lbs.
3/8" and 15/32"	50 lbs.	110 lbs.	140 lbs.
1/2"	50 lbs.	110 lbs.	140 lbs.

① Any belt that has operated for ten minutes or more is considered a used belt.

Drive belt tension specifications.

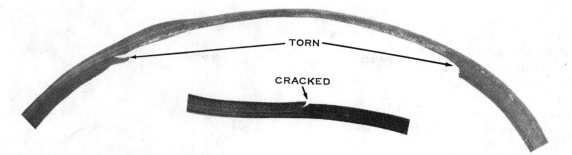

TORN

CRACKED

A worn belt should be replaced to minimize the chances of its breaking while you are miles from any service station.

this condition will cause rapid failure of the bearings in the unit it drives.

If the belt needs to be adjusted, loosen the bolt on the adjusting arm of the alternator or whatever component's belt you are adjusting. Pry outward on the accessory being adjusted until the drive belt depresses about ½", and then tighten the adjusting bolt. Recheck the tension of the belt to be sure it did not change.

Top Tuner Tip

When a new belt is installed, it should be rechecked after 10 minutes of running for the correct tension. New belts always stretch slightly after running a short time and must be adjusted to maintain the normal ½" deflection. After this second adjustment, the belt will not lose its tension as readily.

COOLING SYSTEM

Inspect all cooling system hoses for cracking, rotting, softening, or extreme weathering. Squeeze the hoses. Replace any soft hose or one in questionable condition. It is a lot less trouble to inspect and replace hoses at your convenience than it is to find yourself away from home with a broken hose, lost coolant, and an overheated engine. **CAUTION: All cooling system service should be performed when the engine is cool as it is easy to get severely burned while working on a hot engine.**

Check that all supporting brackets for hoses are in place and that the hoses are correctly installed in the brackets. Make sure the hoses are not twisted or pinched. Check all fittings and clamps to insure that they are tight, in good condition, and installed correctly. **CAUTION: Don't overtighten the clamps.** Check for leakage around the clamps and drain plugs and examine all hoses carefully at the fittings for cuts or weakness.

The drive belt should be adjusted so that there is about ½" free play when depressed in the center of the longest span.

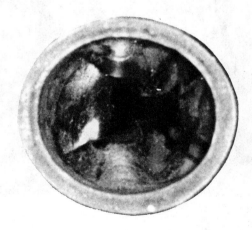

A rusted radiator hose is an indication that the rest of the cooling system is in a similar condition. Overheating and engine damage can result.

CLEANING

If the coolant is rust-colored, you may have problems in the cooling system with rust deposits which restrict circulation. In this case, you can add a can of radiator flush, fill the system with water, and then run the vehicle for the time indicated on the can of radiator flush. Drain the radiator again, and if rust is still there and it appears from looking through the radiator filler cap that considerable deposits remain, then it is desirable to reverse-flush the system.

REVERSE-FLUSHING THE SYSTEM

Reverse-flushing is circulating water through the engine and radiator in a direction opposite to that which it normally circulates, and this forces out the rust deposits loosened by the radiator flush chemical.

The first step in this process is to reverse-flush the block, and this is done by directing water, under pressure, through the block. Take out the thermostat because the cold water will cause it to close and block the passageway. Now disconnect the top hose at the radiator and the bottom hose at the block. Attach a garden hose to the top disconnected radiator hose, pack the space around it tightly with rags, and then turn on the water full force. It will run out of the lower

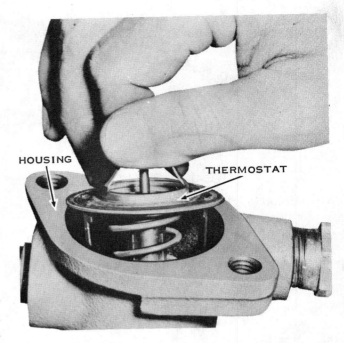

HOUSING   THERMOSTAT

The thermostat must be removed before reverse-flushing the block; otherwise, the cold water will close it and prevent passage of the flushing water.

Rust forms in the coolant passageways of the block and radiator, causing restricted flow of coolant and overheating. This type of deposits must be loosened by a chemical cleaner before reverse-flushing the block and radiator.

radiator hose opening, carrying with it all loose debris.

To reverse flush the radiator, attach the garden hose to the bottom hose of the radiator, and turn on the tap water fully. The water and all loose debris should be coming out of the top radiator hose opening, or through the radiator cap, if you have removed it.

After reverse-flushing the cooling system, replace the thermostat and hoses with new ones. Be sure to tighten the clamps securely to prevent leaks. Fill the radiator with the recommended permanent anti-freeze-and-water mixture to 1" below the bottom of the filler neck or to the cold-fill mark on some radiators.

Install the radiator cap, turning it to the first position (off pressure). This will allow the system to bleed off trapped air. Start and operate the engine for several minutes to warm the coolant and cause the entrapped air to escape. Turn on the heater valve to allow coolant circulation through the heater radiator, and then turn on the fan switch. If the air coming from the heater ducts is cool, then you have air entrapped in this part of the system. To bleed off the air, loosen the top radiator hose clamp and slide off the hose partially until you see that all of the air has escaped, and then reconnect the heater hose.

Recheck the coolent level; replenish if necessary. Tighten the radiator filler cap securely.

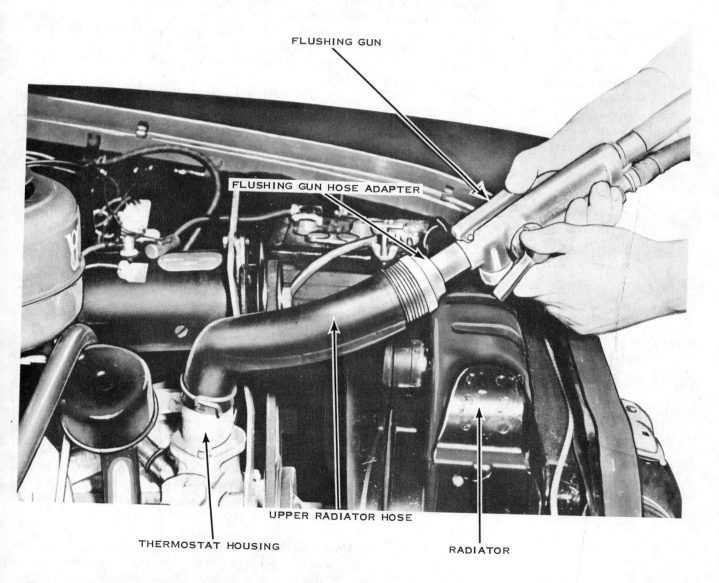

FLUSHING GUN

FLUSHING GUN HOSE ADAPTER

UPPER RADIATOR HOSE

THERMOSTAT HOUSING

RADIATOR

To reverse-flush the block, first remove the thermostat, and then direct water, at full pressure, through the top radiator hose. To reverse-flush the radiator, direct water pressure through the bottom radiator hose.

OIL LEAKS

Oil leaks usually show up as spots on your driveway after the car is parked for a short time. While such spots are usually small, they actually are costing you money. A small leak on your driveway can be a larger leak while your car is moving. With premium oil costing over $1.00 per quart, it doesn't take much of an oil leak to cost you $4-5 a month extra.

There are two types of oil leaks. A pressure-type leak shows up only when the engine is being operated. This type occurs around the oil filter, rear main bearing, pressure sensor in the block, or wherever oil pressure is directed close to the exterior surfaces of the engine. The second type is the non-pressure leak where the oil seeps whether the engine is running or not. This type of leak is usually found around a defective or loose oil pan gasket, rocker arm cover gasket, or around the drain plug of the oil pan.

When an oil leak is noted, the best way to locate its source is by cleaning off the area where the origin of the leak is suspected. This is best done by taking the car to a do-it-yourself car wash and cleaning the engine compartment thoroughly.

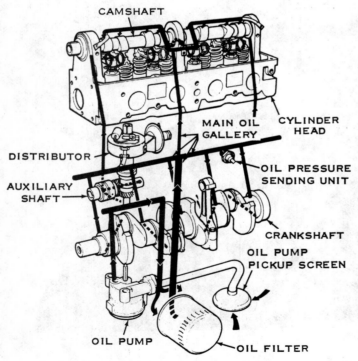

Typical lubrication system. This diagram shows the passage of oil through a Ford four-cylinder engine. The five crankshaft main bearings and the camshaft bearings are force-lubricated.

Top Tuner Tip

Remove the fan drive belt and run the engine without it for a short time to prevent the oil from being blown from the source of the leak. Stop the engine and inspect the area around the rocker arm cover gaskets, which is generally the cause of an engine oil leak, and these gaskets are easily replaceable. Inspect the area around the oil pan where it is fastened to the block; this gasket is also a source of oil leaks.

If an oil leak is noticed shortly after having the oil changed and a new filter installed, there is a possibility that the seal on the new filter is leaking or the filter has not been tightened securely on its base, or over-tightened and distorted. Most oil filters are the easily replaceable canister type, and the oil seal on the mating surface of the filter, where it contacts the mounting pad, must be lubricated with engine oil before the filter is installed. Failure to do this could result in the gasket being pulled loose as the filter is tightened by hand.

An oil leak around a valve cover is usually caused by someone tightening the valve cover too tightly and compressing the gasket until it squeezes out from under the valve cover and then a leak develops. The only way to correct such a leak is to remove the valve cover, clean off all the old gasket, and install a new one. Some manufacturers recommend sealing material on the gasket while others require installing the cover with a dry gasket. **CAUTION: When installing the retaining screws, do not overtighten them.** It takes very little pressure to seal the gasket to the head and excessive pressure will cause distortion and create another leak. Tighten the screws only enough until the gasket is firmly seated and the valve cover is secure.

ELECTRICAL SYSTEM SERVICE

Generally, the repair of alternators and starters requires experience and specialized test equipment. In this section we are going to discuss some troubleshooting procedures to locate the trouble, and then give you the service procedures for doing the work yourself. However, if you feel that you lack the electrical ability to do these jobs, you will still be able to remove and install the unit to save these charges. These same instructions apply to most all manufacturers, but the tool numbers and specifications will vary in most instances.

Money Saving Tip

After removing the starter or alternator, you can take the unit to an automotive electrical repair shop for service or exchange, in which case you will be saving the mechanic's markup of 25-40%.

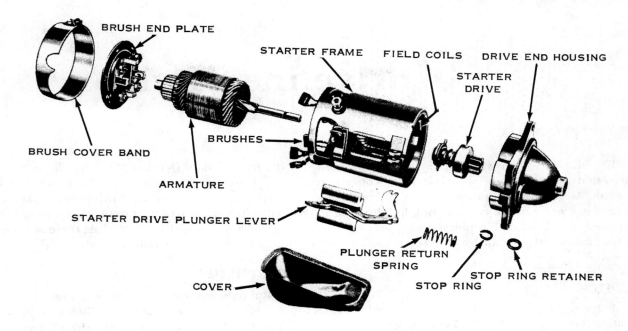

Exploded view of a Ford starter.

To test a G.M. alternator, connect a jumper wire between the BAT and F (field) terminals. If the alternator now charges, with the jumper in place, then the regulator is defective.

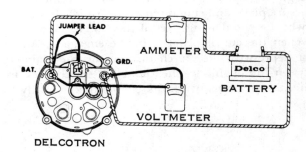

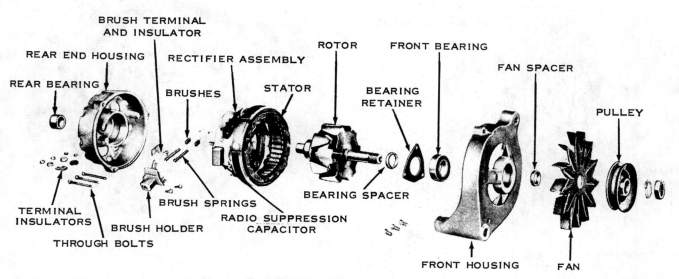

Exploded view of a typical alternator.

6/driveline service

The driveline consists of a clutch, transmission, driveshaft, and rear axle. Because of the complexity and the large numbers of mechanical and automatic transmissions, this subject will not be thoroughly covered in this book. Troubleshooting and external adjustments of the automatic transmission are covered.

CLUTCH

A mechanical clutch is used only in vehicles with a standard-shift transmission. Vehicles with an automatic transmission have a torque converter in place of the conventional clutch.

The clutch is either a diaphragm or spring type, with a single dry disc. The assembly consists of a clutch disc, pressure plate, and clutch release bearing. The engine flywheel is the driving part of the clutch assembly.

When the clutch pedal is in the engaged position (not depressed), the clutch disc facings are clamped between the engine flywheel and the clutch pressure plate, thereby connecting the engine mechanically to the transmission. Depressing the clutch pedal actuates the clutch release lever, which moves the clutch release bearing against the clutch pressure plate fingers. This, in turn, moves the pressure plate away from the flywheel to release the clutch disc, thereby disconnecting engine power from the transmission.

CLUTCH, R&R

Raise the vehicle on a hoist. Remove the driveshaft. To remove the transmission, disconnect the speedometer cable, back-up lamp switch, TCS switch, and the gear shift rods. Support the engine with a jack, and then remove the nuts holding the transmission rear support to the crossmember. Raise the rear of the engine with the jack, and then remove the nuts, washers, and the bolts holding the crossmember to the frame supports. Remove the crossmember.

Remove the bolts that hold the transmission to the flywheel housing, and then pull the transmission rearward until the input shaft clears the housing. **CAUTION: Don't let the transmission hang while**

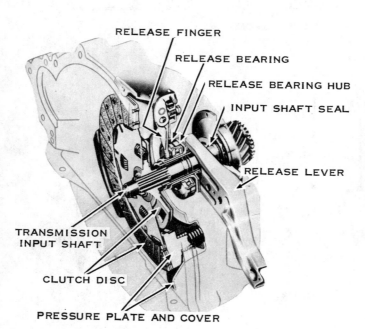

RELEASE FINGER
RELEASE BEARING
RELEASE BEARING HUB
INPUT SHAFT SEAL
RELEASE LEVER
TRANSMISSION INPUT SHAFT
CLUTCH DISC
PRESSURE PLATE AND COVER

Phantom view of the clutch.

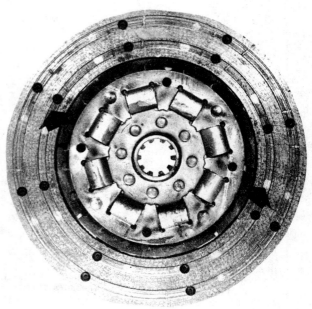

Scored clutch facings indicate that the pressure plate is likewise scored.

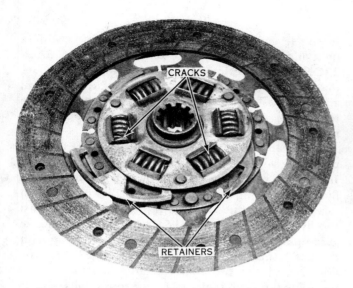

Note the broken retainer, which will cause noisy operation.

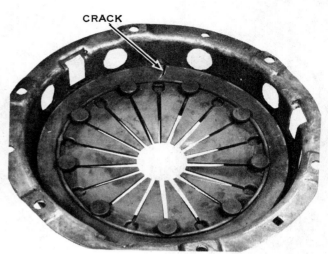

The pressure plate cracks in this fashion.

the end of the clutch shaft is still in the hub of the clutch disc, or you will bend the disc.

Remove the flywheel housing. Slide the clutch fork from the ball stud, and then remove the fork from the dust boot. If the ball stud is worn, it can be screwed out of the housing and a new one installed.

To remove the clutch, install an alignment tool to support the weight of the disc. Mark the cover and the flywheel so that the pressure plate can be installed in the same position in order to maintain balance. Loosen the six pressure plate cover attaching bolts evenly to release the spring tension. **CAUTION: Unless the bolts are released one turn at a time, the pressure plate cover will bend.** Remove the pressure plate assembly and the clutch disc.

INSTALLING

Coat the pilot bushing bore in the crankshaft with

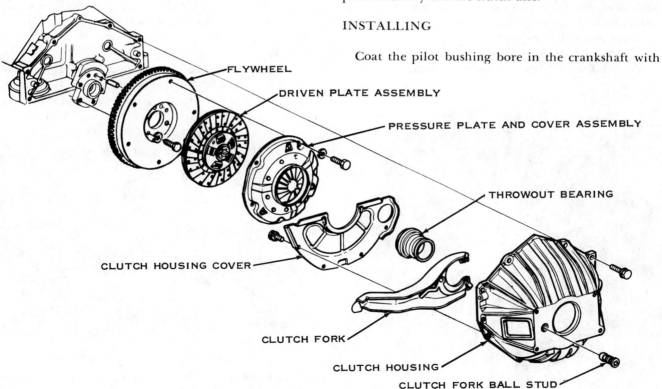

View of a typical clutch. In some cases, the clutch fork ball stud is turned to make the clutch pedal free-play adjustment.

If the release bearing surface is scored, replace the bearing, but also check the diaphragm fingers for similar damage.

a small quantity of wheel bearing lubricant. **CAUTION: Avoid using too much, or it will be thrown onto the clutch disc when the assembly revolves.** Hold a new clutch disc and reconditioned pressure plate in position on the flywheel. **CAUTION: Avoid contaminating the linings with greasy hands.** Start the cover attaching bolts to hold the pieces in place, but do not tighten them. Align the clutch disc with an arbor or an old clutch shaft, and then torque the six pressure plate cover attaching bolts evenly to 12-20 ft-lbs. Remove the arbor tool.

Make sure that the release bearing is in good condition and that the hub is properly installed on the

release lever. Coat the bearing retainer OD with a light film of a grease that contains graphite. **CAUTION: Don't lubricate the bearing hub.** Make sure that the flywheel housing mounting surfaces are clean, and then install the housing. Seat the clutch release rod in the release lever socket, and then install the return spring.

To install the transmission, first make sure that the mounting surfaces are free of dirt, paint, and burrs. Install two guide pins in the lower bolt holes of the flywheel housing, and then slide the transmission forward on the guide pins until it is positioned against the flywheel housing. **CAUTION: In the absence of guide pins, don't allow the transmission to hang with the clutch shaft in the clutch disc, or you will bend the disc.** Install the two upper retaining bolts, remove the guide pins, and then replace the lower bolts.

Raise the rear of the engine enough to permit replacing the crossmember. Remove the jack. Connect the gear shift rods, back-up light switch, and TCS switch. Replace the driveshaft, and then adjust the clutch pedal free play.

CLUTCH PEDAL FREE PLAY ADJUSTMENT

The clutch pedal must have free travel before the throwout bearing engages the clutch diaphragm spring levers. Play is required to prevent clutch slippage, which would occur if the bearing were held against the fingers. It is also required to keep the bearing from running continuously, which would make it fail.

To adjust the play, disconnect the push rod and rotate it until it fits into the gauge hole in the lever. In some cases, a clutch fork ball stud is turned to make the adjustment. The pedal free play should be 3/4 to 1-3/4".

Note the cracked and worn fingers on this diaphragm spring.

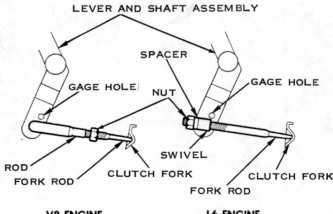

On late-model cars, the clutch pedal free play is determined by the gauge hole in the lever-and-shaft assembly, as discussed in the text. On early models, adjust the rod to give about 1" free play at the pedal.

AUTOMATIC TRANSMISSIONS

It is beyond the scope of this book to show you how to overhaul your automatic transmission because of the complexity of the job and the many types of transmissions. However, we can save you money by showing you how to troubleshoot so that you can determine where the problem lies so that you can discuss the condition intelligently with a service manager, and we can give you instructions for changing the fluid during your car's normal maintenance schedule, and for making some external adjustments: band and linkage.

CHECKING THE FLUID LEVEL

The automatic transmission is designed to operate with the oil level between the ADD and FULL marks on the dipstick at an operating temperature of 150 degrees F to 170 degrees F, and should be checked under these conditions. The operating temperature can be obtained by driving 15 to 20 miles of city type driving with the outside temperature above 50°F.

With the transmission in PARK, engine at curb idle rpm, foot brakes applied, and the vehicle on a level surface, move the transmission selector lever through each range, allowing time in each range to engage transmission units. Return to the PARK position and apply the parking brake.

The automatic transmission fluid level dipstick shows a pair of arrows to indicate the two levels which are acceptable. CAUTION: Don't overfill.

Clean all dirt from the transmission fluid dipstick cap, and then pull the dipstick out of the tube. Wipe it clean, and then push it all the way back into the tube. Be sure it is fully seated.

Pull the dipstick out of the tube again and check the fluid level, which should be between the ADD and FULL marks. If additional fluid is required, add enough through the filler tube to bring the level between the marks. **CAUTION: Do not overfill the transmission, as foaming and loss of fluid through the vent can result in a transmission malfunction. CAUTION: There are several basic types of automatic transmission fluids. Make sure that you are using the correct kind, as the wrong type could destroy the transmission. You will have to check your owner's handbook or the dealer to determine which is the correct fluid for your transmission.**

Install the dipstick, making sure it is fully seated in the tube.

The automatic transmission dipstick is located on the right side of the engine.

CHECKING THE CONDITION OF THE FLUID

When you remove the dipstick for checking the fluid, smell it. If you are having shifting problems, and the oil fluid is black and smells burned, then you have a mechanical problem and there is no need for further testing.

Money Saving Tips

If you are having problems, and you do note the tell-tale signs about the condition of the fluid, then shop around for prices for overhauling your automatic transmission. **CAUTION: Don't enter a shop that advertises a cheap fluid change and band adjustment in the hopes that you can get away from a large repair bill.** Once your vehicle is on a hoist, and the fluid drained, you are at a disadvantage. They have already built up a legitimate service charge for taking the pan down to get to the band adjustments (in most cases) for making an ineffective adjustment that they know will not help the condition at all. Putting the pan back

entails an additional service charge as well as a charge for new fluid and gaskets.

It is much better, in the first case, to shop around legitimate independent repair shops or a dealer of your make of vehicle. There you will get a complete cost estimate without having to go through the extra expense of having the the transmission put back together by the shop using the advertising come-on.

CHANGING THE TRANSMISSION FLUID

Warm the transmission fluid to operating temperature by running the vehicle for five or ten minutes and shifting frequently by stopping and starting.

Raise the front of the car and support it on safety stands. Block the wheels on the ground. **CAUTION: Don't get under any car supported by a jack as it can slip off and cause serious injury.**

Slide a large drain pan under the transmission and remove the drain plug, if there is one. **CAUTION:**

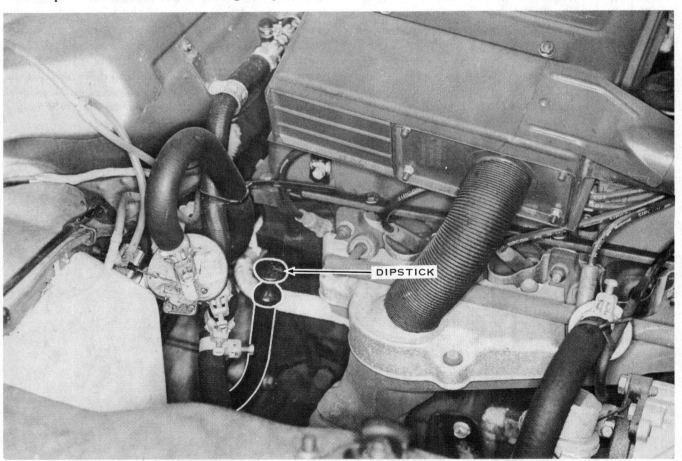

DIPSTICK

The automatic transmission dipstick is located on the right side of the Capri engine. Don't confuse it with the engine oil dipstick.

The fluid is extremely hot and cause severe burns if it contacts your skin, so take proper safety precautions. In most cases there is no drain plug, and it is necessary to remove the pan to drain the fluid. In this case, loosen all of the bolts, and then take them out from three sides of the pan. Pry the pan down slowly so that the fluid can drain out from one side. Finally, remove all of the bolts, and then take down the pan.

Inspect the oil pan for metal particles or segments of clutch material. A small amount of very fine metal particles is normal, due to wear of the internal parts. However, larger pieces indicate the need for repairs. Replace the filter screen at the base of the valve body. **CAUTION: Make no attempt to clean the screen, because it is so fine that you can cause problems of oil flow through it, which can burn out the transmission; always replace the screen.**

Wash the pan in clean solvent and position a new gasket on it. Use gasket cement to hold it in place. Install the pan bolts and lockwashers and tighten them in a criss-cross fashion. **CAUTION: Don't try to tighten them too much as you can easily strip the threads from the aluminum case.**

Jack up the car, remove the safety stands, and lower the vehicle. Use a clean funnel to put in 2-3 quarts of automatic transmission fluid **of the correct type** so that you can start the engine to determine the proper fluid level. **CAUTION: There are several types of automatic transmission fluids and you cannot use certain kinds in some manufacturer's transmissions without burning out the clutches; therefore, check your owner's handbook or ask your car dealer for the proper type of fluid.**

With the parking brakes firmly applied, or the wheels blocked, move the selector lever through all gearing positions to fill the clutches and servos. Then, with the engine idling and the selector lever in PARK, pull the dipstick out of the tube. Wipe it clean, and then push it all the way back into the tube. Be sure it is fully seated.

Pull the dipstick out of the tube again and check the fluid level, which should be between the ADD and FULL marks. If additional fluid is required, add enough through the filler tube to bring the level between the marks. **CAUTION: Do not overfill the transmission, as foaming and loss of fluid through the vent can result in a transmission malfunction.**

Install the dipstick, making sure it is fully seated in the tube.

TROUBLESHOOTING

The routine for diagnosing troubles in an automatic transmission requires you to follow certain procedures. Before any repairs or adjustments are made, certain checks must be made, and then the vehicle must be taken for a road test. For example, the transmission fluid level and the throttle linkage adjustment must be checked before any road test is undertaken.

The sequence in which the diagnosis is performed is most important. It must follow the recommended procedures of the Diagnosis Guide, which lists the steps in the order in which they must be taken. The Guide covers the likeliest causes of troubles first, especially those which do not require opening the transmission.

AUTOMATIC TRANSMISSION DIAGNOSIS GUIDE

1. Transmission fluid. Check the transmission fluid level.   ☐ Full ☐ Overfull ☐ Low

The very first test to make of any automatic transmission complaint is that of the level and condition of the fluid. Too little fluid starves the hydraulic system and causes delay in clutch application, causing slippage. There's also danger of the pump taking in air and causing the fluid to foam, resulting in mushy application of clutches and bands and excessive wear. Too much fluid can be just as bad as too little. The gear train churns it up with the same results as the pump sucking air.

Certain fluid conditions are important to watch for, such as varnish on the dipstick, black fluid with the odor of a burned electrical coil, and friction material in the fluid. Varnish on the dipstick indicates the control valves, clutches, and gears are coated with varnish. Burned, black fluid means overheating and a clutch or band burned out.

Before checking the fluid be sure that it is warmed to operating temperature. Move the selector lever through all ranges to fill the clutches and servos. Then, with the engine idling and the selector lever in PARK, check the fluid level. It should be ¼" below the FULL mark on the dipstick, but never higher than the FULL mark. If there's too much fluid, take some out. If it's low, add some.

2. Engine idle. Too high an engine idle can cause rough initial shifts because of too much control pressure in applying the clutches. Be sure the engine idle speed is set to specifications.   ☐ Performed

3. Linkage. Check the kickdown linkage by driving the vehicle at a road speed of approximately 40 mph and then depressing the accelerator to the floorboard. The transmission should shift back to second gear.
                                    ☐ O.K. ☐ Other

4. Stall test. Perform a stall test to check engine performance and for any sign of transmission slippage. A stall test is made in DRIVE position at full throttle to check engine performance, converter clutch operation, and the holding ability of the clutches and bands. To make a stall test, apply both the parking and service brakes. Connect a tachometer. Start the engine (thoroughly warmed), shift into DRIVE, and then open the accelerator wide. **CAUTION: While making this severe test, don't hold the throttle open for more than five seconds at a time.** After each test, move the selector lever to NEUTRAL and run the engine at about 1000 rpm for 20 seconds in order to cool the converter before making the next test. **CAUTION: If the engine speed exceeds the maximum specified limit, release the accelerator immediately because clutch or band slippage is indicated.** Additional abuse will destroy the slipping unit. If the stall speed is too high, band or clutch slippage is indicated and the transmission must be removed for service. When the stall test speeds are too low, the engine needs turning.   ☐ Performed

5. Road test. Drive the car in each range and through all shifts, including forced downshifts, observing any irregularities of performance. The transmission should shift automatically at approximately the speeds shown. The shifts may occur at somewhat different speeds due to production tolerances and rear axle ratios, but this is not as important as the quality of the shifts, which must be smooth, responsive, and made with little noticeable engine speed-up.   ☐ Road test completed

6. Shift test. The operating conditions shown on the Shift Test Chart should be checked in the order listed; by doing so, you may be able to correct a malfunction with a minor adjustment, thereby making unnecessary a major repair.

7. Pressure tests. CAUTION: The transmission must be at operating temperature. When the linkage is adjusted properly, all of the transmission shifts should occur within or close to the specified speeds. If the shifts do not occur within limits or if the transmission slips during shifts, it is necessary to attach testers to check the pressures. Attach a tachometer gauge to the engine and pressure gauges to the control pressure outlets at the transmission. Firmly apply the parking brake, and then start the engine. Make the tests as indicated according to the type of transmission.

SERVICE PROCEDURES

KICKDOWN LINKAGE ADJUSTMENTS

With the carburetor throttle held at wide-open throttle and the kickdown rod held against the "through detent" stop, adjust the kickdown adjusting screw to obtain 0.010-0.080" clearance between the screw and the throttle arm.

NEUTRAL-START SWITCH ADJUSTMENT

The neutral-start switch is designed to allow the engine to be cranked only when the selector lever is in

Throttle	Range	Shift	OPS–RPM	1	2	3
Closed (Above 17" Vacuum)	D	1-2	370-440	7-9	7-9	7-9
	D	2-3	550-1040	11-21	11-22	11-20
	D	3-1	440 Max.	9 Max.	9 Max.	9 Max.
	1	2-1	2020 Max.	40 Max.	42 Max.	39 Max.
To Detent (Torque Demand)	D	1-2	670-1540	13-31	14-32	13-30
	D	2-3	1425-2275	29-45	30-48	28-44
	D	3-2	1540 Max.	31 Max.	32 Max.	30 Max.
	D	3-1	440 Max.	9 Max.	9 Max.	9 Max.
Through Detent (W.O.T.)	D	1-2	1380-2130	28-43	29-45	27-41
	D	2-3	2610-3450	53-69	56-72	52-66
	D	3-2	3065 Max.	61 Max.	64 Max.	59 Max.
	D	3-1 2-1	1860 Max.	37 Max.	38 Max.	36 Max.

Axle Ratio	Tire Size	Use Column
3.40:1	6.00 x 13, BR70 x 13, A78 x 13 175R x 13, A70 x 13, 175 x 13 BR78 x 13	1
	CR70 x 13, B78 x 13, 185 x 13	2
3.55:1	6.00 x 13, BR70 x 13, A78 x 13 175R x 13, A70 x 13, 175 x 13 BR78 x 13	3
	CR70 x 13, B78 x 13, 185 x 13	1

Typical speed shifts for the Ford C-4 automatic transmission. This is generally the same for all vehicles. However, the quality of the shift is much more important than the actual shift point.

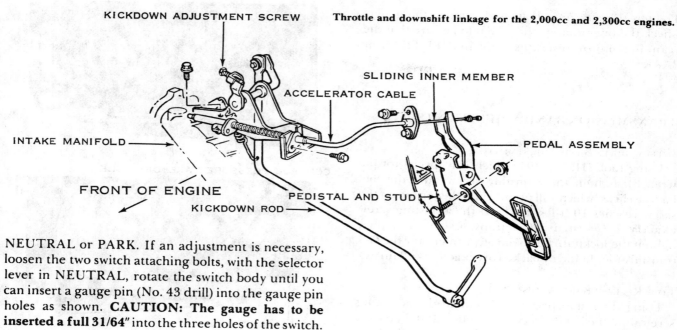

KICKDOWN ADJUSTMENT SCREW

Throttle and downshift linkage for the 2,000cc and 2,300cc engines.

SLIDING INNER MEMBER

ACCELERATOR CABLE

INTAKE MANIFOLD

PEDAL ASSEMBLY

FRONT OF ENGINE

PEDISTAL AND STUD

KICKDOWN ROD

NEUTRAL or PARK. If an adjustment is necessary, loosen the two switch attaching bolts, with the selector lever in NEUTRAL, rotate the switch body until you can insert a gauge pin (No. 43 drill) into the gauge pin holes as shown. **CAUTION: The gauge has to be inserted a full 31/64″** into the three holes of the switch.

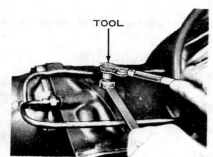

TOOL

Adjusting the band.

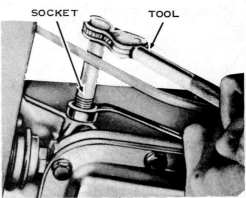

SOCKET   TOOL

Adjusting the low-reverse band.

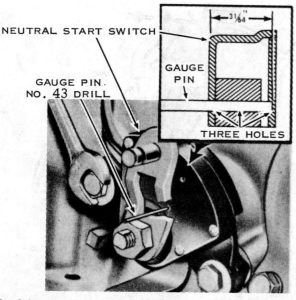

NEUTRAL START SWITCH

GAUGE PIN.
NO. 43 DRILL

GAUGE
PIN

THREE HOLES

Details of the neutral-start switch adjustment, as discussed in the text.

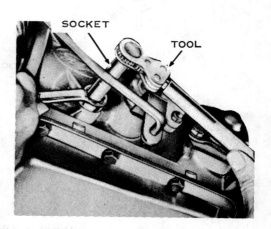

SOCKET

TOOL

Adjusting the intermediate band.

Tighten the attaching bolts and remove the gauge. Check the operation of the switch to be sure that the cranking motor operates only in NEUTRAL or PARK.

TRANSMISSION BAND ADJUSTMENTS

INTERMEDIATE BAND ADJUSTMENT

Using tool 71P-77370H (which is a special torque wrench), tighten the adjusting screw until the tool handle clicks, which will occur when the torque on the screw reaches 10 ft-lbs. Back off the adjusting screw **exactly** 1-3/4 turns, (C-4 transmission), and then tighten the locknut. The band adjustment for the C-3 transmission should be backed off **exactly** 1-1/2 turns

LOW-REVERSE BAND ADJUSTMENT

Using the same special tool, tighten the adjusting screw until the handle clicks (10 ft-lbs.), and then back off the adjusting screw **exactly** 3 full turns. Tighten the locknut.

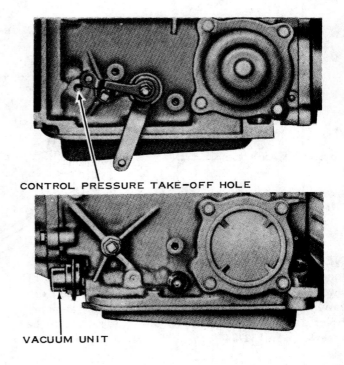

CONTROL PRESSURE TAKE-OFF HOLE

VACUUM UNIT

Control pressure take-off point on the automatic transmission.

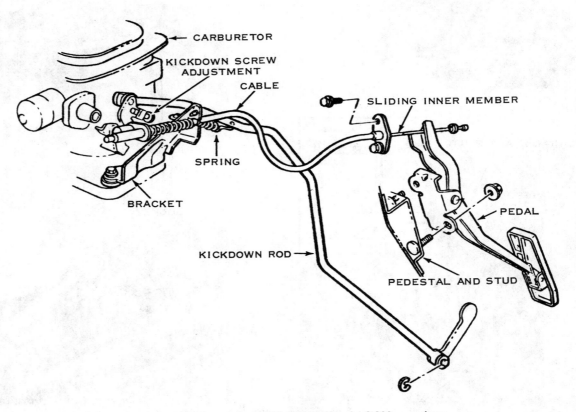

Throttle and downshift linkage for the 2,800cc engine.

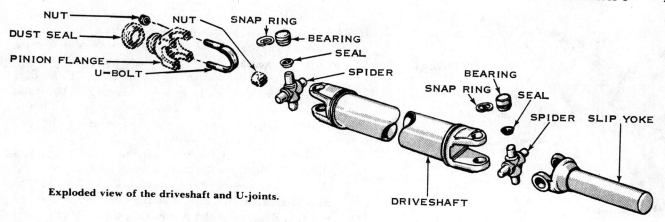

Exploded view of the driveshaft and U-joints.

DRIVESHAFT

The driveshaft receives the power from the engine, through the clutch and transmission, and transfers it to the differential in the rear axle, and then to the rear wheels. The driveshaft incorporates two universal joints and a slip yoke. The splines in the yoke and those on the transmission output shaft permit the driveshaft to move forward and rearward as the axle moves up and down. All driveshafts are balanced. If the vehicle is to be undercoated, cover the driveshaft and the universal joints to protect them from the undercoating material.

REMOVING

Whenever a driveshaft is to be removed, be sure to mark it for correct assembly in order to preserve the balance. Disconnect the rear universal joint from the axle drive pinion flange. Wrap tape around the loose bearing caps to keep them from falling off. Pull the driveshaft toward the rear of the vehicle until the slip yoke clears the transmission extension housing and the seal.

UNIVERSAL JOINT REPLACEMENT

Place the driveshaft in a vise. Remove the snap rings that retain the bearings. Press the bearing out of the slip yoke. Reposition the tool to press on the spider in order to remove the bearing from the opposite side of the yoke, and then take off the yoke.

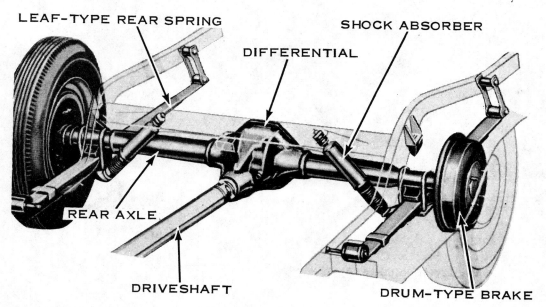

Details of the rear axle and suspension system.

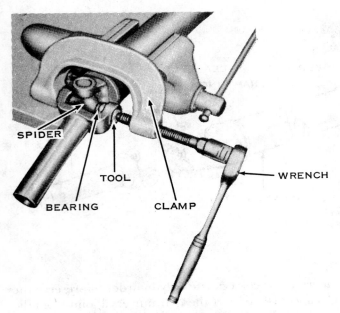

Removing the universal joint bearing.

ASSEMBLING

Start a new bearing into the yoke at the rear of the driveshaft. Insert the thrust bearings into the end of the spider. Position the spider in the rear yoke, and then press the bearing in 1/4″ below the surface. Remove the tool and install a new snap ring. Insert the thrust bearings into the end of the spider. Start a new bearing into the opposite side of the yoke. Install the

tool and press on the bearing until the opposite bearing contacts the snap ring. Remove the tool and install a new snap ring. *NOTE: It may be necessary to dress off the surface of the snap ring to permit easy entry.*

Reposition the driveshaft and install the new spider, thrust bearings, and the two new bearings in the same manner as the rear yoke. Position the slip yoke on the spider, and then install the thrust bearings and two new bearings and snap rings.

Check the joint for free movement. If it binds, a sharp rap on the yokes with a brass hammer will seat the bearing needles and free the joint. **CAUTION: Support the shaft end during this operation to prevent damage to the driveshaft. CAUTION: Don't install the driveshaft assembly in the vehicle unless the universal joints move freely.**

DRIVELINE VIBRATION

If detailed parts of the driveshaft are replaced and shaft vibration is encountered after installation, disconnect the shaft at the slip yoke. Rotate the slip yoke 180 degrees then, reconnect the shaft to the slip yoke. If the vibration persists, disconnect the shaft at the rear axle companion flange. Rotate the companion flange 180 degrees and reconnect the shaft to the flange.

DRIVE LINE ANGLE CHECK

Vibration or shudder which is noticeable either on

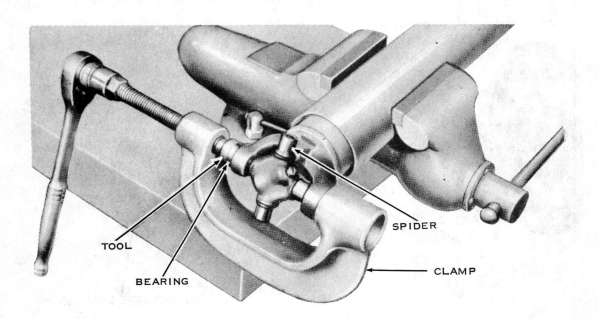

Installing a universal joint bearing with a C-clamp, as discussed in the text.

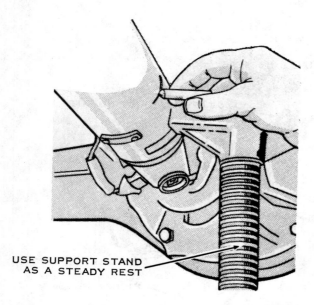

Marking the high point of driveshaft run-out, as discussed in the text.

fast acceleration, when coasting, or when using the engine for braking, may be caused by the rear axle housing being loose on the rear springs or by an improper pinion angle.

DRIVESHAFT RUNOUT CHECK

Using a dial indicator, check the runout at each end and in the middle of the driveshaft. The rear check should be made on the small tube section of the shaft, between the balance weights and the yoke welds.

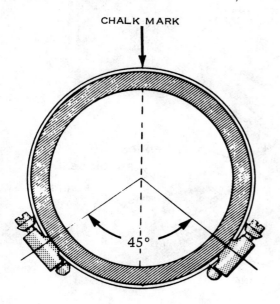

Rotating the clamps to obtain balance, as discussed in the text.

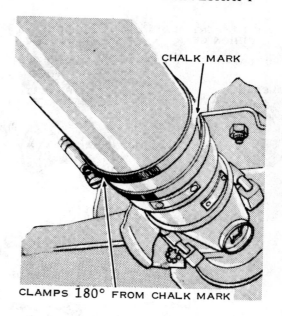

Installing Whittek clamps.

Driveshaft runout should not exceed 0.035 inch at any one point.

DRIVESHAFT BALANCING

If rotating the driveshaft 180 degrees does not eliminate the vibration, the driveshaft may be balanced using the following procedure: Place the vehicle on a twin-post hoist so that the rear of the vehicle is supported on the rear axle housing with the wheels free to rotate.

With the driveshaft rotating at a speedometer speed of 40-50 mph, carefully bring a crayon or colored pencil up until it just barely contacts the rear end of driveshaft. The mark made by the crayon or pencil will indicate the heavy side of the shaft. **CAUTION: Care should be exercised when working near the balance weights to prevent injury to the hands.**

Install two Whittek-type hose clamps on the driveshaft so that the heads are located 180 degrees from the crayon marking. Tighten the clamps.

Run the vehicle up to 65-70 mph speedometer speed. If no vibration is felt, lower the vehicle and road test. If unbalance still exists, rotate the clamp heads approximately 45 degrees away from each other and test for vibration.

Continue to rotate the clamp heads apart in smaller amounts until vibration is eliminated. **CAUTION: To prevent overheating, do not run the vehicle on the hoist for an extended period.** Road test the vehicle.

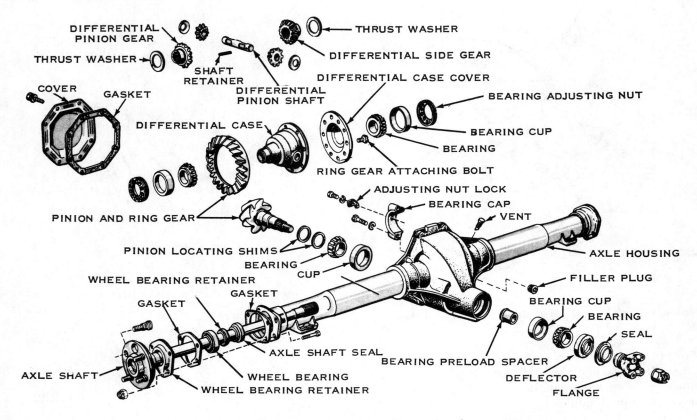

Exploded view of the integral-type rear axle.

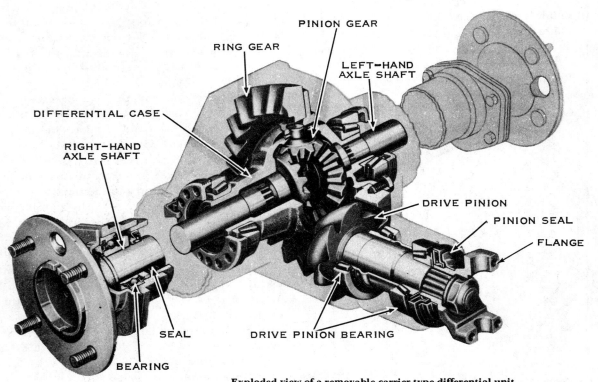

Exploded view of a removable-carrier type differential unit.

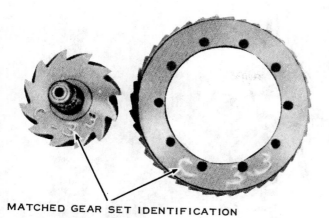

MATCHED GEAR SET IDENTIFICATION

The pinion and ring gears are marked to be used as matched sets.

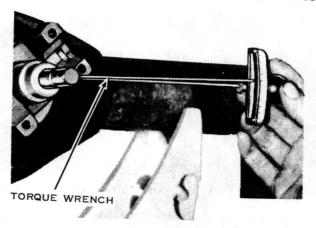

TORQUE WRENCH

Checking the pinion bearing preload adjustment.

REAR AXLE

PINION- POSITIONING SHIM

The pinion-positioning shim is installed just behind the pinion gear, between it and the cone of the rear roller bearing. Changing the thickness of this shim moves the pinion gear in or out in relation to the centerline of the ring gear, which has a decided effect on the gear tooth pattern.

Generally, it requires special tools to determine the correct pinion-positioning shim when starting from scratch. However, the marks on the heads of the old and the replacement pinion gears can be used for selecting the correct shim. If the mark on the replacement pinion gear head is the same as on the one it is to replace, use the original shim. If the mark is more positive (i.e., if it changes from + 1 to + 4), use a 0.003″ thinner shim. If the mark is more negative (i.e., changes from + 1 to -1), use a 0.002″ thicker shim.

PINION BEARING PRELOAD ADJUSTMENT

A collapsible spacer is used to obtain the proper

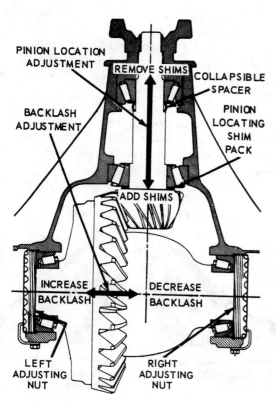

Pinion and ring gear tooth contact adjustments.

PAINT MARKING INDICATES POSITION IN WHICH GEARS WERE LAPPED

Paint marks must be aligned to assure quiet operation.

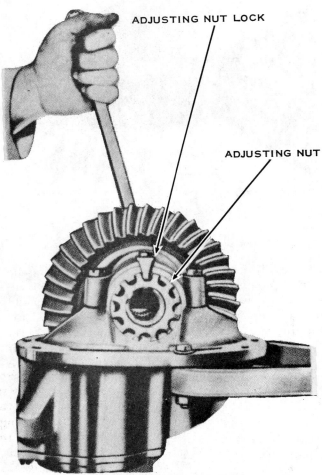

ADJUSTING NUT LOCK

ADJUSTING NUT

Making the differential bearing adjustment.

Checking the backlash.

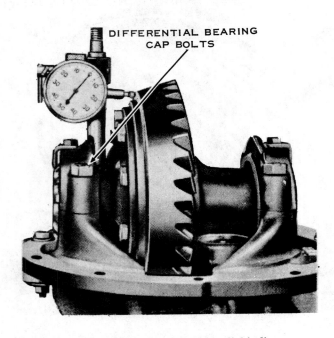

DIFFERENTIAL BEARING
CAP BOLTS

Checking the ring gear run-out with a dial indicator.

preload. To obtain additional bearing preload, tighten the pinion shaft nut a little at a time until the specified preload is obtained. If excessive preload is obtained as a result of overtightening, replace the collapsible bearing spacer. **CAUTION: Don't back off the pinion shaft nut.**

Differential Bearing Preload Adjustment

The differential bearing preload adjustment is made by means of two differential case bearing adjusting nuts.

PATTERN CLOSE TO CENTER

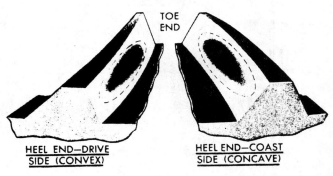

TOE
END

HEEL END—DRIVE
SIDE (CONVEX)

HEEL END—COAST
SIDE (CONCAVE)

Desired ring gear tooth contact patterns under light loading.

INDENTATIONS

SURFACE DEPRESSIONS ON RACE AND ROLLERS
CAUSED BY HARD PARTICLES OF FOREIGN MATERIAL.

CLEAN ALL PARTS AND HOUSINGS. CHECK SEALS
AND REPLACE BEARINGS IF ROUGH OR NOISY.

CAGE WEAR

WEAR AROUND OUTSIDE DIAMETER OF CAGE AND
ROLLER POCKETS CAUSED BY ABRASIVE MATERIAL
AND INEFFICIENT LUBRICATION.

CLEAN RELATED PARTS AND HOUSINGS.
CHECK SEALS AND REPLACE BEARINGS.

MISALIGNMENT

OUTER RACE MISALIGNMENT DUE TO FOREIGN
OBJECT.

CLEAN RELATED PARTS AND REPLACE BEARING.
MAKE SURE RACES ARE PROPERLY SEATED.

Types of roller bearing failure.

Tooth Contact Adjustments

Two separate adjustments affect the pinion and ring gear tooth contact; they are the location of the pinion and the backlash between the gear teeth. When rolling a tooth pattern, use the special compound (tube) packed with each service ring gear and pinion set. Paint all gear teeth and roll a pattern. After diagnosing the tooth pattern as explained here, make the appropriate adjustments.

The drive pattern is rolled on the convex side of the tooth, and the coast pattern is rolled on the concave side. The movement of tooth contact patterns with changes in shimming can be summarized as follows: (1.) Thinner shim with the backlash set to specifications moves the pinion farther from the ring gear. (2.) Thicker shim with the backlash set to specifications moves the pinion closer to the ring gear.

If the patterns are not correct, make the changes as indicated. The differential case and drive pinion will have to be removed from the carrier casting to change a shim.

PATTERN MOVES TOWARD CENTER AND DOWN

TOE END

HEEL END—DRIVE SIDE (CONVEX)

HEEL END—COAST SIDE (CONCAVE)

PATTERN MOVES INWARD AND UP

TOE END

HEEL END—DRIVE SIDE (CONVEX)

HEEL END— COAST SIDE (CONCAVE)

The drawing at the left shows the effect of increasing the thickness of the pinion-positioning shim. The pattern at the right shows the effect of decreasing the shim thickness.

7/running gear service

The material in this chapter will cover, front wheel bearings, shock absorbers, and brakes.

WHEEL SUSPENSION

The front wheels are suspended on coil springs, which are attached to a long-and-short arm type suspension system. The front end incorporates ball joints, which allow the front wheels to move up and down with changes in the road surface. A direct-action shock absorber is bolted to the arm and to the top of the spring housing on each side.

The rear wheels are bolted to axle shafts, which are supported by the rear axle housing by means of wheel bearings. The rear axle housing is supported by two leaf-type springs on light vehicles and station wagons, and on coil springs on most other vehicles.

REPACKING THE FRONT WHEEL BEARINGS

Raise the vehicle until the wheel and tire clear the floor. Remove the wheel cover or hub cap from the wheel. Remove the wheel and tire from the hub and rotor.

Remove 2 bolts and washers that attach the caliper to the spindle. Remove the caliper from the rotor and wire it to the underbody to prevent damage to the brake hose.

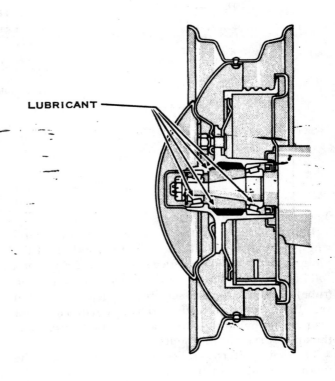

When repacking the bearings, add some lubricant between the bearings to act as a reservoir.

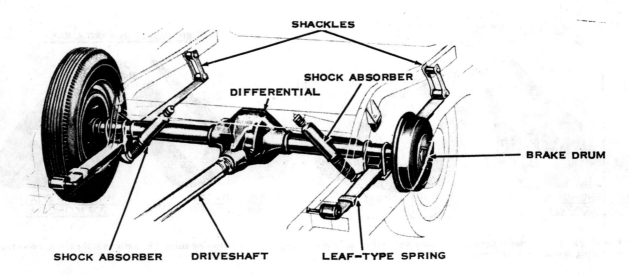

Details of a rear axle suspension using leaf-type rear springs. Note the straddle-mounted shock absorbers.

Remove the grease cap from the hub. Remove the cotter pin, nut lock, adjusting nut, and flat washer from the spindle. Remove the outer bearing cone-and-roller assembly.

Pull the hub and rotor assembly off the wheel spindle. Remove and discard the old grease retainer. Remove the inner bearing cone and roller assembly from the hub.

CLEANING AND INSPECTING

Clean the lubricant off the inner and outer bearing cups with solvent and inspect the cups for scratches,

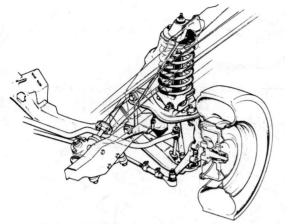

Cross-sectioned view of a front suspension with the front spring mounted on top of the upper support arm.

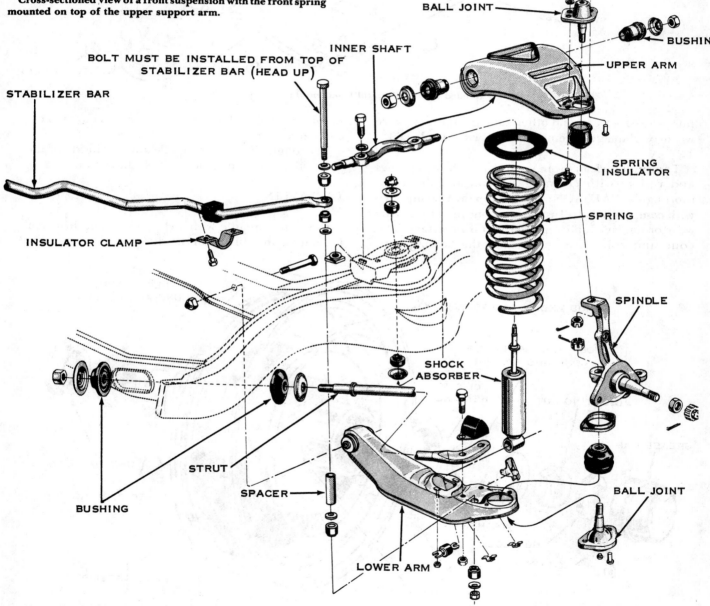

Exploded view of a typical front suspension with the front spring mounted between the upper and lower arms.

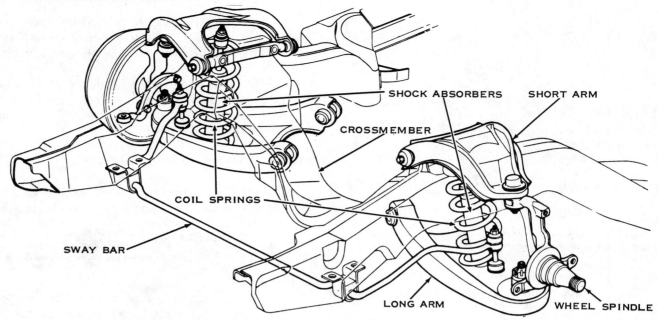

Exploded view of a typical front wheel assembly.

pits, excessive wear, and other damage. If the cups are worn or damaged, remove them with Tool T69L-1102-A.

Thoroughly clean the inner and outer bearing cones and rollers with cleaning solvent, and dry them thoroughly. **CAUTION: Do not spin the bearings dry with compressed air.** Inspect the cones and rollers for wear or damage, and replace them if necessary. The cone and roller assemblies and the bearing cups

should be replaced as a set if damage to either is encountered.

Thoroughly clean the spindle and the inside of the hub with solvent to remove all old lubricant.

INSTALLING

Cover the spindle with a clean cloth and brush all loose dust and dirt from the dust shield. To prevent

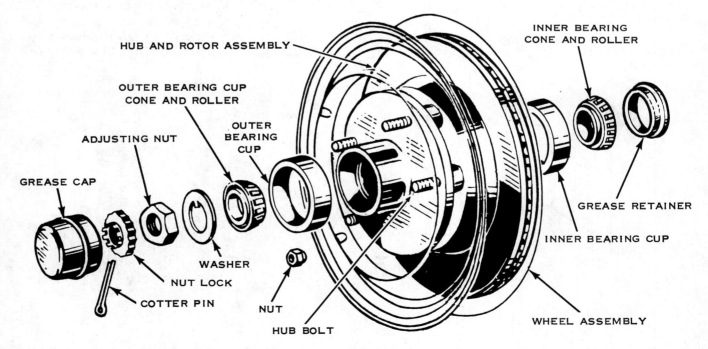

Exploded view of the front wheel and disc assembly.

GREASE

Repacking a wheel bearing, as discussed in the text.

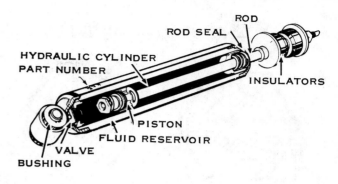

ROD
ROD SEAL
HYDRAULIC CYLINDER
PART NUMBER
INSULATORS
PISTON
FLUID RESERVOIR
VALVE
BUSHING

Details of the shock absorber. Check the action by pushing down on a fender, and then release the pressure suddenly. The car should rebound once or twice, but if it continues to bob up and down, the shock absorbers are weak and need to be replaced. CAUTION: A light film of oil on the shaft is normal.

getting dirt on the spindle, carefully remove the cloth from the spindle.

If the inner and/or outer bearing cup(s) were removed, install the replacement cup(s) in the hub with the tools shown. **CAUTION: Be sure to seat the cups properly in the hub. .**

Pack the inside of the hub with the specified wheel bearing grease. Add lubricant to the hub only until the grease is flush with the inside diameter of both bearing cups. **CAUTION: It is important that all old grease be removed from the wheel bearings and surrounding surfaces because the new Lithium base grease C1AZ19590-B is not compatible with Sodium base grease which may already be present on the bearing surfaces.**

Pack the bearing cone and roller assemblies with wheel bearing grease. A bearing packer is desirable for this operation. If a packer is not available, work as much lubricant as possible between the rollers and cages. Lubricate the cone surfaces with grease.

Place the inner bearing cone-and-roller assembly in the inner cup. Apply a light film of grease to the lips of the grease retainer and install the new grease retainer with the tool shown. **CAUTION: Be sure the retainer is properly seated.**

Install the hub-and-rotor assembly on the wheel spindle. **CAUTION: Keep the hub centered on the spindle to prevent damage to the grease retainer or the spindle threads.** Install the outer bearing cone-and-roller assembly and the flat washer on the spindle, then install the adjusting nut finger-tight. Do not attempt to adjust the wheel bearings at this time.

Install the caliper to the spindle using new bolts, and torque the top attaching bolt, first to 90-120 ft-lbs. and the bottom one to 55-70 ft-lbs. Install the wheel and tire on the hub.

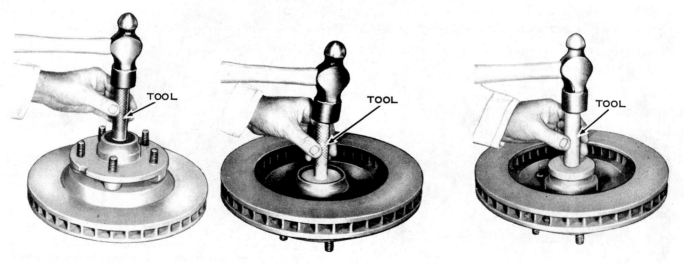

TOOL   TOOL   TOOL

Installing the front wheel bearing cups, outer (left view) and inner (center view). The right view shows the grease retainer being installed.

WITH WHEEL ROTATING, TORQUE ADJUSTING NUT, TO 17-25 FT. LBS.

BACK ADJUSTING NUT OFF 1/2 TURN

TIGHTEN ADJUSTING NUT TO 10-15 IN.-LBS.

INSTALL THE LOCK AND A NEW COTTER PIN

Details for making the front wheel bearing adjustments.

ADJUSTING THE FRONT WHEEL BEARINGS—FORD & A.M.

Rock the wheel, hub, and rotor assembly in and out several times to push the shoe and linings away from the rotor.

While rotating the wheel, hub, and rotor assembly, torque the adjusting nut to 17-25 ft-lbs to seat the bearings. Back the adjusting nut off one half turn. Retighten the adjusting nut to 10-15 **in-lbs** with a torque wrench or just finger-tight.

Locate the nut lock on the adjusting nut so that the castellations on the lock are aligned with the cotter pin hole in the spindle, as shown. Install a new cotter pin, and bend the ends of the cotter pin around the castellated flange of the nut lock.

Check the front wheel rotation. If the wheel rotates properly, install the grease cap and the hub cap or wheel cover.

ADJUSTING THE FRONT WHEEL BEARINGS—CHRYSLER & G.M.

Jack up the front of the vehicle. Remove the wheel cover and dust cap. Take out the cotter pin, and then tighten the spindle nut to seat the bearings fully while you spin the wheel.

Back off the adjusting nut 1/4-1/2 turn until it is just loose, and then hand-snug the nut. Loosen the nut until either hole in the spindle lines up with the slot in the nut, and then insert a new cotter pin. When the bearing is properly adjusted, there must be 0.001-0.008″ end play. **CAUTION? Under no circumstances should the bearing adjustment be even finger-tight, or you will burn out the bearings.**

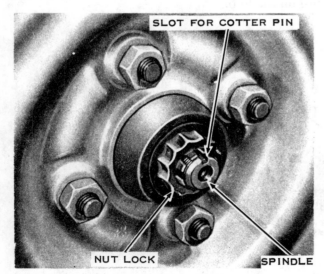

Illustration to show the correct position of the nut lock aligned with the adjusting nut.

All too frequently, the small race spindle surface galls when the vehicle is run with a defective front wheel bearing. Naturally, such a spindle must be replaced to restore the finely ground surface necessary for long bearing life.

SHOCK ABSORBERS

Most vehicles have a double-action hydraulic shock absorber at each wheel. The shock absorber must be replaced if defective. It cannot be serviced. Worn shock absorbers are evidenced by a bouncy ride or unusual tire wear.

CHECKING

Park the vehicle on a level surface, and then bounce each corner of the car several times by depressing the fender with all of your weight. Let go after a depression stroke and the corner of the vehicle must not bounce over 1-1/2 times before coming to rest.

If one corner of the car continues to bounce, it is a sure sign that the shock absorber is worn out.

Making a front wheel bearing adjustment on G.M. and Chrysler vehicles.

Money Saving Tip

Shock absorbers are long-mileage units and are often changed even though they are not defective. Typically, a tire service salesman will suggest that you replace your shock absorbers whenever you replace the tires, explaining that they wear out together. Other salesmen will try to sell you shock absorbers by pointing to an oil-moistened cover (normal seal leakage), explaining that the shock absorber is leaking, therefore defective. Still others will have a demonstration unit available for you to check the resistance of two shock absorbers, one like the one that was sold with your car and another alongside of it to show a heavy duty part which has much more resistance. Most of these sales pitches are outright frauds, unless you are seeking to buy a heavy duty shock absorber for a so-called "Handling package," which is designed to minimize vehicle front end roll when speeding around s sharp corner. If you intend to race the vehicle, you do need stiffer shock absorbers (heavy duty types). But, if you're an average driver, you are buying a product that will make your vehicle ride harsher. If your backside skin is tender, don't buy heavy-duty shock absorbers.

REPLACING A SHOCK ABSORBER

If one of your shock absorbers is defective, it is wise to purchase two as a matched set for the front or rear. You can buy them cheaper in an automotive parts house than when you have them installed.

To replace a shock absorber, jack up the front or rear of the vehicle and position it on safety stands, or use a hoist. **CAUTION: Don't work under the vehicle while it is on a jack. The vehicle can slide off the jack and you can be crushed. Block both sides of one wheel on the ground for safety reasons.**

Most shock absorbers have a threaded bolt protruding from the upper end, and this is secured to the upper suspension or the floor pan with a nut, spacers, and a rubber washer. Remove the nut to unfasten the upper part of the shock absorber. The bottom end is secured to the rear axle or front suspension with a bolt and nut, with compression rubber bushings. Remove the bolt and nut to unfasten the lower end. Slide the old shock absorber from the vehicle.

Install the new shock absorber in place of the damaged unit, using new rubber bushings. Tighten the nut only enough to bulge the rubber spacers slightly; the end must have no side play.

BRAKING SYSTEMS

Almost all American cars are equipped with Bendix, Due-servo, drum-type brakes; self-adjusting devices were added in 1963. Since 1968, all vehicles have a split braking system, using a dual master cylinder with two sections; one for the front wheel brakes and the other for the rear wheels.

Disc brakes have been used on the front wheels of many models since 1967. Initially most cars used four-piston type brake assemblies. Most models now use single-piston, sliding-caliper type brake units on the front wheels.

Money Saving Tips

If you do the work of removing the brake shoes or pads, you can take them to your automotive parts house where you can exchange them for relined shoes at a fraction of the cost. In the event your drums or rotors need to be turned to remove scores, you can have this work done at the parts house's machine shop and thus avoid the mechanic's usual markup of 25-40%.

DUAL BRAKING SYSTEM

The system is designed with separate hydraulic systems for the front and rear brakes, using a dual master cylinder. The split system consists basically of two separate brake systems. When failure is encountered in either, the other is adequate to stop the vehicle. If one system is not functioning, it is normal for the brake pedal lash and pedal effort to increase. This occurs because of the design of the master cylinder,

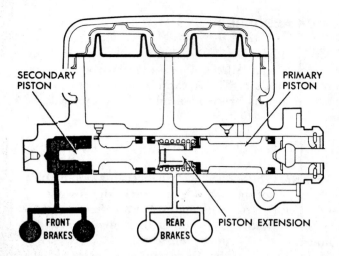

When the rear hydraulic system loses fluid through a leak, the primary piston bottoms on the end of the secondary piston, and sufficient pressure is built up to stop the vehicle.

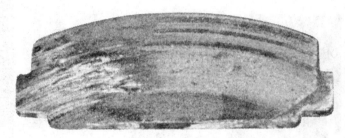

When the disc brake pads are worn this much, you can slip in a new set with a minimum of tools and skills.

which incorporates an actuating piston for each system. When the rear system loses fluid, its piston will bottom against the front piston. When the front system loses

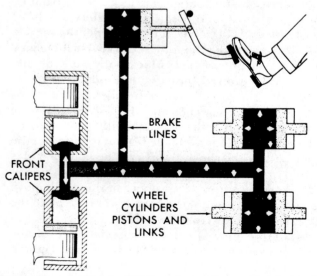

Hydraulic pressure is distributed equally to the hydraulic cylinders at all four wheels.

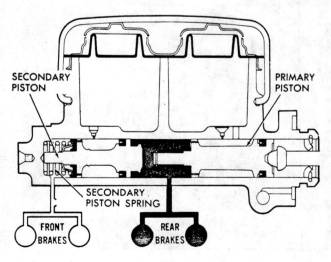

When the front system loses hydraulic pressure, the secondary piston bottoms in the end of the master cylinder, and then the primary piston develops sufficient pressure to stop the vehicle.

fluid, its piston will bottom on the end of the master cylinder body. The pressure differential in one of the systems causes an uneven hydraulic pressure balance between the front and rear systems. The brake pipe distribution and switch assembly, or combination valve, near the master cylinder detects the loss of pressure and illuminates the brake alarm indicator light on the instrument panel. The pressure loss is felt at the brake pedal by an apparent lack of brakes for most of the brake pedal travel and then, when the failed chamber has bottomed, the pedal effort will harden.

DUAL MASTER CYLINDER

The master cylinder contains two fluid reservoirs and two cylindrical pressure chambers in which the brake pedal force is transmitted to the fluid to actuate the brake shoes. Breather ports and compensating ports permit passage of fluid between each of the pressure chambers and its fluid reservoir during certain operating conditions. A vented cover and flexible rubber diaphragm at the top seal the hydraulic system against the entrance of dirt and, at the same time, permit expansion and contraction of the hydraulic fluid within the system without direct venting to the atmosphere.

VALVES

FRONT DRUM BRAKES

A brake pipe distribution-and-switch (combination valve) assembly is mounted below the master cylinder. The front and rear hydraulic brake lines are routed from the master cylinder, through the brake pipe distribution-and-switch assembly, to the front and rear brakes. The switch is wired electrically to the brake alarm indicator light on the instrument panel. If a leak in either the front or rear system should occur, the pressure differential during brake application will cause the piston to compress the springs and move in the bore until it touches the electrical contact, which causes the parking brake lamp on the instrument panel to light. This lamp is also illuminated when the parking brake is applied.

FRONT DISC BRAKES

Disc brake vehicles have a combination valve below the master cylinder, which houses the brake-failure warning switch, metering valve, and proportioning valve in one assembly (some models do **not** have a proportioning section of the valve).

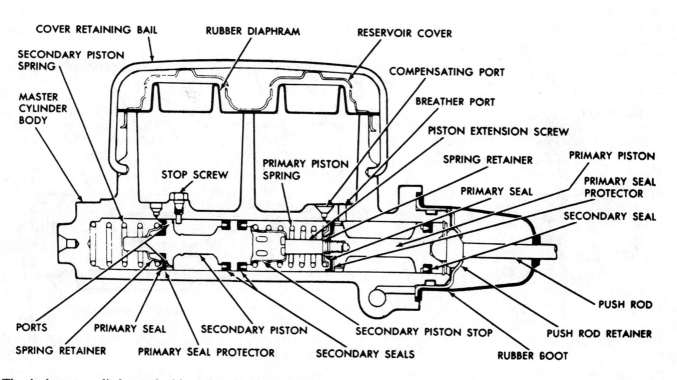

The dual master cylinder used with modern braking systems has two reservoirs and two pistons to develop pressure in each of the braking systems. A vented cover and flexible rubber diaphragm at the top of the reservoirs seal the system from contamination.

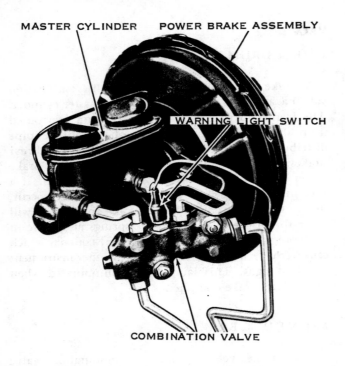

MASTER CYLINDER   POWER BRAKE ASSEMBLY

WARNING LIGHT SWITCH

COMBINATION VALVE

A brake distribution-and-switch (combination valve) assembly is mounted below the master cylinder.

COMBINATION VALVE

The combination valve contains a metering valve, failure-warning switch, and proportioner valve combined into an assembly which also serves as the front junction block. This valve is used on all disc brake applications. The input-output characteristics of the valve vary with vehicle usage.

Metering Valve

This valve delays front disc brake application until the shoes of the rear drum brakes contact the drum. The action is needed because of the return springs on the rear wheel brake shoes. Disc brake shoes have no return springs.

Brakes Not Applied

The metering valve allows free flow of brake fluid through the valve when the brakes are not applied. This allows the fluid to expand and contract with temperature changes.

Shut-Off Point (Initial Brake Apply)

The metering valve stem moves to the left and, at

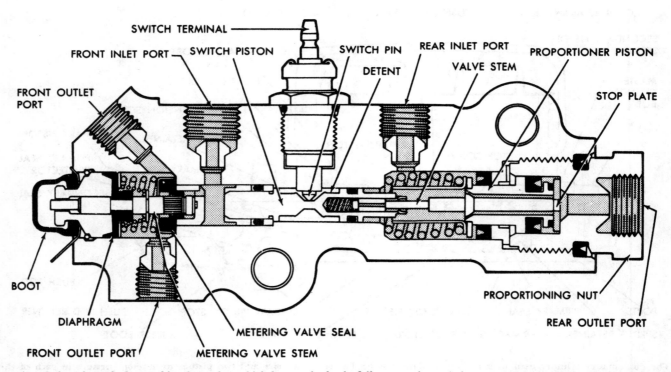

SWITCH TERMINAL

FRONT INLET PORT   SWITCH PISTON   SWITCH PIN   REAR INLET PORT   PROPORTIONER PISTON

FRONT OUTLET PORT   DETENT   VALVE STEM   STOP PLATE

BOOT

DIAPHRAGM   METERING VALVE SEAL   PROPORTIONING NUT

FRONT OUTLET PORT   METERING VALVE STEM   REAR OUTLET PORT

Sectioned view through the combination valve, which houses the brake-failure warning switch, metering valve, and proportioning valve.

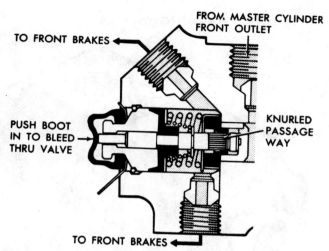

The metering valve keeps the disc brake pads from operating until the shoes of the rear drum brake contact the drum. In this non-applied position, free passage of brake fluid is allowed through the knurled passageway.

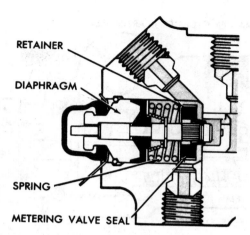

As pressure builds up in the system, the metering valve allows pressure through the valve to the front disc braking system.

4 to 30 psi, the smooth end of the stem is in a sealing position with the metering valve seal lip, and this is the shut-off point.

Hold-Off Bend Pressure

The metering valve stem continues to the left on initial brake apply and stops on the knurl at the metal retainer. The metering valve spring holds the retainer against the seal until a predetermined pressure is produced at the inlet of the valve. This pressure overcomes the spring and allows pressure through the valve to the front brakes. A continued increase of pressure into the valve is metered through the metering

valve seal (through to the front brakes) and produces an increasing force on the diaphragm. The diaphragm pulls the pin and the pin, in turn, pulls the retainer, thus reducing the spring load on the metering valve seal. Eventually, the pressure reaches a point where the spring is completely pulled away by the diaphragm pin and retainer, leaving the metering valve seal free to pass unrestricted pressure through the valve.

FAILURE-WARNING SWITCH

The failure-warning switch is activated if either the

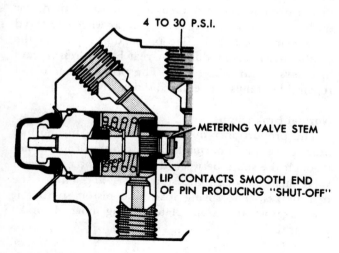

On initial brake apply, the metering valve stem moves to the left and shuts off hydraulic pressure to the front disc brakes.

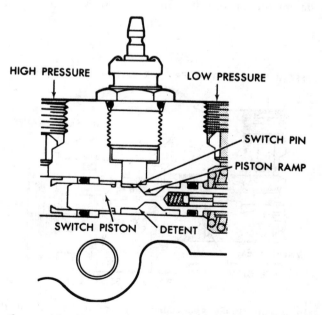

In the combination valve used on late models, the failure-warning switch action is in the center section, and this diagram shows a rear-wheel braking system failure.

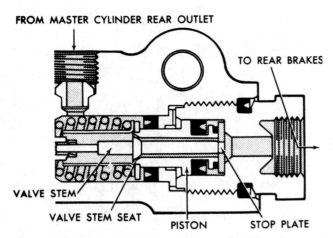

The combination valve has a proportioner valve at the right end to improve front-to-rear brake balance during sudden stops. This valve is necessary to prevent rear-wheel lock-up and skids during emergency stops. During normal stops, fluid flows through the space between the piston center hole and the valve stem, and the valve has no effect on brake operation.

front or rear brake system fails and, when activated, completes a circuit to the dash warning lamp. If the rear hydraulic system fails, the pressure of the good front system forces the switch piston to the right. The switch pin is forced up into the switch by the piston ramp and completes the electrical circuit, lighting the dash lamp; it is held in this position by the piston. When repairs are made and pressure is returned to the rear system by bleeding, the piston moves to the left and resets the switch to the OFF position. The detent on the piston typically requires 100 to 450 psi

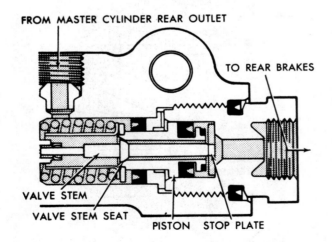

On a hard brake application, pressure pushes against the large end of the piston, and when sufficient to overcome the spring load, moves the piston to the left so that pressure flow through the valve is restricted.

FAILURE-WARNING SWITCH

Since the split hydraulic brake system was introduced in 1968, this brake failure-warning switch was used in the pipe distribution block of early models. Loss of hydraulic pressure in either system activates the switch to light a warning lamp on the dash.

pressure before allowing full reset (centering) of the piston. The same condition exists if the front hydraulic system fails, except the piston moves to the left.

PROPORTIONER

The rear brake proportioner improves front-to-rear brake balance at high deceleration. During quick stops, a percentage of the rear weight is transferred to the front wheels. Compensation must be made for the resultant loss of weight to the rear wheels to avoid early rear wheel skid. The proportioner part of the combination valve reduces the rear brake pressure and so delays a rear wheel skid. The proportioner is not repairable; it must be replaced if defective.

Normal Brake Stops

The proportioner does not operate during normal brake stops. Fluid normally flows into the proportioner through the space between the piston center hole and valve stem, through the stop plate, and out to the rear brakes. The spring loads the piston so that it rests against the stop plate during normal brake pressures.

Proportioning Action

Pressure developed within the valve pushes against

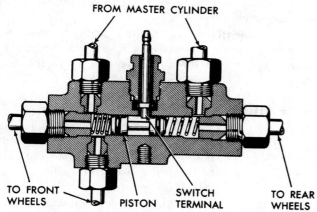

FROM MASTER CYLINDER

TO FRONT WHEELS   PISTON   SWITCH TERMINAL   TO REAR WHEELS

On early models, the brake distribution switch was a separate unit, and this sectioned view shows it in a "failed" position. Note how the right-side contact has moved forward to contact the stem of the switch terminal because of low pressure in the front-wheel braking system.

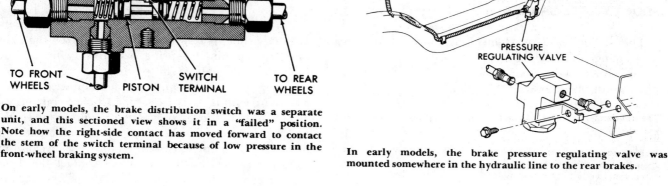

FRAME

PRESSURE REGULATING VALVE

In early models, the brake pressure regulating valve was mounted somewhere in the hydraulic line to the rear brakes.

the large end of the piston and, when sufficient to overcome the spring load, moves the piston to the left. The piston contacts the spherical stem seat and starts proportioning by restricting pressure through the valve.

BRAKE DISTRIBUTION SWITCH

This switch assembly is used on all front drum-type braking systems since 1968. It is a pressure-differential type, designed to light a brake-warning lamp on the instrument panel if either the front or rear hydraulic system fails. The lamp provides the driver a visible warning that part of the car's brake system has failed.

When hydraulic pressure is equal in both the front and rear hydraulic systems, the switch piston remains centered and does not contact the terminal in the switch cylinder bore. The switch includes a spring on each side of the piston to hold the piston in the centered position. If pressure fails in one of the systems, hydraulic pressure moves the piston toward the inoperative side. The shoulder of the piston then contacts the switch terminal to provide a ground for the warning lamp circuit and lights the warning lamp.

This switch is a non-adjustable, non-serviceable component. If defective, it must be replaced. **CAUTION: The brake warning light will come on when the brakes are applied in a defective system. It must not remain on when the brakes are released.**

DRUM-TYPE BRAKES

The brakes are the Duo-Servo, single-anchor pin type, which utilize the momentum of the vehicle to assist in the brake application. The self-energizing force is applied to both brake shoes at each wheel in both forward and reverse directions.

Wheel cylinders are the double-piston type. To keep out dust and moisture, both ends are sealed with a rubber boot. The wheel cylinders have no adjustments.

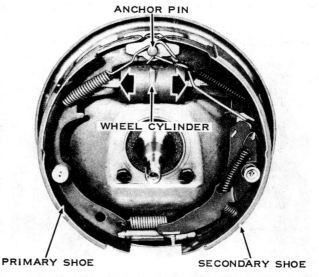

ANCHOR PIN

WHEEL CYLINDER

PRIMARY SHOE   SECONDARY SHOE

The front-wheel braking mechanism is mounted on the brake flange plate, which is bolted directly to the front wheel steering knuckle.

All parking brakes have a foot-operated, ratchet-type pedal, mounted to the left of the steering column. A cable assembly connects the pedal to an intermediate cable by means of an equalizer, where the adjustment for the parking brake is incorporated. The intermediate cable attaches to the two rear cables, which operate the rear service brakes.

FRONT WHEEL BRAKES

The wheel brake mechanism is mounted on the brake flange plate, which is bolted directly to the front wheel steering knuckle. The anchor pin is the upper pivot point of the brake shoes, and it is located above the wheel cylinder. Two brake shoes are used, a primary shoe toward the front of the car and a secondary shoe toward the rear. The primary shoe lining is always shorter than the secondary. The two brake shoes are held to the anchor pin at the top by color-coded retracting springs.

SELF-ENERGIZING ACTION

When the driver applies pressure to the brake pedal, fluid pressure is applied to the two pistons at each of the four wheel cylinders. This action forces the shoes outward at the top, causing the shoes to expand, pivoting on the adjusting screw. As they contact the drum, friction forces them to rotate with it. The primary shoe (front one) moves away from the anchor pin and exerts a rearward force on the adjusting screw, and this forces the secondary shoe upward, tightly against the anchor pin, so that the force applied to the secondary shoe is the sum of the original application force and the rotational force applied by the primary shoe.

When the brakes are applied while the vehicle is reversing, the rear shoe becomes, in effect, the primary shoe, applying its forces in like manner to the front shoe.

SELF-ADJUSTING ACTION

A self-adjusting actuating lever is mounted on the secondary shoe; it is attached to the shoe by the hold-down spring pin-and-spring assembly, which allows the lever to pivot about this point.

During a forward stop, the shoes contact the drum and rotate with it until the secondary shoe contacts the anchor pin; it moves only far enough to place the lining in contact with the drum. The small amount of movement does not activate the adjusting mechanism.

During a reverse stop, the shoes contact the drum and rotate with it until the primary shoe contacts the anchor pin. If there is excessive clearance because of brake lining wear, secondary shoe movement is enough to activate the adjusting mechanism by pulling the top of the actuating lever inward. As the lever pivots on the hold-down spring-and-pin assembly, the pawl end rocks down on the star wheel and turns it one notch to increase the length of the adjusting screw and so makes a take-up adjustment.

When the brakes are released, the retracting springs return the brake shoes to their normal positions, and the actuating lever return spring raises the pawl end of the activating lever to return it to its normal position. The pawl slips back over the teeth of the star wheel and takes a new "bite" on another tooth.

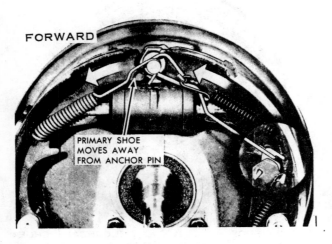

During forward stops, friction between the brake lining and drum causes the primary shoe to move away from the anchor pin, and this exerts a rearward force on the adjusting screw to force the secondary shoe into tighter contact with the drum.

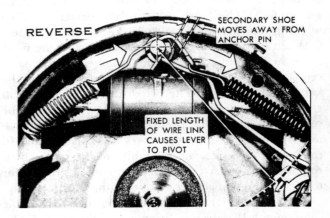

During a reverse stop, the secondary shoe moves away from the anchor pin, and the action is reversed. If there is excessive clearance because of brake lining wear, secondary shoe movement is enough to activate the adjusting mechanism by pulling the top of the actuating lever inward (arrow).

When there is only a slight clearance between the shoes and drum, such as might occur when the brake linings are near their proper adjustment, the brake shoes rotate only a small amount before they contact the anchor pin, and this is not enough movement to cause the actuating lever to advance the star wheel.

REAR WHEEL BRAKES

The rear wheel brake mechanism is the same as the front, except for the additional parking brake activating mechanism, which consists of an operating lever located in back of the secondary shoe and attached to the shoe by a pivot at the upper end. A strut rod, located a few inches below the pivot point, extends forward from this lever to the primary shoe.

The parking brake cable is connected to the lower end of the operating lever. When the parking brake is applied, the cable pulls the lower end of the operating lever forward, causing the strut rod to push the primary shoe forward. At the same time, the upper end of the lever pushes the secondary shoe rearward. The combined action of the lever and the strut rod drives the primary and secondary shoes apart and into contact with the drums.

SINGLE-PISTON TYPE DISC BRAKES

When pressure is applied to a hydraulic system, it acts equally in all directions. In the single-piston mechanism, the pressure acts on two surfaces. The first is the piston. The second is in the opposite direction, against the bottom of the bore of the caliper housing.

Since the area of the piston and bottom of the caliper bore are equal, equal forces are developed.

Hydraulic force in the caliper bore is exerted against the piston which is transmitted to the inner brake shoe and lining assembly and to the inner surface of the disc. This tends to pull the caliper assembly inboard, sliding on the four rubber bushings. The outer lining, which rests on the caliper housing, then applies a force on the outer surface of the disc and together the two linings slow the car. Since an equal hydraulic force is applied both to the caliper housing and the piston, the force created against the outer surface of the disc is the same as the inner. Since there are equal forces on the linings, no flexing or distortion of the disc occurs regardless of the severity or length of application, and lining wear tends to be equal.

As the brake linings wear, the caliper assembly moves inboard and fluid fills the area behind the piston, so that there is no pedal travel increase. As the driver releases the brake pedal, the piston and caliper merely relax into the released position, and braking effort is removed.

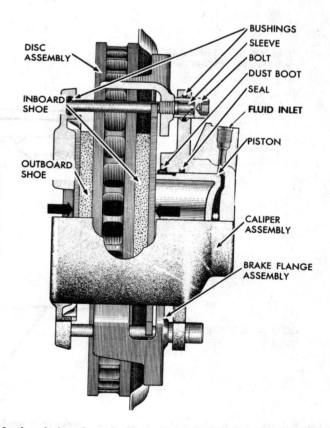

Sectioned view through the single-piston type caliper disc brake assembly.

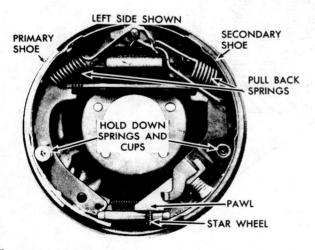

The rear-wheel brake mechanism is the same as the front, except for the parking brake actuating strut rod between the shoes, located just under the hydraulic cylinder.

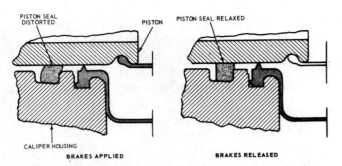

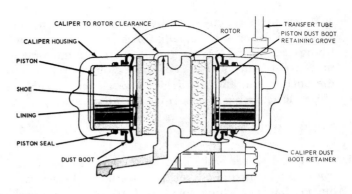

The piston seals distort when the brakes are applied, and this forces the piston back slightly from the rotor for running clearance when brake pedal pressure is released. As the linings wear, the seals slip in the bore to take up a new position so that the adjustment is automatically made.

An important thing about disc brakes is that the lining is in constant contact with the disc, giving the advantages of improved brake response, reduced pedal travel, and faster generation of line pressure. The shoe, being at zero clearance, also wipes the disc free of foreign matter.

Sectioned view through the caliper assembly to show how the pistons force the linings into contact with the rotor, which is secured to the hub.

FOUR-PISTON TYPE DISC BRAKES

The caliper contains two pairs of directly-opposed pistons. When installed on the vehicle, the caliper straddles the disc so that, on application, the pistons, through the shoes and linings, clamp the disc an equal amount on each side. The caliper housing consists of an inboard and outboard half that is bolted together. The outboard half has the extension that straddles the disc. The caliper is of nodular iron and is machined to receive two pistons in each half.

The two piston bores in each half are connected

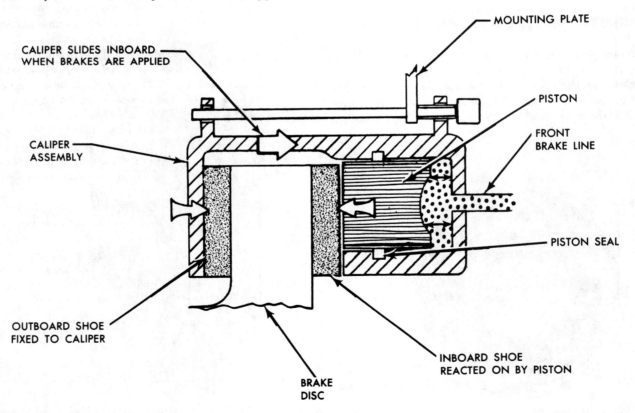

When fluid is contained in a closed system and pressure is applied, it is exerted equally in all directions and, in the single-piston assembly, it acts on two surfaces: (1) the piston, and (2) in the opposite direction against the caliper housing, which pulls the housing inboard, sliding on the four rubber bushings.

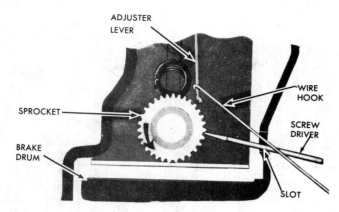

Some brake drums have a lanced area which can be knocked out in order to insert a screwdriver for retracting the star wheel adjuster.

hydraulically by internal passages. The two halves are connected hydraulically by means of a crossover passage. Each piston bore has a groove that accepts the outer lip of a dust boot. Each piston has two grooves. The inner groove is tapered slightly and accepts the hydraulic seal. The outer groove accepts the inner lip of the dust boot, so that the caliper bore and piston are completely sealed from external contamination.

In this system, pressure is applied to the rear of the pistons and to the disc through the shoes and linings. A major difference between this and the single-piston brake system is that the caliper stays stationary. When the brake pedal is released, the system returns to a relaxed position and pressure on the disc is removed.

The four-piston caliper straddles the disc, and four pistons apply pressure equally to both sides of the rotor when the brakes are applied.

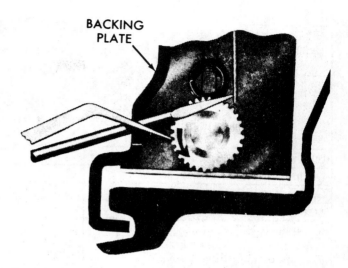

On most models, it is possible to pry out the rubber cover in the backing plate to gain access to the star adjusting wheel.

DRUM BRAKE SERVICE PROCEDURES,

RELINING

If the brake drums are worn severely, it may be necessary to retract the adjusting screws in order to remove the drums. To gain access to the adjusting screw star wheel, knock out the lanced area in the brake drum or flange plate, using a chisel or similar tool. Release the actuator from the star wheel with a small screwdriver on models with an access hole in the flange plate or with a wire hook on models with a hole in the drum. Back off the star wheel with a second screwdriver, as shown. **CAUTION: After knocking out the metal, be sure to remove it from the inside of the drum and clean all metal from the brake compartment. A new metal hole cover must be installed when the drum is replaced.**

The brake lining can be inspected through slots in the flange plate. The portion of lining visible through the slot will not necessarily be the area of maximum wear, and extra caution is necessary to make sure the lining is replaced prior to the point where the remaining thickness is 1/16″. Riveted linings should be replaced when worn within 1/32″ of the rivet heads.

REMOVING

Raise the vehicle on a hoist. Loosen the check nuts at the forward end of the parking brake equalizer enough to remove all tension from the brake cable. Remove the brake drums. **CAUTION: The brake pedal must not be depressed while the drums are removed.**

⊛ Most probable cause(s)

	Brake Tell-Tale Glows During Stop	Brakes Chatter (Roughness)	Brakes Squeak During Application	Scraping Noise from Brakes	Uneven Braking Action (Front to Rear)	Uneven Braking Action (Pulls to Side)	Brakes Drag	Brakes Slow to Release	Brakes Slow to Respond	Excessive Braking Action	Excessive Brake Pedal Effort	Pedal Travel Gradually Increases	Excessive Brake Pedal Travel
Leaking Brake Line or Connection	⊛				●							⊛	●
Leaking Wheel Cylinder or Piston Seal	●					●					●	⊛	●
Leaking Master Cylinder	●											⊛	●
Restricted Brake Fluid Passage					●	●	●	●	●		●	●	
Air In Brake System	⊛				●								⊛
Contaminated or Improper Brake Fluid	●						●	●	●				
Faulty Metering Valve (Disc Only)	●					●		●	●	●	●		●
Sticking Wheel Cylinder or Caliper Pistons					●	●	●	●			●		
Improperly Adjusted Master Cylinder Push Rod	●						⊛	●					●
Leaking Vacuum System									●		⊛		
Restricted Air Passage In Power Unit									●	⊛	●		
Improperly Assembled Power Unit							⊛	●	●	●	●		
Damaged Power Unit							●	●	●	●	●		
Brake Assembly Attachments – Missing or Loose		●		●	●	●	●						●
Brake Pedal Linkage Interference or Binding							⊛	⊛	●		●		
Worn Out Brake Lining – Replace			●	●	●	●					●		
Uneven Brake Lining Wear – Replace	●		●	●	●	●							●
Glazed Brake Lining – Sand Lightly			●		●	●			●		⊛		
Incorrect Lining Material – Replace		●	⊛		●	●			●	●	●		
Contaminated Brake Lining – Replace		●	●	●	⊛	⊛			●	⊛			
Linings Damaged By Abusive Use – Replace			●	●	●	●				⊛	●		
Excessive Brake Lining Dust – Remove with Air			●		⊛	⊛				⊛	●		
Brake Drums or Rotors Heat Spotted or Scored		⊛	●		●	●				●			
Out-of-Round or Vibrating Brake Drums		⊛											
Out-of-Parallel Brake Rotors		⊛											
Excessive Rotor Run-Out		●											
Faulty Automatic Adjusters	●				●	●		●				⊛	●
Weak or Incorrect Brake Shoe Return Springs			●	⊛	●	●	⊛	●			●		
Drums Tapered or Threaded				⊛									
Incorrect Wheel Cylinder Sizes					●	●					●	●	
Improperly Adjusted Parking Brake							●						
Incorrect Front End Alignment						⊛							
Incorrect Tire Pressure					●	●							
Incorrect Wheel Bearing Adjustment		●		●									●
Loose Front Suspension Attachments		●		⊛		●							
Out-of-Balance Wheel Assemblies		⊛											
Driver Riding Brake Pedal					●		●				●	●	●
Faulty Proportioning Valve							●	●	●		●		
Insufficient Brake Shoe Pad Lubricant			⊛	⊛	●		●	●					

Brake system diagnosis chart.

Unhook the brake shoe retracting springs from the anchor pin and link end. Remove the actuator return spring. Disengage the link end from the anchor pin and then from the secondary shoe. Remove the hold-down pins and springs.

Remove the actuator assembly. The actuator, pivot, and override spring are an assembly and should not be disassembled for service, unless they are broken. It is much easier to assemble the brakes by leaving them intact. Separate the brake shoes by removing the adjusting screw and spring. **CAUTION: Mark the shoe and lining positions if they are to be reinstalled.** Remove the parking brake lever from the secondary brake shoe.

INSPECTING

Clean all dirt out of the brake drum. Inspect the drums for roughness, scoring, or out-of-round. Replace or recondition the drums as necessary.

Carefully pull the lower edges of the wheel cylinder boots away from the cylinders and note whether the interior is wet with brake fluid. Excessive fluid at this point indicates leakage past piston cups, requiring an overhaul of the wheel cylinder. *NOTE: A slight amount of fluid is nearly always present to act as lubricant for the piston.* **CAUTION: If one wheel cylinder is leaking, all hydraulic cylinders should be overhauled at the same time because all have had** equal wear and will be leaking in a short time if not repaired.

Inspect the flange plate for oil leakage past the axle shaft oil seals. Install new seals if necessary.

Check all brake flange plate attaching bolts to make sure they are tight. Clean all rust and dirt from the shoe contact faces on the flange plate, using fine emery cloth.

INSTALLING

Inspect the new linings and make sure there are no nicks, burrs, or bonding material on the shoe edges where contact is made with the brake flange plate or on any of the contact surfaces. **CAUTION: Keep your hands clean while handling brake shoes. Do not permit oil or grease to come in contact with linings.** Lubricate the parking brake cable with Delco Brake Lube No. 5450032. Lubricate the fulcrum end of the parking brake lever and the bolt, and then attach the lever to the secondary shoe with a bolt, spring washer, lockwasher, and nut. Make sure that the lever moves freely.

Put a light coat of lube on the pads, flange plate, and threads of the adjusting screw. **CAUTION: A loose adjustment can occur from an adjusting screw that is not properly operating. CAUTION: Be careful**

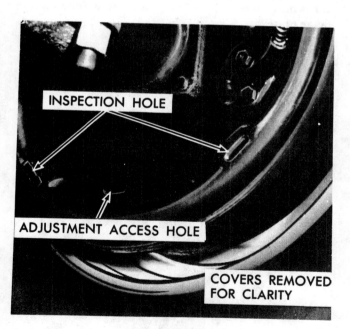

Inspection holes in the backing plate provide means to determine the brake lining thickness without removing the wheel and drum.

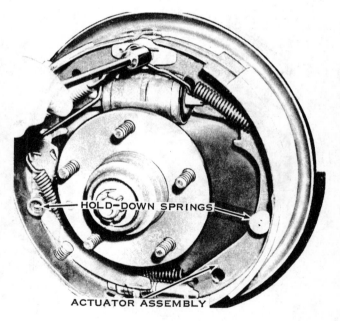

Unhook the brake shoe retracting spring from the anchor pin with this tool, and then depress each of the hold-down spring retainers to disengage them. Take off the actuator assembly, and then remove both brake shoes.

Lightly lubricate the brake shoe support surfaces (arrows) on the backing plate. **CAUTION:** Don't get any lubricant on the brake linings, or they will grab.

to keep lubricant off the brake linings.

Connect the brake shoes together with the adjusting screw spring, and then place the adjusting screw, socket, and nut in position. **CAUTION: Make sure**

On rear-wheel brakes, connect the parking brake strut, and then secure the brake shoes with the hold-down pin and spring. Connect the return springs to the anchor bolt at the top of the backing plate.

the proper adjusting screw is used ("L" for the left side of the vehicle, "R" for the right side). The star wheel should be installed with the wheel nearest the secondary shoe and the adjusting screw spring inserted to prevent interference with the star wheel. Make sure the right-hand thread adjusting screw is on the left side of the car and the left-hand thread adjusting screw is on the right side of the car. Make certain the star wheel lines up with the adjusting hole in the flange plate.

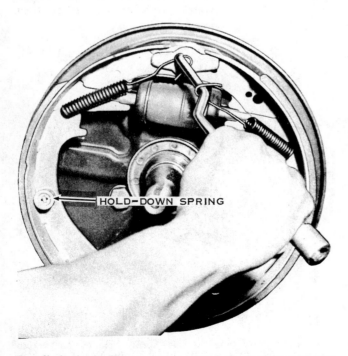

HOLD-DOWN SPRING

Install the brake shoes, and then insert the hold-down springs and retainers. Pull the retracting springs over the anchor pin with the illustrated tool.

A special brake drum gauge is available to measure the inside diameter of the drum.

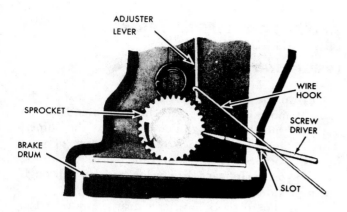

This diagram shows how a wire hook can be used to keep the adjuster lever from interfering with the brake adjusting tool when the adjustment is made through the slot in the brake drum.

On rear wheels, connect the parking brake cable to the lever. Secure the primary brake shoe (short lining —faces forward) first, with the hold-down pin and spring. At the same time, engage the shoes with the wheel cylinder connecting links. Install and secure the actuator assembly and secondary brake shoe with the hold-down pin and spring. On rear wheels, position the parking brake strut and strut spring. Install the guide plate over the anchor pin. Install the wire link. **CAUTION: Do not hook the wire link over the anchor pin stud with a regular spring hook tool or you will stretch it. Fasten the wire link to the actuator assembly first, then place it over the anchor pin stud by hand, while holding the adjuster assembly in the full-down**

position. Install the actuator return spring. **CAUTION: Do not pry on the actuator lever to install the return spring. Ease it into place, using the end of a screwdriver.**

If the old brake retracting springs are nicked, distorted, or if their strength is doubtful, install new ones. Hook the springs into the shoes by installing the primary spring from the shoe over the anchor pin and then the spring from the secondary shoe over the wire link end. **CAUTION: Make certain the actuator lever functions easily by hand, operating the self-adjusting feature.** Adjust the service brake and parking brake. Install the drum and the wheel. Lower the vehicle to the floor.

ADJUSTING DRUM-TYPE BRAKES

After installing new brake linings, it is necessary to make an adjustment to the star wheel in order to be able to install the brake drums. A special drum-to-brake shoe clearance gauge is available to check the diameter of the brake drum, and then the tool is reversed to straddle the brake shoes. To make a preliminary adjustment, turn the star wheel until the gauge just goes over the brake shoes, and then install the brake drum.

Alternatively, the star wheel can be backed off enough to install the drums, and then a preliminary adjustment can be made by holding the ratchet off the

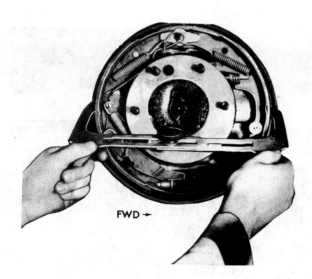

Note how the gauge is reversed in this diagram to set the brake shoes to the diameter of the drum.

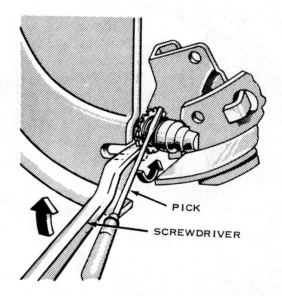

When making a brake shoe adjustment from the backing plate side, a pointed tool can be used to hold the adjuster lever away from the star adjusting wheel, which can then be turned with a screwdriver.

When properly adjusted, the brake pedal should have about 1/4" free play.

SINGLE-PISTON TYPE DISC BRAKE SERVICE PROCEDURES

INSPECTING

Jack up the front end of the vehicle to inspect the pads. Remove the wheels and check both ends of the outboard shoe by looking in at each end of the caliper. This is the point at which the highest rate of wear normally occurs. At the same time, check the lining thickness on the inboard shoe by looking down through the inspection hole in the top of the caliper.

The outboard shoes have ears near the outer edge, which are bent over at right angles to the shoe. The top ends of the shoe have looped ears with holes in them, which the caliper retaining bolts fit through. The large tab at the bottom of the shoe is bent over at a right angle and fits in the cut-out in the outboard section of the caliper. The inboard shoe and lining has ears on the top ends, which fit over the caliper retaining bolts. A special spring inside the hollow piston supports the bottom edge of the inboard shoe. *NOTE: Outboard shoes (with formed ears) are designed for original installation only and are fitted to the caliper. The shoes should never be relined or reconditioned.*

star wheel with a thin-bladed screwdriver through the access hole in the backing plate while you make the adjustment.

The final adjustment must be made by making numerous forward and reverse stops, spplying the brakes with firm pedal effort until a satisfactory pedal height results. **CAUTION: Frequent shifting of an automatic transmission into the forward range to halt reverse vehicle motion can prevent the automatic adjusters from functioning properly, thereby inducing a low pedal height.**

REMOVING THE BRAKE SHOES

Remove the master cylinder cover and observe the brake fluid level in the reservoirs. If a reservoir is more than 1/3 full, siphon the necessary amount out.

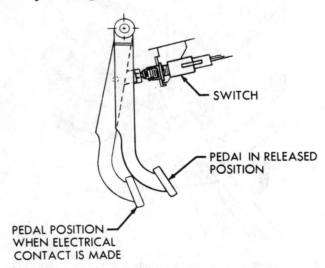

The stop light switch can be adjusted by rotating it in its bracket. The lamp should light when the pedal is depressed about 1/2".

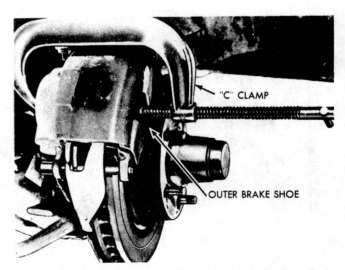

Use a C-clamp to push the piston into its bore to assist in removing the caliper. **CAUTION: The master cylinder reservoir must not be more than 1/3 full, or the excess will overflow.**

CAUTION: This step is taken to avoid reservoir overflow when the caliper piston is pushed back into its bore. Discard the brake fluid you removed. CAUTION: Never reuse brake fluid.

Push the piston back into its bore. This can be accomplished by using a C-clamp, as shown. Remove the two mounting bolts which attach the caliper to the support. Lift the caliper off the disc. Remove the inboard shoe, dislodge the outboard shoe, and position the caliper on the front suspension arm so that the brake hose does not support the weight of the caliper. CAUTION: Mark the shoe positions if they are to be reinstalled.

Remove the shoe support spring from the piston, the two sleeves from the inboard ears of the caliper, and the four rubber bushings from the grooves in each of the caliper ears.

CLEANING AND INSPECTING

The shoes should be replaced when the lining is worn to approximately 1/32″ thickness over the rivet heads. CAUTION: Always replace the shoes in axle sets.

Thoroughly clean the holes and the bushing grooves in the caliper ears and wipe any dirt from the mounting bolts. CAUTION: Do not use abrasives on the bolts, since this can damage the plating. If the bolts are damaged or corroded, they should be replaced.

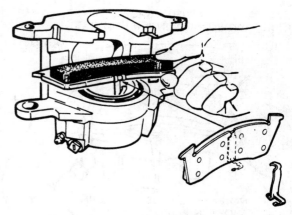

Installing the shoe support spring and the inboard shoe in the center of the piston cavity.

Examine the inside of the caliper for evidence of fluid leakage. If leakage is noted, the caliper should be overhauled. Wipe the inside of the caliper clean, including the exterior of the dust boot. Check the boot for cuts, cracks, or other damage. CAUTION: Do not use compressed air to clean the inside of the caliper. This can unseat the dust boot.

INSTALLING

Lubricate new sleeves, new rubber bushings, the bushing grooves, and the end of the mounting bolts with Delco Silicone Lube No. 5459912. CAUTION: It is essential that new sleeves and rubber bushings

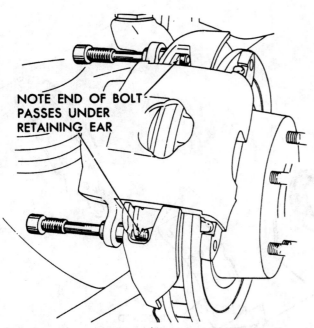

Removing the two mounting bolts which hold the caliper to the support.

NOTE END OF BOLT PASSES UNDER RETAINING EAR

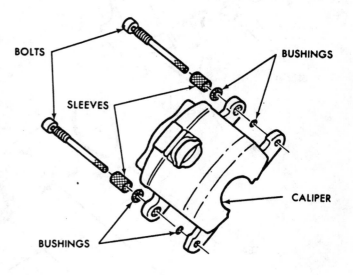

BOLTS

BUSHINGS

SLEEVES

CALIPER

BUSHINGS

▨ LUBRICATE AREAS INDICATED

Lubricate these parts with Silicone Lube No. 5459912. CAUTION: Never use mineral oil on any parts of the brake system, or the rubber parts will swell.

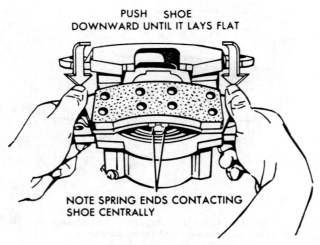

Installing the inboard brake shoe.

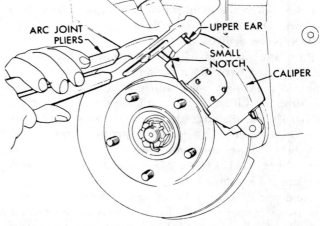

Use arc-joint pliers to bend both upper ears of the outboard shoe until all radial clearance is removed, as discussed in the text.

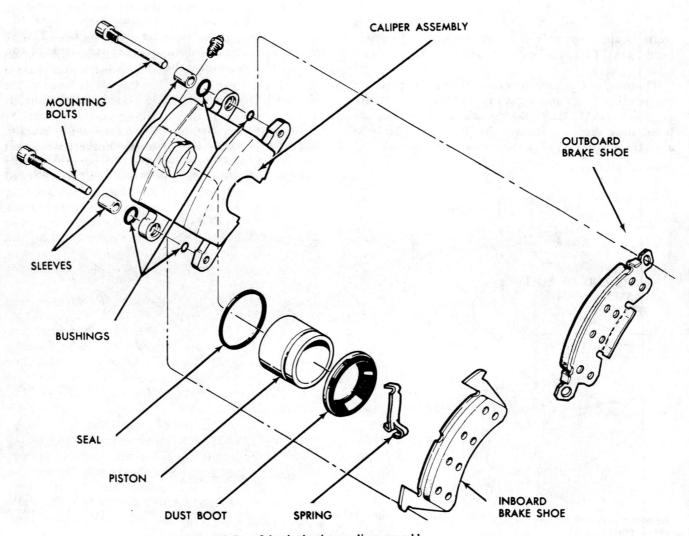

Exploded view of the single-piston caliper assembly.

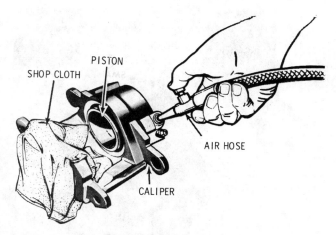

If the piston needs to be removed from the caliper, use air pressure to force it out.

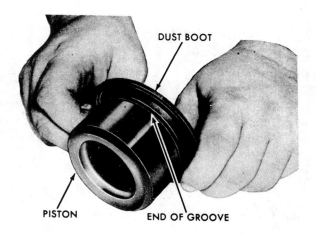

Installing a new dust boot on the piston.

be used and that lubrication instructions be followed in order to ensure the proper functioning of the sliding caliper design. Install the new rubber bushings in the caliper ears. Install the new sleeves to the inboard ears of the caliper. *NOTE: Position the sleeve so that the end toward the shoe-and-lining assembly is flush with the machined surface of the ear.*

Install the shoe support spring and the inboard shoe in the center of the piston cavity, as shown. **CAUTION: If the original shoes are being reinstalled, they must be replaced in the original positions (as marked at removal).** Push down until the shoe lies

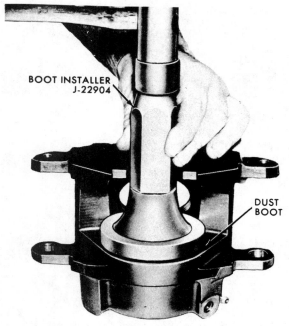

Driving the piston into the caliper. Use the illustrated tool to make sure that the dust boot seats properly.

flat against the caliper. Position the outboard shoe in the caliper, with the ears at the top of the shoe over the caliper ears and the tab at the bottom of the shoe engaged in the caliper cut-out.

With both shoes installed, lift up the caliper assembly and rest the bottom edge of the outboard lining on the outer edge of the brake disc to make sure there is no clearance between the tab at the bottom of the outboard shoe and the caliper abutment. Position the caliper over the brake disc, lining up the hole in the caliper ears with the holes in the mounting bracket. **CAUTION: Make sure that the brake hose is not twisted or kinked.** Start the caliper-to-mounting bracket bolts through the sleeves in the inboard caliper ears and through the mounting bracket, making sure that the ends of the bolts pass under the retaining ears on the inboard shoe. Push the mounting bolts through to engage the holes in the outboard shoes and the outboard caliper ears, threading the mounting bolts into the mounting bracket. Torque the mounting bolts to 35 ft-lbs.

Pump the brake pedal to seat the linings against the rotors. Using arc-joint pliers, as shown, bend both upper ears of the outboard shoe until no radial clearance exists between the shoe and the caliper housing. Locate the pliers on the small notch of the caliper housing during the clinching procedure. **CAUTION: If radial clearance exists after the initial clinching, repeat the process.**

Reinstall the front wheel and lower the vehicle. Add brake fluid to the master cylinder reservoir to bring the fluid level up to within 1/4" of the top. **CAUTION: Before moving the vehicle, pump the brake pedal several times to make sure that it is firm. Do not move the vehicle until a firm pedal is obtained. Check the master cylinder fluid level again after pumping the brake pedal.**

FOUR-PISTON TYPE DISC BRAKE SERVICE PROCEDURES

INSPECTING

Jack up the front of the vehicle and remove the wheel. Shoes with bonded linings should be replaced when the lining is worn to approximately 1/16" thickness. Shoes with linings retained by rivets should be replaced when the lining is worn to approximately 1/32" thickness over the rivet heads.

REMOVING THE BRAKE SHOES

Syphon 2/3 of the brake fluid from the master cylinder reservoirs to prevent the fluid from overflowing when the thicker linings are installed. **CAUTION: Do not drain the reservoirs completely or air will be sucked into the system.** Remove and discard the cotter pin from the inboard end of the shoe retaining pin, and then slide out the retaining pin. Remove the inboard shoe by pulling it up. **CAUTION: If the shoes are to be reused, identify their location.**

INSTALLING NEW SHOES

Insert the new shoe and lining into position. Use two screwdrivers to push the pistons back as the shoe is inserted. Replace the outboard shoe in the same

To install new brake shoes, use two screwdrivers to push the pistons back as the shoe is inserted. **CAUTION: Make sure that the master cylinder reservoir is not over 1/3 full, or the excess will overflow.**

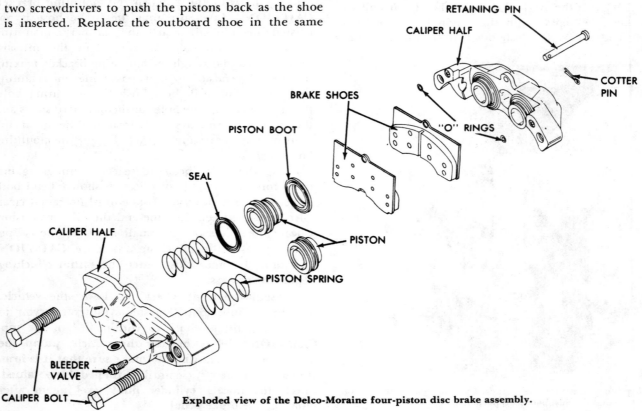

Exploded view of the Delco-Moraine four-piston disc brake assembly.

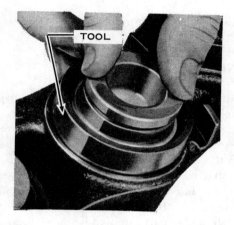

Installing the piston in the caliper with the aid of a special tool.

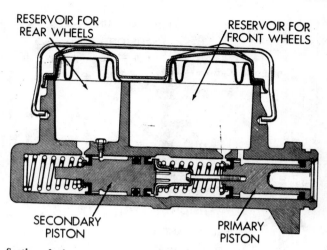

Sectioned view through the Bendix master cylinder used in the split braking system. Note that the front wheel reservoir is at the rear of the master cylinder. Also note the stop bolt in the bottom of the front reservoir to keep the secondary piston from moving back too far.

manner. When both shoes have been replaced, install the shoe-retaining pin through the outboard caliper half, outboard shoe, inboard shoe, and inboard caliper half. Insert a new 3/32 × 5/8" plated cotter pin through the retaining pin, and then bend back the ends of the cotter pin.

Refill the master cylinder fluid level to within 1/4" of the top. If necessary, bleed the brake system. Install the wheels and lower the vehicle. **CAUTION: Do not move the car until a firm pedal is obtained.**

MASTER CYLINDER SERVICE PROCEDURES

REMOVING

Wipe the master cylinder and lines clean with a clean cloth. Place dry cloths below the master cylinder area to absorb any fluid spillage. Disconnect the hydraulic lines at the master cylinder. Cover the line ends with clean lint-free material to prevent foreign matter from entering the system.

Disconnect the push rod from the brake pedal. Unbolt and remove the master cylinder from the dash panel or power brake booster.

Use the illustrated tool to seat a new boot seal in the caliper.

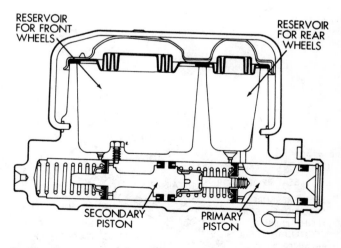

Sectioned view through the Delco-Moraine master cylinder. Note the reversal of the reservoirs from the Bendix. Also note the stop bolt in the bottom of the front reservoir to keep the secondary piston from moving back too far.

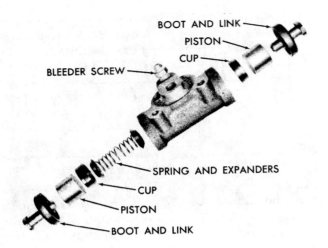

Exploded view of a wheel cylinder used with drum-type brakes.

DISASSEMBLING

Remove the small secondary piston stop screw from the bottom of the front fluid reservoir of the master cylinder. Place the master cylinder in the vise so that the lock ring can be removed from the small groove in the I.D. of the bore. Remove the lock ring-and-primary piston assembly. Remove the secondary piston, secondary piston spring, and retainer by blowing air through the stop screw hole. Remove the primary seal, primary seal protector, and secondary seals from the secondary piston.

The brass tube fitting insert should not be removed unless visual inspection indicates the insert is damaged. To replace a defective insert, thread a No. 6=32 x 5|8″ self-tapping screw into the tube-fitting insert. Using

the claw end of a hammer, remove the screw and insert.

CLEANING AND INSPECTING

Remove the casting from the vise and inspect the bore for corrosion, pits, and foreign matter. Be sure the outlet ports are clean. Inspect the fluid reservoirs for foreign matter. Check the bypass and compensating ports to the master cylinder bore to determine if they are unrestricted.

Use clean brake fluid to clean all reusable brake parts thoroughly. Immerse them in the cleaning fluid and brush metal parts to remove all foreign matter. Blow out all passages, orifices, and valve holes. Place cleaned parts on clean paper or lint-free clean cloth. If slight rust is found inside of either the front or rear half housing assemblies, polish with crocus cloth or fine emery paper, washing clean afterwards. **CAUTION: Be sure to keep parts clean until assembly. Rewash if there is any doubt of cleanliness. If there is any suspicion of contamination or any evidence of corrosion, completely flush the entire hydraulic brake system. Failure to clean the hydraulic brake system can result in early repetition of trouble. Use of gasoline, kerosene, anti-freeze, alcohol, or any other cleaner, with even a trace of mineral oil, will damage rubber parts.**

Always replace all rubber parts.

ASSEMBLING

If the brass tube inserts were removed, place the

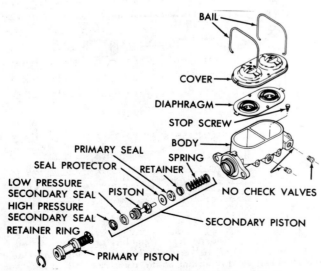

Exploded view of the split-braking system master cylinder.

The wheel cylinder must be replaced if there is over 0.003″ clearance between the piston and cylinder bore.

master cylinder in a vise so that the outlet holes are facing up. Position the new brass tube inserts in the outlet holes, making sure they are not cocked. Thread a spare brake line tube nut into each outlet and turn the nuts down until the insert bottoms. Remove the tube nut and check the outlet hole for loose brass burrs, which might have been turned up when the insert was pressed into position.

Place new secondary seals in the two grooves in the flat end of the secondary piston assembly. The seal which is nearest the flat end must have its lip facing toward this flat end. On Delco units, the seal in the second groove should have its lip facing toward the end of the secondary piston which contains the small compensating holes. On Bendix units, the seal in the second groove is an O-ring seal. Assemble a new primary seal and primary seal protector over the end of the secondary piston, opposite the secondary seals, so that the flat side of the seal seats against the flange of the piston which contains the small compensating holes.

In order to ensure a correct assembly of the primary piston assembly, a complete primary piston assembly is included in the repair kit.

Coat the bore of the master cylinder and the primary and secondary seals on the secondary piston with clean brake fluid. Insert the secondary piston spring retainer into the secondary piston spring. Place the retainer and spring down over the end of the secondary piston so that the retainer locates inside the lips of the primary seal. Holding the master cylinder with the open end of the bore up, push the secondary piston into the bore so that the spring seats against the closed end of the bore. Use a small wooden rod to push the secondary piston into its seat.

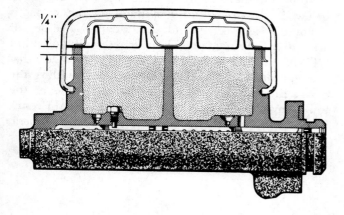

The master cylinder should be kept full of brake fluid during the bleeding process. The correct level is 1/4" below the top of the reservoir.

Coat the primary and secondary seals on the primary piston with clean brake fluid. Push the primary piston (secondary piston stop first) into the bore. Hold the piston down and snap the lock ring into position in the small groove in the I.D. of the bore. Continue to hold the primary piston down, which will also move the secondary piston forward and will insure that the secondary piston will be forward far enough to clear the stop screw hole, which is in the bottom of the front fluid reservoir. Install the stop screw and tighten it to a torque of 33 in-lbs.

Install the reservoir diaphragm in the reservoir cover and position the cover on the master cylinder. Assemble the bail wires into position to retain the reservoir cover. The master cylinder is now ready for "bench bleeding."

BENCH BLEEDING

Install plastic plugs in both outlet ports. Clamp the master cylinder in a bench vise, with the front end tilted down slightly. **CAUTION: Tighten the vise only enough to hold the reservoir securely; too much pressure will damage the master cylinder.** Fill both reservoirs with clean brake fluid.

Insert a rod with a smooth round end into the primary piston, and then press in to compress the piston return spring. Release pressure on the rod. Watch for air bubbles in the reservoir fluid. Repeat as long as bubbles appear.

INSTALLING

Assemble the push rod through the push rod retainer, if it has been disassembled. Push the retainer over the end of the master cylinder. Assemble a new boot over the push rod and press it down over the push rod retainer. Slide a new mounting gasket into position.

Secure the master cylinder to the dash panel with the mounting bolts. Connect the push rod clevis to the brake pedal with a pin and retainer. Connect the brake lines to the master cylinder.

BLEEDING THE HYDRAULIC SYSTEM

The hydraulic brake system must be bled whenever any line has been disconnected or air has entered the system. Bleeding of the brake system may be performed by one of two methods—either pressure or manual. Bleeder valves are provided at the calipers, wheel cylinders, and on some master cylinders.

It is advisable to bleed one valve at a time to avoid

allowing the fluid level in the reservoir to become dangerously low. The correct sequence is to bleed the valve (either front or rear system) nearest the master cylinder first. This sequence expels air from the lines and calipers or wheel cylinders nearest the master cylinder first and eliminates the possibility that air in a line close to the master cylinder may enter a line farther away after it has been bled.

To bleed the system, clean all dirt from the top of the master cylinder, and then remove the cylinder cover and rubber diaphragm. If pressure-bleeding equipment is to be used, install the brake bleeder adaptor on the master cylinder. *NOTE: Pressure-bleeding equipment must be of the diaphragm type. That is, it must have a rubber diaphragm between the air supply and the brake fluid to prevent air, moisture, oil, and dirt from entering the hydraulic system.* Connect a hose from the bleeder equipment to the bleeder adaptor, and then open the release valve on the bleeder equipment. On disc-brake cars, a combination metering, proportioning, and failure-warning switch is in the hydraulic system. It is mounted either on the frame rail or under the master cylinder. **CAUTION: This valve must be held in the open position while bleeding.** This can be accomplished by installing Tool J-23709, with the open slot under the mounting bolt and pushing in on the pin in the end of the valve, as shown.

Install a bleeder wrench on the caliper bleeder valve nearest the master cylinder, and then install one end of a bleeder hose on the bleeder valve. *NOTE: If the master cylinder is equipped with bleeder valves, bleed these first.* Pour enough brake fluid into a transparent container to ensure that the end of the bleeder hose will remain submerged. Place the loose end of the hose in the container. **CAUTION: Make sure the hose end is always submerged in fluid.**

Open the bleeder valve approximately 3/4 of a turn and observe the flow of fluid at the end of the bleeder hose. To assist in the bleeding operation, a rawhide mallet can be used to tap the caliper while fluid is flowing. Close the bleeder valve tight as soon as bubbles stop, and the brake fluid flows in a solid stream from the bleeder hose.

If you are not using pressure-bleeding equipment, have a helper depress the brake pedal. Just before the brake pedal reaches the end of its travel, close the bleeder valve tightly and allow the brake pedal to return slowly to the released position. Repeat until the expelled brake fluid flows in a solid stream, without air bubbles, and then close the bleeder valve tightly. **CAUTION: Carefully monitor the fluid level in the master cylinder. Do not allow the level to drop enough to expose the ports, which would allow air to enter the system.** Remove the wrench and hose from the bleeder valve. Repeat on the remaining bleeder valves.

Disconnect the bleeder equipment from the brake bleeder adaptor. **CAUTION: The master cylinder on some models is tilted. When removing the bleeder adaptor on these models, place a clean, dry cloth below it to absorb fluid spillage as the cover is removed.** Remove the bleeder adaptor. Wipe all areas dry. Fill the master cylinder reservoirs to within 1/4" of the rims. Install the master cylinder diaphragm and cover. **CAUTION: When installing the cover, the retaining bail must be slipped over the lower cover bosses. Incorrect installation could result in bail tension loss and fluid leakage.** Test the operation of the brake pedal before moving the vehicle.

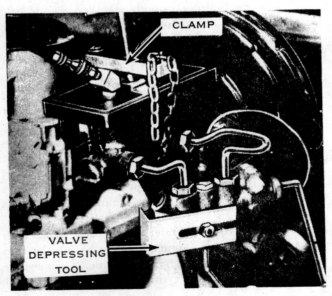

This illustration shows pressure-bleeding equipment in place and use of the tool J-23709 to hold the metering valve depressed during the bleeding operation.